Black Performance and Cultural Criticism
Valerie Lee and E. Patrick Johnson, Series Editors

Secrecy, Magic, the One-Act Plays

of Harlem Renaissance Women Writers

TAYLOR HAGOOD

THE OHIO STATE UNIVERSITY PRESS
Columbus

Library of Congress Cataloging-in-Publication Data
Hagood, Taylor, 1975–
    Secrecy, magic, and the one-act plays of Harlem Renaissance women writers / Taylor
Hagood.
        p. cm. — (Black performance and cultural criticism)
    Includes bibliographical references and index.
    ISBN-13: 978-0-8142-1121-2 (cloth : alk. paper)
    ISBN-10: 0-8142-1121-6 (cloth : alk. paper)
    ISBN-13: 978-0-8142-9219-8 (cd-rom)
    1. American drama—African American authors—History and criticism. 2.
American drama—Women authors—History and criticism. 3. American drama—20th
century—History and criticism. 4. One-act plays, American—History and criticism. 5.
Secrecy in literature. 6. Magic in literature. 7. Harlem Renaissance. I. Title. II. Series:
Black performance and cultural criticism.
    PS153.N5H2 2010
    812'.04109896073—dc22

                                                                      2009032693
This book is available in the following editions:
Cloth (ISBN 978–0-8142–1121–2)
CD-ROM (ISBN 978–0-8142–9219–8)

Cover design by Janna Thompson-Chordas.
Type set in Adobe Minion Pro.
Text design by Jennifer Shoffey Forsythe.
Printed by Thomson-Shore, Inc.

♾ The paper used in this publication meets the minimum requirements of the American National Standard for Information Sciences—Permanence of Paper for Printed
Library Materials. ANSI Z39.48–1992.

9 8 7 6 5 4 3 2 1

For Virginia Azalee Jackson Hagood

Contents

List of Abbreviations

BFP   *Black Female Playwrights*, edited by Kathy A. Perkins
FSE   *Frye Street and Environs*, Marita Bonner
NHTP   *Negro History in Thirteen Plays*, edited by
         Willis Richardson and May Miller
PGDJ   *The Plays of Georgia Douglas Johnson*,
         Georgia Douglas Johnson
PNL   *Plays of Negro Life*, edited by Alain Locke and
         Montgomery Gregory
SCRBC   Schomburg Center for Research in Black Culture
SF   *Strange Fruit*, edited by Kathy A. Perkins and
         Judith L. Stephens
WW   *Wines in the Wilderness*, edited by
         Elizabeth Brown-Guillory

Acknowledgments

THERE ARE two people I would acknowledge first as being of crucial help to me on this book. One is Ethel A. Young-Minor, who first introduced me to these one-act plays in her graduate seminar on African American writers in the South. Her encouragement and enthusiasm have been and continue to be great boosts for me as a scholar. The second person to whom I owe much thanks is Kathy A. Perkins: where Ethel started me on this journey, Kathy kindly aided me at crucial points along the road by offering important help and information about Eulalie Spence, May Miller, Georgia Douglas Johnson, and the other writers discussed herein. I also want to acknowledge her importance in bringing these writers and their one-act plays to critical attention; she (and Judith L. Stephens, who has also kindly helped me) has done a tremendous and heroic service to the field in her textual work.

 ´ If these brought me on the journey toward writing this book, Sandy Crooms, of The Ohio State University Press, has been the one to help bring it to fruition. She showed enthusiasm from the moment I first mentioned the project to her, and it has been wonderful to work with her. Open, energetic, enthusiastic, efficient—such are only a few words that describe her. I am thankful also to Malcolm Litchfield, director of the press, for his support of this project and for his friendliness, and to Eugene O'Connor, whose attentive editing, deft administration, and warm correspondence have been so important to its realization. Thank you to Jennifer Shoffey Forsythe and Janna Thompson-Chordas for the wonderful cover design and text layout. Thank you to the anonymous readers whose amazingly nuanced responses engaged my argument: I feel very fortunate to have had such brilliant and sensitive people responding to this text. Thank you to E. Patrick Johnson and Valerie Lee for including it in the Black Performance and Cultural Criticism Series.

I want to acknowledge also certain other people and institutions. Thank you to Josephine Beoku-Betts for inviting me to present on Eulalie Spence's *Hot Stuff* in Florida Atlantic University's Women, Gender, and Sexuality Studies Colloquium Series; I am grateful to Josephine, Jane Caputi, and Jan Hokenson for their feedback and support. Thank you to Florida Atlantic University's Division of Sponsored Research for awarding me a Creative and Scholarly Activities Grant, which provided funds and course release time for research and writing. Thank you to the various planners of MELUS conferences for giving me the opportunities to present various parts of this volume. My discussion of Zora Neale Hurston's *The First One* and May Miller's *Riding the Goat* first appeared as an essay entitled "Dramatic Deception and Black Identity in *The First One* and *Riding the Goat*" and is reprinted from *African American Review* 39, no. 1–2 (Spring–Summer 2005). Also, I want to thank Diana Lachatanere, Curator of Manuscripts, for permission to cite materials from the Eulalie Spence Papers, Sc MG 552, Manuscripts, Archives and Rare Books Division, Schomburg Center for Research in Black Culture, The New York Public Library.

My colleagues in various disciplines at Florida Atlantic University have been so very helpful to me in thinking through the pathways of this book. Karen Chinander, of Business, patiently helped me with the intricacies of game theory (even if the book does not at all exhibit those intricacies). Psychology professor Natalie Ciarocco asked penetrating questions about my ideas on secrecy which have been very helpful in sharpening my thinking. Arthur Sementelli has pointed me in fruitful theoretical directions regarding secrecy and public administration. My dear friend and history professor Douglass T. McGetchin continually converses with me on secrecy and its functions in various contexts. The late biologist Hank T. Smith was an encouragement always, and one who himself understood the crushing weight of secrecy. In the English Department, Elena Machada Sáez and Raphael Dalleo offered provocative feedback on my thinking about *Christophe's Daughters,* and Jonathan Goldman has consistently shown interest in this project.

Certain students have been especially inspiring in regard to this undertaking. Amber Estlund was the first student whose M.A. thesis I was privileged to guide to completion, and it was a very thought-provoking reevaluation of the term "folk drama" and its relation to Hurston's *Color Struck*. Likewise, Tinea Williams's thesis on female lynching included excellent treatments of Mary P. Burrill's plays. It is gratifying to know that these two fine scholars will be going on to write about these one-acts in rich and provocative ways, and I consider it a distinct honor to be associated with them.

There are also certain people who are colleagues but who are also friends, and I am incredibly thankful for their support, be it general or specific to this book. Some of them I have mentioned already. To these I would add Mary Faraci, my mentor, whom I hold dear to my heart. Andrew Furman has been wonderfully encouraging both as department chair and as civilian. Reverse that order for Wenying Xu, who has believed in me both before and since her becoming the current chair of FAU's English Department. Sika Dagbovie has been so warm and welcoming. Mark Scroggins and Jennifer Low maintain standards of scholarly excellence I always admire and strive for. Oliver Buckton does the same, and like them has been a great and patient friend to me. Johnnie Stover has been always the sweetest. Don Adams, Eric Berlatsky, Steve Blakemore, John Childrey, Jeff Galin, John Leeds, Tom Martin, Carol McGuirk, Dan Murtaugh, and Emily Stockard have all gone out of their way to befriend and guide me and each is very special to me. Kristen Murtaugh has been a support in so many ways as have Clevis Headley and Marina Banchetti. Neil Santaniello has steadfastly encouraged. Suzanne Deffendall has been a constant throughout the various stages of this project, both morally and materially.

Some have helped me to believe in myself and my work for a long time, and I close by thanking them. Christopher B. Bundrick, Scott Henkel, Randall J. Jasmine, Travis Montgomery, Suzanne Penuel, and David Ramm, bless their hearts, have been tireless in their support. Thomas Flynn and Howard Wisch have no idea how important they have been to me. David Noble I hope does. Marsha Dutton has been there for me at all moments. Thadious Davis, Donald Kartiganer, Annette Trefzer, Jay Watson, Benjamin F. Fisher, Ann Fisher-Wirth, and Joan Wylie Hall have all been constant and true. Thanks are always due to Joseph R. Urgo for patient guidance. Crystal Lorimor always bestows enthusiasm. Laura Cade always listens, always responds, always assures. My grandmother unflaggingly promotes my scribbling. No words can ever adequately thank my mother, father, and sister for each and every big and small thing they do.

If we were a people much given to revealing secrets, we might raise monuments and sacrifice to the memories of our poets, but slavery cured us of that weakness. It may be enough, however, to have it said that we survive in exact relationship to the dedication of our poets (include preachers, musicians and blues singers).

—Maya Angelou, *I Know Why the Caged Bird Sings*

Nineteen judges, all of whom are crowded with their own literary duties, have consented promptly and eagerly to pass upon the merits of the contributions of Negroes to OPPORTUNITY's contest. Their consent is both a gesture of friendliness toward a long submerged and virtually inarticulate group, and a recognition of the rich stores of material in Negro life to be exploited in the interest of American literature generally.

—*Opportunity: A Journal of Negro Life* (October 1924, 291)

I who am visible to you must also protect a certain reserve. Within the intention of appearing to you, there must also exist the intention of remaining invisible, of covering life and love with the shadow of a secret.

—Luce Irigaray, *To Be Two*

Yes I can lay my head on the rocks of Nowhere.

—Marita Bonner, *The Purple Flower*

Induction:
JOYCE HETH

P. T. BARNUM'S first "exhibit" was a black woman named Joice Heth. She was the alleged 160+-year-old former slave nurse of George Washington. In her performances, she sat on display, addressing and interacting with spectators to confirm her authenticity. According to the advertisement that first announced her in August of 1835, she was "The Greatest Natural and National Curiosity in The World," and when one visited her, one would find that she "retains her faculties in an unparalleled degree, converses freely, sings numerous hymns, relates many interesting anecdotes of *the boy* Washington and often laughs heartily at her own remarks, or those of the spectators" (qtd. in Wallace 4). The advertisement also stressed that she "is a Baptist and takes great pleasure in conversing with ministers and religious persons" (4). Above all, the ad proclaimed, the "appearance of this marvelous relic of antiquity strikes the beholder with amazement, and convinces him that his eyes are resting on the oldest specimen of mortality they ever before beheld. Original, authentic, and indisputable documents accompanying her prove," the ad concluded, "however astonishing the fact may appear, that Joice Heth is in every respect the person she is represented" (4).

There is much to be gleaned from the performances of and connections between Heth and Barnum, the most significant for this volume being that both individuals were involved in their respective ways in theatrical performances that operated within a poetics of deception that created, negotiated, maintained, and revealed secrets. For Barnum, this performance was the auspicious start to an auspicious career in chicanery and trickery. As James W. Cook has recently argued, even in this first foray into staging hoaxes Barnum already understood that the way to generate the most interest was to invite the possibility that the very thing he was passing off as authentic was inauthentic, so that in posing the two viewpoints simultaneously he generated even greater controversy (and ticket sales) than if he had simply defended Heth's authenticity. In subsequent advertising, Barnum layered this controversy carefully—not only did he actually invite speculation as to whether Heth really was Washington's nurse, he also introduced the possibility that she might not even be a real person at all but rather a cleverly constructed automaton, a stage magician's machine designed to create a fabulous illusion. To arrive at the central secret of who Joice Heth *was* required penetrating multiple walls of the fortress of trickery Barnum built around her.

Where for Barnum Heth was a product to be exploited, this black woman's own attitude about her involvement with the showman and her performance is unknown to history. As there is practically no known record of her perspective, one must speculate as to what *her* secrets were. It is tempting to see her as participating in the act as a way of empowering herself at a moment when black women's mobility and economic opportunities were severely restricted. It is possible that she was playing the system in order to obtain status otherwise unattainable for her. Yet the fact is that she was to some extent Barnum's property, purchased as an "act" from another white male performer.[1] Thus controlled and in a sense enslaved, she seems not to have achieved any real independence, especially in light of the fact that it was Barnum who evidently pocketed the revenue generated by the performance and who went on to fame and wealth. Whatever the case, Heth took the secrets of her own reasons for and goals in participating in the show to her grave, leaving an inscrutable narrative behind.

What emerges from the Heth-Barnum case is that both figures were tricksters, for it was revealed after Heth's death (as if it were not already obvious) that she had not lived much past eighty years. Both were perpetrating a hoax, a fact that makes their interconnection highly difficult to read. In the sticky dynamics of their relationship, they apparently played off of one another as well as the public: one wonders what their conversations must have been like, for even as it is patently clear that Barnum was exploiting her, she was herself clearly performing a sophisticated and convincing role. It could be that their relationship exemplified a kind of Hegelian interdependence with Barnum realizing that he needed her in order to make his fortune. She, meanwhile, was clearly limited in her economic mobilities and was thus to some degree compelled to participate in the performance. Both Heth and Barnum were embroiled—in voluntary as well as involuntary ways—in the highly complex, flexible, and multivalent thing that is secrecy.

The power of the web of secrecy is immense, and Heth and Barnum's "relationship" is a theatrical example of the ways that both white and black people in the nineteenth century maneuvered or were maneuvered by, the need to keep things hidden about their lives, their identities, their pasts. Thomas Jefferson's interracial relationship is now well known, and many such affairs of prominent white southern men who promoted sharp racial division have emerged since, while male slaveowners' rape of black women has been much documented. While these relationships featured varied degrees of exploitation—perhaps it was possible that in some cases both parties willingly participated in them with something closer to equal amounts of affection—the dynamics of secrecy connected with them were pernicious and invariably put the parties involved in compromising positions. Moreover, these relationships say nothing of the other kinds of activities that both white and black people kept hidden during the nineteenth century, whether it was their involvement with the Underground Railroad or racial passing.

If the nineteenth century was characterized by such fraught matters of hiddenness and race, the twentieth was hardly different. If African Americans possessed greater mobility by the time of the Harlem Renaissance, passing remained a necessity in realizing a mobility as free as that of white people. If slavery was no more, segregation created spaces of division that were the essence of the principle of secrecy. Racist-driven persecution was carried out under the hooded cloak of the Ku Klux Klan, yet for a white person openly to defend interracial mixing of any kind could lead to social ostracism and even physical harm in many parts of the United States. Relationships of whatever kind between men and women of different races continued to be tortured, as writers as diverse as Richard Wright and Erskine Caldwell showed in *Uncle Tom's Children* and *Trouble in July*, respectively.

This book is about the ways in which people on both sides of the color line have been and are interpolated in and performing in secrecy by considering a body of work that is exemplary in its treatment of these matters. The body of work is a group of one-act plays written during the Harlem Renaissance by Marita Bonner, Mary P. Burrill, Thelma Duncan, Shirley Graham, Zora Neale Hurston, Georgia Douglas Johnson, May Miller, and Eulalie Spence. Their plays provide a fitting site for such an exploration because they portray the intricate inner workings of secrecy, and they do so because the playwrights were themselves embroiled in secrecy as black women struggling to negotiate a white patriarchal-dominated society. For them secrecy was a part of their lives that they could also wield as a mode of social negotiation both in and beyond their writing of one-act plays.

The book will proceed in three phases. First, I will discuss the machinery of secrecy in the context of African American culture, paying particular attention to magic (both secular and religious) as the prime theatrical mode of performing a poetics of secrecy in an interracial context. In the second section, I will explore secrecy and magic in a selected group of the one-acts by these women, showing the interconnections among these works within the context of the multiply interpolated tapestry of secrecy of which they are a part. The volume's final section is labeled "Exeunt" to counterbalance this "Induction," and in it I will ponder the book's implications and problems regarding the politics of performance in interracial interaction, primarily in the academy.

The final section and its aims are grandiose and tortured, the highly problematic conclusion to a highly problematic book. One problem with this volume is that the probing of secrets itself is a tenuous endeavor, a groping about for something that is by its nature elusive. This elusiveness leads to another problem, which is that once secrecy is introduced as a site of investigation, the avenues it touches proliferate rapidly and exponentially. For example, as one reads these one-acts and sees their similarities, one may not be able to help but wonder if these women together created a sort of in-group coding, producing a body of work intentionally designed to keep and reveal certain secrets. Yet the fact is that although these women knew each other, they did not form a formal writing group with any strict aesthetic principles or goals. Indeed, the very grouping of these women (who were not the only ones writing one-acts at the time) in this volume, which is really my own grouping, is arbitrary and even artificial. Or, at least it probably is—perhaps what history has no record of is that these women *did* secretly collaborate in inculcating their plays with shared imagery precisely to have it decoded by a scholar. Probably not.

And there is one other problem, a big one that I will address explicitly at the end of the book although I have already introduced it and will touch on it throughout. For now, let me conclude this induction by saying that my goal in this book is to bring these plays, which have been heretofore largely unknown (in a sense secret), greater attention from readers and scholars, and I hope that in the process secrecy will be more generally recognized as the fundamental aspect of social interaction that it is. At the same time, this book is designed to bring illusion into visibility, to foreground the vexing threat of trickery and the final unresolvability of magic and the ways that such unresolvability touches everything from the writing of drama to the writing of literary criticism, especially in the context of the politics of interracial involvement, which at the time I am writing (during the 2008 presidential election year) are clearly of as crucial significance as ever in the United States. Ultimately, these one-acts offer a highly fecund site for a multitude of investigations, and this volume hopefully takes a step toward manifesting the entire dimensions of that site by modeling a way that these largely forgotten plays can speak to culture not only in their historical moment but in our own.[2]

On Secrecy, Magic,
& BLACK WOMEN
PLAYWRIGHTS

BONNER, BURRILL, Duncan, Graham, Hurston, Johnson, Miller, and Spence wrote about and themselves participated in black women's negotiations of the hegemony of white men, white women, and even black men in the United States.[1] They did so by drawing upon and generating techniques of secrecy through forms of both secular and religious magic. These techniques were necessary because the groups that stood in opposition to them to various degrees and in various ways themselves were embroiled in and operated through and within secrecy. In order to understand how these black women writers worked in this mode, it is necessary to articulate the specifics of secrecy and magic in their lives and the ways that from their perspective these other groups as well as they themselves were interpolated in a widespread web of secrecy.

That secrecy has been central to African American performance has been noted by numerous scholars. During the era of slavery, secret tactics were utilized in multiple ways. Frederick Douglass explains that slaves would "universally say they are contented, and that their masters are kind" when asked about such things by white people (even strangers) because the "slaveholders have been known to send in spies among their slaves, to ascertain their views and feelings in regard to their condition," creating the slave maxim "that a still tongue makes a wise head" (*Narrative* 62). Additionally, as

Albert J. Raboteau has explained, slaves met in "hush harbors" to practice their own forms of religion in secret, while passing was a distinctly theatrical way for light-skinned African Americans to keep secret their race in order to enter white spaces and participate to some degree in the privilege found there.[2] In a more subtle vein, as Henry Louis Gates Jr. has famously argued, games of Signifyin[g] permitted (and has since permitted) African Americans to speak in coded ways to protect their secrets while providing a deceptive text for white outsiders. Such coding also characterized slave spirituals, which were crucial to African American survival, as Eileen Southern has argued.

As slavery drew to an end and the Jim Crow era began, additional forms of secrecy developed. The Underground Railroad had been a mode of secret escape, and now Black Masons and other secret societies provided protective and empowering spaces, a form of segregation that was community-confirming as opposed to the oppressive segregation developing primarily in the southern states.[3] This time period also saw more black people donning minstrel masks, which could be a move designed to counteract white-defined notions of essentialized blackness.[4] Houston A. Baker Jr. (in *Modernism and the Harlem Renaissance*) as well as Gates (in *Figures in Black*) have shown the subversive capabilities of such appropriations of masks, with Baker taking things a step further by identifying a "phaneric" as well as a "cryptic" mask; where the latter was essentially a minstrel mask worn by Booker T. Washington and others, the former was worn by W. E. B. Du Bois and was "meant to advertise. It distinguishes rather than conceals. It secures territorial advantage and heightens a group's survival possibilities" (51).

These techniques of protecting secrets depended on and operated within the multiply interpolated machinery of secrecy. Although not often theorized or evoked in literary criticism, secrecy is fundamental to social negotiation, identity formation, and even writing itself.[5] It can incarnate as a space, a function, a condition, a situation, or a strategy. Most important, theorizing secrecy is necessary to understand the resplendent complexity of African American performance and its functions in responding to white oppression and its own secrets, and to deepening our grasp of those secrecy tactics already mentioned and exposing additional ones as written about by the black women whose work is this volume's focus.

I

Sissela Bok, in her voluminous *Secrets: On the Ethics of Concealment and Revelation,* perhaps best explains the fluid nature of secrecy as a mode of social negotiation. She begins her exploration by discussing the signifiers that denote secrecy in various languages, citing the Latin words *secretum* and *arcanum*, which signify the ideas of "something hidden, set apart" and "the daunting and the fascinating, dread and allure" (6), respectively. From the frightening she turns to the warm and cozy, noting that the German word *heimlich* originally signified "the home, the hearth, the intimate; later, it took on the added meaning of something kept from the view of strangers and finally also of all that is secret" (7). Meanwhile, the Swedish word *lönn* refers to "lying, denial, and every form of deceit" (7). The overtones of these various words are subtle, and while, after discussing several additional ones, Bok sums up by suggesting that "the hidden is part of the meaning of all" of them, she also acknowledges that "the different shadings of each one—whether of something sacred, intimate, private, unspoken, silent, prohibited, shameful, stealthy, or deceitful—come together in our understanding of the meanings of the secret and of secrecy" (7). She also notes that "[w]e cannot encompass all these meanings in a single definition; for while they form a family of related meanings, they are not always present together in any one instance of secrecy" (7). Actually, just how tight-knit that "family of related meanings" is itself looms as a large question, as Bok proceeds to develop an intriguing discussion of secrecy that traces the various situations in which it is used, from espionage to secret societies.

For Bok, secrecy is an ethical necessity for individual or group autonomy but its use must be a measured balance of hiddenness and unhiddenness. In order to maintain the privacy essential to individuality, one must have the freedom to have one's secrets. Secrets, in this sense, are thus implicitly figured as property, a vital aspect of the concept of private ownership, illustrated by the fact that secret information can be purchased. Yet, at the same time that secrecy is necessary and too much openness threatens individual or even group rights, too much secrecy can be both intentionally and unintentionally harmful. For instance, withholding important health information can protect an individual's privacy regarding her having a sexually transmitted disease, but if she keeps that information secret she violates a partner's rights to information and she can physically harm that person. In the ethics of concealment and revelation, there must be a constant search for the most proper and/or effective possible balance of hiddenness.

It is in the regulation of what can be an uneasy balancing act that the true complexities of secrecy emerge; part of this complexity is due to the paradoxical machinery of hiddenness itself. Malcolm Bull describes this subtlety, exploring what he calls the "coming into hiddenness" that accompanies a thing's very existence, its very coming into visibility. He argues that things feature an "inescapable hiddenness" that is the simultaneous other side of what is unhidden, so that the one is constituted by the other in perception even though the hidden aspect or aspects can never be perceived simultaneously with the unhidden. He takes, for example, the word *port:* in a certain context it "means the place where ships dock" and "even though the inscription itself is right in front of you it will not even suggest a fortified wine, and nothing of its other meaning(s) will be perceived" (25). "However," he explains, "provided that you are conversant with both meanings of the word, there is no reason why, in an appropriate context, you should not alternate between the two" (25). It is the impossibility of simultaneity of perception that constitutes hiddenness and causes secrecy to emerge as a fundamental part of constituting a thing. The perceiver may even be aware of the other sides of things, but is limited by perception. Thus Wittgenstein's rabbit and duck can only ever be a rabbit or a duck in a single act of perception even if the perceiver is aware of both readings of the image. Indeed, as Bull points out, nothing could be more unhidden than Poe's purloined letter, which is so effectively concealed in plain sight.

Because of the machinery of perception, therefore, things are inscribed within a necessary secrecy, and this principle includes people and the processes of identity-formation. Bull cites Walt Whitman's evocation of multiple selves in "Song of Myself" to show that each recognition of a self highlights a self not previously seen. Identity itself is a coming into hiddenness as the other perceives one aspect of the multilayered thing that is the self. In this economy of seeing (Bull stresses that hiddenness is inextricably bound to sight, even when connected with other senses), the subject-forming in the mirror stage itself alienates certain constitutions of the self in the recognition of and by the other so that not only does the perceiving other split the self into hiddenness and unhiddenness in that other's perception, but presumably nonperceived parts of the self become hidden even to the perceiving self. The subject herself is thus vexed by the hidden, and it is precisely this fear of the secret self that Leslie Fiedler argues is the dreadful fascination and repulsion of the "freak." The self is thus interpolated in secrecy, both externally (from the perceiving other) and internally (in the sense of the self as externally constructed).

The ineluctable presence of secrecy within perception and its role in identity formation is especially helpful in considering the multiply interpolated role of perception in African American identity. Du Bois's Veil is dense with the aura of secrecy. It is a divider, something that stands between, keeps separate, and hides, but as a figure it also signals the nuances of perception. In the Hegelian-influenced dynamic of this figure in black identity, the white denial of recognition is a form of secreting, hiding, making opaque. At the same time, as Fanon would later argue, life within the Veil would at certain points in history make a number of black people's own cultures and concerns secret even to themselves, denied as they could be of self-consciousness and continually groping for white consciousness and experience. Moreover, Du Bois assigns to the Veil specific folk cultural elements of perception by casting it as the caul which gives its wearer the gift of second sight, the ability literally to see things which are hidden but nonetheless present—ghosts invisibly haunting consciousness.

This presentness of the hidden is significant, for not only is the self formed in perception, but that very perceiving self grows out of a state of secrecy that remains immanent even as it is invisible. Resurrecting the *chora* (receptacle) from Plato's *Timaeus,* Julia Kristeva identifies it as the realm of the primal semiotic. An "essentially mobile and extremely provisional articulation constituted by movements and their ephemeral stases" (*Revolution in Poetic Language* 25), the *chora* is the deeply articulated space of the drives that is presymbolic, which is to say that it is unregulated by and not translated into the order, which is itself patriarchal. Kristeva addresses language as representative of this symbolic order, a "logical" system of signification. Unlike the symbolic, the semiotic expresses differently, responding organically to deep bodily inflections. Thus the "*chora* is a modality of significance in which the linguistic sign is not yet articulated as the absence of an object and as the distinction between real and symbolic" (26). It is rather the realm of "concrete operations" which "precede the acquisition of language, and organize preverbal semiotic space according to logical categories, which are thereby shown to precede or transcend language" (27). The *chora* therefore is "a preverbal functional state that governs the connections between the body (in the process of constituting itself as body proper), objects, and the protagonists of family structure," a functioning different from the "symbolic operations that depend on language as a sign system—whether the language [*langue*] is vocalized or gestural (as with deaf-mutes)" (27). Because it precedes and transcends the symbolic order, the *chora* is even more "unknown" than the unconscious, which is the space of repressed memories that were at least once known and can return to consciousness. As Kristeva writes, the semiotic

> is not, therefore, cognitive in the sense of being assumed by a knowing, already constituted subject. The genesis of the *functions* organizing the semiotic process can be accurately elucidated only within a theory of the subject that does not reduce the subject to one of understanding, but instead opens up within the subject this other scene of presymbolic functions. (27)

I am reading the *chora* as the somatic-psychic space of secrecy in which the multivalent self (a proliferation of selves) is ensconced.[6] The *chora* is the ultimate secret self, the soft body encased in the carapace of consciousness, the supreme testimony to the fact that the subject is always already ensconced and interpolated in secrecy. Beyond perception of the self by either the other or the self, secrecy is thus a fundamental aspect of being-in-the-world (to continue this shift from the Husserlian to the Heideggerian) and is inextricably linked to identity formation not only in terms of perception but even in the very miasmic churnings that spew forth the multivalent subject. This inaccessible and invisible space's immanence haunts consciousness, being part of what insulates the individual as individual, because its unpredictable and inscrutable nature is the indispensable secret core of autonomy.

This space of secrecy, deeply embedded within the subject (or perhaps it is the secret ocean upon which the self floats—the source of the "oceanic" that so obsesses Freud in *Civilization and Its Discontents*) as a kind of ghost space immanent but necessarily unknown—might be thought of as a figure applicable in a large sense to the color line itself and to black people as a body. The white Western imagination has considered African Americans as unknown in the same sense as the *chora* is, and white stereotypes have throughout history cast black people as animalistic, spinal, earthly, and characterized by excessive corporeality and sexuality—in short, as denizens of libidinal drives. There is an inherent mystery in stereotypes of the descendants of the "Dark Continent." Moving to the other side of this double interpolation, African Americans have at times bolstered this mystery for their own protection and empowerment. Kristeva observes that the moment when a concept, emotion, or reaction originating in the *chora* is spoken, it has entered the symbolic order and is no longer semiotic, the *chora* erupting instead in nonsymbolic ways and thus in its persistent unknowableness refuses to signify, at least and again, within the economy of the symbolic. Certain forms of Signifyin(g) can be seen as this kind of semiotic breach in the symbolic.

Because the *chora* erupts as an inscrutable presence, presenting itself as the unknowable, it makes the interesting move of making that unknowability known precisely as unknowability—a revelation of the fact of hiddenness. To evoke the cliché that the only thing to fear is fear itself is to observe that one must create the awareness of the existence of fear in order for fear to be generated. Likewise, it is with the awareness of the fact that something is hidden that a secret is born as a player in social interaction. In what might seem a surprising reversal, secrecy may as readily be seen as a participant in the *visible* and *accessible* as it is the *invisible* and *inaccessible*. Whether in terms of the dynamics of seeing or in the unknowableness of the *chora*, secrecy registers a poetic of *presence* rather than *absence*. It marks a point on a scale of hiddenness and unhiddenness, visibility and invisibility, the known and the unknown. This marked point is that of balance within a given situation, and it is important to remember that what is seeable is just as crucial in this balance as what is not.

Where secrecy *as a process* marks this point of balance, the secret *as an item* is the concretization of that process—the marker itself. A secret is, in a sense, itself a type of receptacle, a kind of cardboard box marked not with the words "dishes" or "boxes" or even "fragile" or "handle with care," but rather simply "unknown," announcing itself precisely as a species of interaction, communication, and expression that signifies as resisting revelation despite the fact that the revelation of its very existence is a revelation. To say "I have a secret" is to say that "I have something to say but am not saying it," thus striking a pose within a dialectic of avowal and disavowal.

The secret as an item of social exchange can in fact be seen as fetishistic. Signifying the aura of the unknown, metonymically standing in for all figures of unknowableness, a secret as such can generate and/or contain a complex of desires by the very fact that it is pregnant with inaccessible content made conspicuous by its very inaccessibility. Claiming to possess a secret creates conspicuousness—hence the appeal of a "mysterious" person or situation. It is this sort of fetishistic dynamic that D. A. Miller evidently has in mind when venturing that "I have had to intimate my secret, if only not to tell it and conversely, in theatrically continuing to keep my secret, I have already *given it away*" (194). Barthes makes a similar point in regard to the "ultimate triangle" of the stripper's G-string, which is "the irrefutable symbol of the absolute object" that is a part of the nakedness that is itself the "*natural* vesture of woman, which amounts in the end to regaining a perfectly chaste state of the flesh" (85) in what is, for Barthes, a performance that brings about a supreme coming into hiddenness. In the radical division between secrets as details kept hidden and the secret as a type of communicative object, the latter functions as a visible and well-known figure with a specific mode of referentiality, and this dynamic can be seen at work, for example, in the sort of minstrel and phaneric masking that Baker identifies in Washington's and Du Bois's rhetoric, respectively.[7]

Not to say that this dialectic of concealment and revelation is always or ever entirely intentional. There is validity to Miller's assertion that "secrecy would seem to be a mode whose ultimate meaning lies in the subject's formal insistence that he is radically inaccessible to the culture that would otherwise entirely determine him" (195). But, as I observed earlier, the multivalent subject is presumably no more capable of perceiving her own hiddenness than is the perceiving other. Additionally, the *chora* is incapable of articulation within the symbolic, and even the unconscious is a space and function of secrecy that operates in ways that escape and compromise intention. Fur-

thermore, the act of secreting responds to complex situations that are themselves inflected with secrecy, as Luise White observes that keeping a "secret
isn't something a self does, it's something that continually has to be reconsti-
tuted and renegotiated through changing political and discursive practices"
(22). Because subtle and varied forces surround, affect, and contain the multivalent subject, subtle and varied responses to those forces are required. The
subject is therefore interpolated in secrecy not only within pereception and
that subject's somatic-psychic makeup but also within situation.[8]

Some attention should therefore be given to secrecy in and as situation.
Stanton K. Tefft well defines the situational incarnations of secrecy through
his application of conflict theory. He writes that "[c]onflicts of interest
between individuals and groups over values, prestige, power, wealth, control
of resources, or political goals initiate processes of social interaction which
include information control (secrecy)" ("Secrecy, Disclosure, and Social
Theory" 63). This situational model is, for Tefft, one that is largely based on
the participants' conscious intentions, although it is intriguing to consider
the role of the unconscious in utilizing this "social resource which oppo-
nents can use defensively or offensively during social conflicts" (63). The
particular directions of this offensive-defensive maneuvering vary in their
goals depending on whether groups oppose other groups, individuals oppose
those of the out-group, or individuals oppose others in their in-group. As
Tefft argues, the "actions and reactions of individuals, organizations, and
political communities to each other depends not only [on] how they perceive
these to be threatened by outsiders" for "[i]ndividuals and the organizations
to which they belong determine the rewards or costs of secrecy or disclosure
in terms of their own self-interest as the conflict with outsiders intensifies or
dissipates" (63). Thus whatever "the structural sources of conflict, and they
may be many and varied, secrecy plays a role in conflict-group formation
and the dynamics of conflict itself" so that the "more intense the conflict
the greater the efforts to conceal information from antagonists" while the
conflict "also leads to in-group cohesion by setting group boundaries and
strengthening group cohesiveness. Often secrecy norms help maintain such
social boundaries and contribute to group cohesiveness" (51).

However intentional this "information control" may be, again, secrecy
takes on a situational life of its own. Secrets begin to be used to counteract
other secrets, as "[a]ntagonists who keep secrets from one another, must
employ security devices to protect such secrets" (63). This interaction is
influenced by factors far beyond individual control, since the "nature as well
as the effectiveness of such security systems are determined by social structural, cultural, economic, ecological, and political factors" (63). What seems
evident is that secrecy is constituted as a discursive form, a mode of dis-

course that, like language itself, is externally and socially constructed. To ply secrets is to participate in an overarching framework of discursivity. This is not to say that secrets cannot be connected to or based in material, but rather that the various forces within situations of secrecy are mediated by discursive measures of secreting. Even hiding material evidence is accompanied by discursive strategy (if only implicitly and covertly) and is ensconced in a discursive context that makes that secreting meaningful.

Tefft's nomenclature signals the game aspects of this situation, and one might think of such situations as games of what could be labeled "secrecy-discourse." Game theory, in its most basic sense, provides a helpful way of thinking such situations because it provides explanations and vocabulary to make sense of them: players in game situations enact certain strategic moves in order to achieve their desired payoffs.[9] Game play is dictated by the necessity of achieving a situational equilibrium that posits levels and types of payoffs, and this balancing is, as has been noted, crucial to secreting. Moreover the applicability of game theory to the dynamics of secrecy is well reflected in the gaming aspect of African American Signifyin(g), passing, and the kinds of masking that have already been mentioned.

Games of secrecy-discourse are necessarily inscribed within specific cultural situations, making them difficult to describe in a general way; nevertheless, certain principles of secrecy-discourse game situations can be discerned. Specifically, such situations are played out by means of certain "secrecy-moves." These moves may take one or more of the following forms: silence, lying, and coding.[10] The shadings of difference among these types of moves are slight, and one can often enact the function of others. But each features a distinct type of principle. Silence, for instance, does not necessarily deceive but can nevertheless be a form of lying. By lying, I mean a performance of signs deliberately designed to deceive an opponent; as Bok writes, a lie is "any intentionally deceptive message which is stated, but can of course also be conveyed" as she drolly puts it, "via smoke signals, Morse Code, sign language, and the like" (*Lying* 13). What I am not including in lying (although it can be a form of lying) is a form of signage that uses double-signification intelligible to an ally but unintelligible to the enemy. Such double-signifying is coding, and coding operates in especially subtle ways interconnected with in-group/out-group dynamics.[11]

In addition to these general principles of secrecy-moves, it should be noted that, perhaps in accord with its Hegelian aspect, secrecy is often connected with situations of social inequity. While it can certainly be the case that people of equal social status, gender, race, and so on can come into conflict that requires information control, it is usually the case that, as Tefft notes, secrecy "enables the powerful to escape accountability for their exploitation and manipulation of the weak and enables the weak to escape coercion by the powerful and to oppose them" (76). Carol Warren and Barbara Laslett address this difference between the secrets of the empowered and those of the unempowered. The former they refer to as "public-life secrets," which they define as "secrecy on the part of those in power and their agents, acting purportedly in the public interest" (29). These secrets are those of empowered institutions, and Warren and Laslett identify their agents as including "FBI and CIA officers, plainclothes police officers, and government bureaucrats of various types. They may also include human behavior researchers and journalists" (29). Governmental investigations are top secret because they have to be: FBI agents, CIA officers, journalists, and so on "are secretive by virtue of their political role" for the "ideological justification of public-life secrecy is the seeking out and elimination of 'undesirable elements' in society—elements that might threaten the control of the powerful" (29). Thus, Warren and Laslett provocatively add, "the object of public-life secrecy is the discovery of how the ostensibly private roles of others are in fact relevant to public life" (29). Public-life secrets are precisely the sorts of government-affirming secrets that Socrates believed are necessary for the establishment of a republic, and in a moment when racial and ethnic profiling have entered into official and unofficial policies of US governmental institutions and officers (and have especially touched African Americans), it is easy to see their function.[12]

Opposed to public-life secrets are "private-life secrets." This term refers to "secrecy about one's personal life rather than to secrecy in relation to political roles of other persons" and in action it "is the concealment of attributes, actions, or relationships that, if discovered, might bring harm to the individuals or groups engaged in them" (29). Warren and Laslett explain that this form of secrecy's "justification is less an independent ideological one than a response to ideology: a desire to avert the full wrath of whatever powerful groups are in control of the definition of 'undesirable elements'" (29). Moreover, where public-life secrets are "active and directed at the lives of others," private-life secrets are "passive and protective of the self" (30) and "would most likely be [used] where persons are morally stigmatized or where they have inadequate financial or other resources to provide themselves with privacy" (31). Although these private-life secrets would seem to apply to African Americans, Warren and Laslett do not consider race as a factor in secrecy, yet their assigning this kind of secrecy to the "morally stigmatized" and financially inadequate is revealing. They conclude that they "expect that secrecy would be utilized more by lower than higher status persons, by children and the institutionalized elderly rather than adults, by the mentally and physically ill more than the healthy, and by the morally stigmatized more

than the 'normal'" (31). Of course they would, for "normal" signifies confor-
mity, voluntarily and/or coincidentally, to dominant ideology, which seeks to
weed out nonconformity under the rapacious cloak of public-life secrecy.

Along with these game situation-defined *functions* of secrecy, the actual
content-types of secrets dictate their value and role in social exchange.
Robert E. Regan identifies three types of secrets: first, there is the *natural
secret,* so called because "the obligation of secrecy which it imposes arises
directly from the natural law; no contract, expressed or implied, is needed
to make it binding" (5). The second is the *promised secret,* designated by
the fact that "the obligation of maintaining secrecy is begotten by a *promise*
given and accepted" (6). Third in the list is the *entrusted* (also referred to as
a *committed) secret* "whose obligation arises from an agreement, given and
received antecedently to any disclosure, that the secret matter will be rigor-
ously guarded" (7).[13] Regan observes that these types of secrets possess an
"obliging force" resulting from "the specific malice involved in their violation" (20); the "moral obligation of guarding a *natural* secret is, in general, a
serious one" while that of "guarding a merely *promised* secret is, generally, a
slight one . . . due to the fact that a merely promised secret binds according
to the intention of the one promising" except in the case of "a serious obligation in justice" or when a promised secret is also a natural one (20–21).
The moral obligation of an entrusted secret is "a serious one, and generally
more serious than that attaching to the natural or merely promised secret"
(21).

The varying degrees of moral and ethical weight attached to natural, promised, and entrusted secrets are affected if not determined by the culturally
specific circumscriptions of secrecy-discourse game situations within which
ethical distinctions emerge, and these situations are generally not monolithic
but rather are sites of overlapping situations each with its own ethical hierarchy. Not only do multiple players adopt multiple strategies, they are also
playing in multiple games simultaneously and the different game situations
they encounter can be tinged by the other game situations in which they are
operating. This intersecting is another reason why multiple players or groups
of players are interpolated in secrecy, for in the unhiddenness of playing one
game, other games become hidden but no less related or present.

This situational intersection can be found painfully enacted in Claude
Lévi-Strauss's encounter with a Nambikwara village in *Tristes Tropiques.*
Lévi-Strauss relates the way that he tricks a group of girls into telling him the
names of the people in the tribe—which was information the tribe had been
keeping secret apparently to maintain a protective space from the anthropologist, although Lévi-Strauss simply asserts that "the use of proper names
was taboo" (335). Lévi-Strauss explains that upon one occasion when he is

playing with the children of the village, one of the little girls hits another one, and the assaulted girl goes to him "to confide what seemed to be solemn secret" (336), which turns out to be the girl's name. "From then on," Lévi-Strauss writes, "it was very easy, although rather unscrupulous, to incite the children against each other and get to know all their names. After which, having created a certain atmosphere of complicity, I had little difficulty in getting them to tell me the names of the adults" (336).[14] This account manifests multiple games of secrecy-discourse. Lévi-Strauss as the white European anthropologist is an emissary of public-life secrecy, an upholder of Western dominant ideology, who plays a game of learning about (and arguably colonizing) another culture with that learning (colonizing) being his payoff. The Nambikwarans may or may not be fully aware of the nature of his game, but whether they are or not he is frustrated in his game by the fact that the Nambikwarans keep their names hidden (he has even begun to give them names of his own making to distinguish them). In the meantime, the girls have their own literal unnamed game, and when one of them loses, she quits playing it and begins her own game in which she gives away a natural (and possibly entrusted) private life secret, which in turn leads Lévi-Strauss to establish a new coercive game.

Intersecting games situations thus generate additional ones as secrecy-moves and countermoves proliferate, and these new secrecy-discourse games can be created in a couple of ways. In the case of the Nambikwara girl, when she leaves her own game and starts a new one she is behaving as what Johan Huizinga calls a "spoil-sport." This figure "is not the same as the false player, the cheat; for the latter pretends to be playing the game and, on the face of it, still acknowledges the magic circle" of the game (30). A spoil-sport tends to receive harsh retribution from the other players (and indeed the girl is heavily chastised for her behavior by the other Nambikwarans) because such a figure "shatters the play-world itself. By withdrawing from the game he reveals the relativity and fragility of the play-world in which he had temporarily shut himself with others. He robs play of its *illusion*" (30). Such a Bartleby-esque figure "must be cast out, for he threatens the existence of the play-community. . . . The spoil-sport breaks the magic world, therefore he is a coward and must be ejected" (30). Huizinga goes on to note that sometimes "spoil-sports in their turn make a new community with rules of its own. The outlaw, the revolutionary, the cabbalist or member of a secret society, indeed heretics of all kinds are of a highly associative if not sociable disposition, and a certain element of play is prominent in all their doings" (30).

A new secrecy-discourse game can be established also when a player actually plays to lose. Such a tactic, according to Michael Beaujour, implies a victory on some other level. . . . The desire to play a game in reverse [to lose] usually arises when the straight way of playing has become a bore, or when the usual kind of victory appears self-defeating. The rules of the game which, although arbitrary, had somewhere become "natural" to the players, now seem "artificial," tyrannical and dead: the system does not allow for sufficient *play* or freedom within it, and must be discarded. (62)

The important thing to note is that such "discarding" in a certain game field means migrating to another field, which operates on the very same rules, however different the situation may be, for "only a system can replace a system . . . it is but the moment of a 'new deal'" (62). Beaujour adds the observation that "playing a serious game in order to lose is a very sophisticated behavior" and it "will be felt to be a return to nature and to whatever is fundamental, universal and spontaneous in man. This is merely the illusion attendant on the break-down of old rules, when the new ones are not yet formulated" (62).

The briar-patch quality of these strategies for deconstructing oppressive secrecy-discourse game situations are clearly discernable in the recognized African American secrecy-discourse moves that have already been noted. The silence tactics of slaves mentioned by Douglass and Raboteau and the interpretation-based coding Baker and Gates recognize are secrecy-moves, with Du Bois's form of masking arguably being a form of rule breaking that realigns racial performance that powerfully paves the way for the artistic and cultural blossoming that was the Harlem Renaissance. What the foregoing discussion of the game aspect of secrecy hopefully helps further do is accentuate the reciprocally constitutive nature of secrecy, its dialectic functioning within which multiple players, both white and black, male and female, are interpolated. P. T. Barnum, it should now be evident, was an agent and purveyor of public-life secrecy, for the core of his hoax confirmed white racism, however much he may have encouraged other forms of debate. The problematic thing about his rhetoric is that he was negotiating two different in-groups—that of other whites in the United States but also the one he at least tacitly formed with Heth, which was further complicated by his own individual goals. Heth herself remains inscrutable: complicitous with Barnum to some degree, she aided in his promulgation of public-life secrecy, managing a skillful game of outright lying in order to negotiate a hegemonic but also, to some degree, vulnerable white out-group in the process of what might be seen as a heroic playing of white expectations were it not for the fact that she seems to have been regrettably cut off from her own in-group. By simply making a living within interconnecting spheres of secrecy she appears to have ended up in a final sad isolation, buried in ultimate secrecy.

II

In order fully to parse secrecy and the ways that multiple groups and individuals are interpolated in and wielding it in interracial interaction in the United States, it must be understood how secrecy is also theatrical and how that theatricality incarnates in the form of magic which itself is multivalent and complexly interpolated. I have already hinted at the reciprocities between secrecy and theater. The space of secrecy-discourse is a theatrical space as well as a game-space, and Tefft acknowledges that just as conflict theory may be used to describe the social functions of secrecy, so can the "dramaturgical model" be applied, which sees "the social world [as] structured in terms of the interactions of individuals, scripts, other players (team members) and various audiences" (40–41). African American culture has been tinged by both formal theater and *theatrum mundi* from its origins, for Carol Allen notes that "the slave auction and the plantation fashion a 'show business' of sorts" (1), and alongside this theater of cruelty (and not the liberating and positive revolutionary kind Antonin Artaud envisioned) emerged minstrelsy, in which black bodies serving as fetishes turned performance into a tour de force. I have already mentioned the theatricality of passing and black minstrelsy as an obvious subversion of a theatrical tradition just as much as it is a form of game play. But a deeper look into theatricality and its spatial overtones helps expose additional aspects of secrecy in African American experience and performance.

I should first note why I evoke "theatricality" instead of, or at least along with, "performance" as a concept for discussing secrecy. Both concepts make unhidden the fact that "playing" is also performing (actors as players/gamers as players), that the "seeing" of selves outlined earlier is the other side of "performance" of selves, and that game moves are the same things as performance "strategies" discussed by such theorists as Bourdieu and Certeau. The matter of performance in the context of theater, however, grows particularly attenuated, for the term then takes on, if possible, an ever greater opacity. Indeed, I want to focus on theatricality not only because this volume ultimately focuses on playwrights, but because theatricality necessitates more concrete structures of display and makes imperative the act and manipulation of seeing in ways that performance does not necessarily do. Theater scholars have eyed "performance theory" as it is appropriated by multiple disciplines with some doubt, with Thomas Postlewait and Tracy C. Davis wryly observing that the

> idea of performance, certainly, is a compelling explanatory construct. Its many facets are exciting for those to whom, apparently, this is a new idea.

> But the desire to characterize performance as a comprehensive idea, even a system, has often been done not only in ignorance of the complicated history of the concept but also in disregard for its capacity to be imprecise. (33–34)

Performance cannot be abandoned as foundational in examining subjectivity and social interaction, but thinking in terms of theatricality allows for thinking through the connections between theater proper and the world.[15]

Theatricality in the context of conscious performance refers to all aspects of drama beyond and including the written text. As Bernard Beckerman observes in *Dynamics of Drama,* the written script of a play "is a mere skeleton; performance fleshes out the bones. Reading an 'unfinished' play script depends upon the governing vision of one's spectacles" (3). In theater's poetics of "occurring," what "happens" is what "finishes" the play. "Activity is the basic medium of theater," Beckerman explains. "It is the only channel through which presentational ideas can be projected and so the art of the theater is the art of manipulating activity" (13). Theater, however, includes more than just performance. As Ric Knowles observes in developing his theory of what he calls "material semiotics" of theater, the phenomenon of theater includes the performance text, the conditions of the production, and the conditions of reception. Knowles points out that "each pole of this triangle is constituted by multiple and multiply encoded systems of production, systems of communication, and systems of reception, all working in concert or tension both within their own 'corner,' and along the axes that hold the poles together and in tension with one another" (19).[16] It is this attention to factors such as the structures of space, situational variables, and audience makeup that make theatricality a more useful concept than performance because such elements take into account the architecture and machinery, whether material or not, that undergird performativity.

Theater/theatricality has historically carried its own issues of secrecy, often with negative connotations. Theater throws into relief the problems of artifice and mimesis that have drawn the ire of thinkers from Plato to Nietzsche because it raises the same sorts of vexed issues of subjectivity with which postmodernism, most recently, has grappled. But it does so by creating yet another level of performance (i.e., performing selves performing), a situation that creates a plane of Baudrillardian precession of simulacra that might, such thinkers have feared, merely point to another lying beneath it. The sort of coming into hiddenness that Bull describes thus transfers to the stage and its setting, the actors and the audience, all of which appear and perform not only in their already established multivalence as selves but also in their roles as prescribed by the given theatrical moment. Some forms of theater actually keep themselves secret, an example being Augusto Baol's

"Invisible Theater," in which the actors perform in an informal public setting such as a restaurant without revealing that they are in fact actors and that their activities are part of a preestablished script, even though surrounding "non-actors" are being drawn into the performance and themselves turned into actors as well as spectators.

This matter of visibility is especially trenchant when considering secrecy and theater. As Joseph Roach points out, the word "theater" derives "from the Greek word for seeing and sight" (46), and while he goes on to champion performance as a more expansive and useful concept, it is worth considering the matter of seeing and its attendant issues of visibility and invisibility and their connections with secrecy as a product of seeing. Seeing, or to adopt a more utilized term *the gaze*, signals a theatricality that registers constitutive forces of power as described by Hegel, Lacan, Fanon, and others. In *Discipline and Punish: The Birth of the Prison,* Foucault traces the theatricality of the public spectacle and its subsequent movement into a very different form of invisibility. "The theatre of punishment of which the eighteenth century dreamed and which would have acted essentially on the minds of the general public," Foucault writes, "was replaced by the great uniform machinery of prisons" which in the nineteenth century were characterized by the "high wall, no longer the wall that surrounds and protects, no longer the wall that stands for power and wealth, but the meticulously sealed wall, uncrossable in either direction, closed in upon the now mysterious work of punishment" (116). Within those walls—inside the secret of the prisons—a new visibility prevailed, exemplified in the Panopticon, which was itself designed "to induce in the inmate the conscious and permanent visibility that assures the automatic functioning of power" (21) in which two aspects worked together to establish and maintain power: "Visible: the inmate will constantly have before his eyes the tall outline of the central tower from which he is spied upon. Unverifiable: the inmate must never know whether he is being looked at at any moment; but he must be sure that he may always be so" (201).

In fact, a highly visible and multiply interpolated spectacle drenched with secrecy in an African American context is that of lynching. Kirk W. Fuoss discusses lynching as theater, and this display of black bodies represents a spectacle in which, according to Trudier Harris, whites exorcised their fear of the "Black Beast" stereotype. It is also the case that lynching was touched by secrecy in multiple ways; when the Ku Klux Klan was doing the lynching, the event was obviously being perpetrated by masked members of a secret society, but Jacqueline Goldsby has recently argued that a much wider and insidious secrecy surrounded lynching, for it was not simply an epidemic of the racist US South but rather of a nationwide "cultural logic." She explains that lynching made certain cultural developments and tensions visible for Americans to confront. On the other hand, because lynching's violence was so unspeakably brutal—and crucially, since the lives and bodies of African American people were negligible concerns for the country for so long a time—cultural logic also describes how we have disavowed lynching's normative relation to modernism's history over the last century. Hence, I speak of lynching's "secrecy" as an historical event. (6)[17]

Spatiality is central to these theatrical aspects of secrecy, particularly the fluidity of spatial divides. The visibility of theaters of punishment is manipulated by changing the spaces of these theaters. What Foucault so effectively shows are the ways secret spaces are pragmatically made to signify just as the secret as an item can signify as an object of social negotiation. For Foucault, the high wall itself emerges as a spotlit curtain, the V/veil itself being foregrounded for its secreting function. Yet, again, secrecy and theatrical space can be much more immediately fluid, as is the case in Baol's theater which has no material curtain at all nor even any spatial divide between the actors and the audience, as all present are enlisted as players as well as spectators. Even in conventional formal theater, space and visibility are fluid; at the same time that offstage and hidden sounds and "events" accommodate the rigid dimensions of a stage, dramatic irony results from an audience's "seeing" what a given character cannot.

The technique par excellence of manipulating visibility in fluid theatrical spaces is magic. Explaining the necessity of "activities" in "finishing" the written aspect of the play, Beckerman identifies three different kinds of activities: natural, artificial, and virtual. Natural activities include those that imitate real-life actions. Artificial activities are "made by human skill" and include such skills as "juggling, tap dancing, acrobatics, that are so distinctive in character and so specialized in form that they cannot be recognized as stemming from familiar patterns of behavior. They exist wholly for the purpose of presentation as activities devised and practiced by men to astonish and delight others" (14). Virtual activities, however, involve illusory acts, or acts of "magic" that differ from artificial activities in that the person performing virtual activities "does one thing while trying to create the illusion that he is doing another" while the one performing artificial activities "is actually doing what he appears to be doing" (16). The actor performing magic thus creates in the very space of visibility an invisibility, and the stage magician's expertise lies in his or her ability to make the visible invisible through sleight of hand.

This creation of secrecy within an overarching openness amounts to what Barbara Maria Stafford calls the "visible invisible." Exploring forms of

Enlightenment-era entertainment, Stafford discusses the dialectic of rationality and irrationality at work among the devices of prestidigitators and other creators of illusion. The term *visible invisible* signifies the balancing of revelation and concealment but does so in the specific context of stage magic and the particular ethics of that particular theatricality. Drawing on the reciprocities between game play and theater, Stafford observes that on "one hand, the *invisible* or concealed imposition of artificial patterns could change the world into a toy and the players into tools of the hidden juggler," the effect of which was to make objects "appear to exist 'objectively,' as if emitted 'naturally' or automatically," while on "the other hand, the illusionists could make instrumentality *visible* by informing the viewer of the tactics used in the performance" (129–30). This sort of avowal-disavowal is exactly the kind of technique that Barnum used to promulgate the Heth hoax. What is particularly subtle in such sleight of hand is that "the performer created the illusion of eyewitnessing without informing the beholder how the action was done" (79). This sort of illusion of witnessing is a kind of false seeing resulting from a manipulation of perception, and it is this maneuvering that constitutes "the visible invisible [which during the Enlightenment could have] . . . the technologist . . . condemned as a cheap trickster and his product judged as sophisticated flimflam. The total experience added up to commodified wonder selling base stupefaction" (79).

This sort of stage magic visible invisible appears in Ralph Ellison's *Invisible Man*. Explaining what he means when he refers to himself as being invisible, the novel's narrator states:

> I am an invisible man. No, I am not a spook like those who haunted Edgar Allan Poe; nor am I one of your Hollywood-movie ectoplasms. I am a man of substance, of flesh and bone, fiber and liquids—and I might even be said to possess a mind. I am invisible, understand, simply because people refuse to see me. Like the bodiless heads you see sometimes in circus sideshows, it is as though I have been surrounded by mirrors of hard, distorting glass. When they approach me they see only my surroundings, themselves, or figments of their imagination—indeed, everything and anything except me. (3)

The "bodiless heads" illusion Ellison refers to is one that usually features a table with a box on top of it that contains a head that addresses the people who file by—the illusion is achieved by having the person playing the role of the talking head sit beneath the table with his or her head thrust through a hole in the table and the bottom of the box on top of the table. Mirrors are placed in between the table's legs and the lighting is adjusted so that it seems that there is no body under the table. When constructed correctly, the spectator sees nothing but darkness under the table, as it is customary for a "black-on-black" (the irony of the statement is intended) effect to be used. There is an interesting paradox of success and failure, concealment and revelation in Ellison's image, for even as he gives the trick away the trick remains powerfully effective. Such paradox lies at the heart of secrecy and the African American body and especially secrecy and the black women playwrights whose one-acts will be discussed later.

But magic and theatricality are significant not merely in the context of stage sleight of hand but also in that of supernatural magic, which is inextricably linked with stage magic. In *Modern Enchantments: The Cultural Power of Secular Magic,* Simon During writes that stage magic, or what he calls "secular" magic, "cannot be disentangled from its opposing twin, magic with a supernatural punch[;] . . . there is no difference between the truth-content of secular and supernatural magics. One is as illusory as the other, and always was entangled with the other" (2). Indeed, as During goes on, "entertainment-and-fictional magic refers back to its 'real' double even when departing from it. Thus the logic of secular magic is describable only in relation to a magic with supernatural purpose" (3). Magic is therefore a liminal, fluid form of theatrical performance ensconced in complex systems of belief all of which rely upon a unifying mode of secrecy. Both secular and religious magic are interpolated within the multivalent medium of secrecy, working reciprocally to create effects that are simulations of one another.

Marcel Mauss addresses this fluid reciprocity when he raises the thorny question, "[H]ow is it possible for a sorcerer to believe in magic, when he must constantly come face to face with the true nature of his methods and their results?" (93). As he notes, here "we must confront the serious problem of fraud and simulation in magic" (93), and after discussing cases of magicians who simultaneously realize the simulation of their practice while also believing in magic as a "real" phenomenon, Mauss observes that "the magician's simulations are of the same nature as those observed in nervous conditions. As a result, it is both voluntary and involuntary at the same time. Even when it starts off as a self-imposed state, the simulation recedes into the background and we end up with perfect hallucinatory states" (96). In this magical performance, the performer, if Mauss is to be believed, becomes fraught by his or her own hiddenness, which is the mysterious presence of magic. "The magician then becomes his own dupe," Mauss writes, "in the same way as an actor when he forgets that he is playing a role" (96). Ultimately, this magician, unlike stage magicians who are self-conscious actors, stands as a purveyor of public life secrets who "pretends because pretence is demanded of him, because people seek him out and beseech him to act. He is not a free agent" but rather "is forced to play either a role demanded by tradition or one which comes up to his client's expectations. . . . He is a kind of official, vested by society with authority, and it is incumbent upon the society to believe in him" (97). And so, Mauss continues, "what a magician believes and what the public believes are two sides of the same coin. . . . It is this belief which the magician shares with the rest, which means that neither his sleights of hand nor his failures will raise any doubts as to the genuineness of the magic itself" (97).

Thus even "religious" magic is theatrical. Mauss posits a three-part structure of magical performance reminiscent of Beckerman's theatrical construct, writing that in

> magic we have officers, actions and representations: we call a person who accomplishes magical actions a magician, even if he is not a professional; magical representations are those ideas and beliefs which correspond to magical actions; as for these actions, with regard to which we have defined the other elements of the magic, we call them magical rites. (18)

Mauss's structure obviously resembles Beckerman's theatrical construct, with the magician as the actor/performer, the magical rites being the virtual actions, and the magical representations the manipulation of ideas and expectations which are assigned the phoneme "illusions." But Mauss's construct must be understood to perform in a different remove of theatrical space, for the professional secular magician is actually performing the role of magician, or, more accurately, a synthesis of various magician roles assembled from this "previous" theatrical space in an assemblage that resembles Lévi-Strauss's notion of bricolage, with the actor serving as a bricoleur.[18] In this recycling of signifiers, the rites and representations equally recreate those already established in previous theaters so that the magician creates and operates within a palimpsestic mythic place made of several layers largely transparent but each bearing a unique opaque trace of cultural-historic specificity.

Magic, religion, and African American subjectivity and performance interrelate in ways that again reveal secrecy's multiple interpolating. Since the time of Christianity's beginning, magic has taken on a dubious position in Western culture. "Early Christianity darkened magic," During writes, tracing the development of magic throughout Western history. "From the beginning of the Christian era, learned and popular magics were persecuted by religious authorities who associated them not just with paganism but with the devil" (7). This diabolic coloring of magic took on a hue rife with ethnocentrism with the initiation of European colonizing practices. In fact, During goes on to assert that

European expansion, especially into Africa, perpetuated the old division between "white" magic and pagan or diabolic magics. A patina of racism intruded into the blackness of "black" magic, which now also connoted skin color. The old terms "necromancy" (literally, magic conjuring up the dead) and "negromancy" (black or malevolent divination) had been used interchangeably in the medieval period, and the linguistic accident which tied death to blackness would be exploited, perhaps unknowingly, by colonialist discourse. Certainly, after about 1780, African varieties of supernaturalism (often called "mumbo-jumbo," "voodoo," "zombie-ism" and so on) were invoked for a diversity of white agendas. (10)

While these negative connotations of magic and African-originated religion were expounded by white people, such magical forms actually served black peoples as ways of subverting those very colonial forces. Not only voodoo but also other forms of religion, including Yorùbá religious practices and Islam, contributed to the rich religious texture the slaves carried across the Atlantic and combined/stuffed-into various forms of Christianity.[19] This amalgamation of religion was inundated with secrecy that struck terror in white slaveholders but helped unify slaves and articulate their oppressive situation. As Raboteau explains, most slaveholders feared that converting slaves to Christianity would incite revolt despite the fact that the precepts it offered were essentially antirevolutionary. Moreover, conversion implied that blacks were humans with souls to save rather than chattel, an obviously problematic idea for those white people involved in the Peculiar Institution who also saw themselves as upstanding Christians.

The threat of subversion was heightened by the fact that African American religious practices were often carried out in secret. Even though controlled instruction and worship finally became generally established in plantation culture, Raboteau notes that the

religious experience of the slaves was by no means fully contained in the visible structures of the institutional church. From the abundant testimony of fugitive and freed slaves it is clear that the slave community had an extensive religious life of its own, hidden from the eyes of the master. In the secrecy of the quarters or the seclusion of the brush arbors ("hush harbors") the slaves made Christianity truly their own. (212)

Hush harbors thus made the familiar strange, outside of visibility and therefore outside of control. The fear of such covert religious activity is thoroughly registered, for example, in white aristocratic Virginia writer Thomas Nelson Page's story "No Haid Pawn" in which black people whose religion stresses visceral "belief" over cerebral "reason" are metaphorically linked with an abolitionist- and ghost-haunted plantation.

Where hush harbors infuse the familiar with secrecy, the traces of African religions signify that which was unknown and therefore fearful to the white community. For African Americans, Anthony B. Pinn insists, the religious experience reached beyond Christianity to include herbalism, witchcraft, and conjure, which was "a theory for explaining the mystery of evil [as well as] . . . a practice for doing something about it. . . . [And the] ultimate source of the conjurer's power was either God or the devil" (277). At the same time, voodoo as both cult and system of magic persisted in the United States as well as in Haiti, where in addition to its saturation in magic and secrecy it also served as the realm in which secret societies were formed as early as the revolution of 1804 and which have continued to play a critical role in politics there to the present.[20] Certainly the separation of white and black religious practices did not end with the abolition of slavery: Yvonne Patricia Chireau makes the point that where conjure has always been kept secret from white people, after Emancipation new notions of "respectability" among African Americans drove it further underground as "part of a hidden tradition, obscured from public view, but still deeply embedded within Black-American culture" (87).[21] By the time of the Harlem Renaissance, religion was central to secret (meaning unavailable for white viewing) African American life.

III

The interconnections between secrecy and magic in African American performance and theater grow deeper and exceptional when considered in light of gender—specifically, when considering the positionality and experiences peculiar to black women. Both secrecy and magic are especially significant in theorizations of women, generally. In *This Sex which Is Not One*, Luce Irigaray shows that for male thinkers and masculine-dominated discourses "the woman" has conventionally been a mystery and her body a secret. Focusing on biological difference (however problematic Judith Butler has shown that doing so can be), Irigaray observes that where "man needs an instrument: his hand, a woman's body, language . . . [and] this self-caressing requires at least a minimum of activity," a woman "touches herself in and of herself without any need for mediation, and before there is any way to distinguish activity from passivity" (24). Where a man is sexually characterized by "*one* of form, of the individual, of the (male) sexual organ, of the proper name, of the proper meaning," the woman is "*at least two* (lips) which keeps woman in touch with herself, but without any possibility of distinguishing what is touching from what is touched" (26). The woman "within herself . . . is already two—but not divisible into one(s)—that caress each other" because "her genitals are formed of two lips in continuous contact" (24), and she operates in both active and passive sexual roles, a doubleness that informs a distinct poetic of presence and hiddenness in her body and sexuality, for she

> takes pleasure more from touching than from looking, and her entry into a dominant scopic economy signifies, again, her consignment to passivity: she is to be the beautiful object of contemplation. While her body finds itself thus eroticized, and called to a double-movement of exhibition and of chaste retreat in order to stimulate the drives of the "subject," her sexual organ represents the horror of nothing to see. A defect in this systematics of representation and desire. A "hole" in its scoptophilic lens. It is already evident in Greek statuary that this nothing-to-see has to be excluded, rejected, from such a scene of representation. Woman's genitals are simply absent, masked, sewn back up inside their "crack." (26)

This condition of hiddenness describes a poetic of concealment and secrecy, for a woman's body is, according to Irigaray, simply unknowable and indescribable even to herself. Her possession, maintaining, and revealing of secrets is ambivalent, uncontrolled, uncontrollable even, for "the 'thickness' of that 'form,' the layering of its volume, its expansions and contractions and even the spacing of the moments in which it produces itself as form—all this the feminine keeps secret. Without knowing it" (27). Such socially constructed and negotiated dynamics appear in Irigaray's observation that

> if woman is asked to sustain, to revive, man's desire, the request neglects to spell out what it implies as to the value of her own desire. A desire of which she is not aware, moreover, at least not explicitly. But one whose force and continuity are capable of nurturing repeatedly and at length all the masquerades of "femininity" that are expected of her. (27)

Just as secrecy haunts a female identification, so have women been linked in unique ways to magic. In classifying different types of figures who may be magicians or associated with magic, Mauss observes that such persons bear bodily, organic markings. "Nobody can become a magician at will," he explains; "there are qualities which distinguish a magician from the layman. Some are acquired, some inherited; to some the qualities are lent while others actually possess them" (27). Although Mauss does not distinguish race as a

mark of the magician, he does point to the marginal, those marked by variation, noting that in "the Middle Ages people looked for the devil's mark"
and that all "over the world there are people who have a peculiarly cun-
ning look, who appear odd or untrustworthy, who blink at one strangely"
and who "are all lumped together as magicians, along with nervous and
jumpy individuals or subnormal peoples" (27). After further enumeration,
he makes the striking observation "that all these individuals—the disabled
and the ecstatic, the pedlars, hawkers, jugglers and neurotics—actually form
kinds of social classes. They possess magical powers not through their individual peculiarities but as a consequence of society's attitude towards them
and their kind" (28). To this group Mauss adds yet another: women. I quote
at length.

> They are everywhere recognized as being more prone to magic than men,
> not so much because of their physical characteristics, but because of the
> social attitudes these characteristics provide. The critical periods of their life
> cycle lead to bemusement and apprehension, which place them in a special
> position. And it is precisely at periods such as puberty, menstruation, preg-
> nancy and childbirth that a woman's attributes reach their greatest intensity.
> It is usually at such times that women are supposed to provide subjects or
> act as agents for magical action. Old women are witches; virgins are valuable
> auxiliaries; menstrual blood and other like products are common specifics.
> Moreover, it is true that women are particularly disposed to hysteria, and
> their nervous crises make them susceptible to superhuman forces, which
> endow them with special powers. However, even outside of these critical
> periods, which occupy a not insignificant part of their life, women are the
> butt of superstitions and jural and religious taboos, which clearly mark them
> off as a separate class in society. They are made out to be more different
> than men than they are in fact. They are said to be the fount of mysterious
> activities, the sources of magical power. On the other hand, since women
> are excluded from most religious cults—or if admitted, reduced to a passive
> role—the only practices left to them on their own initiative are magical ones.
> The magical attributes of women derive primarily from their social position
> and consequently are more talked about than real. In fact, there are fewer
> female practitioners of magic than public opinion would have us believe.
> The curious result is that on the whole, it is the men who perform the magic
> while women are accused of it. (28)

The layering of seeing illustrated in Mauss's comments is important, for
women "are seen" by men as magical in both active and passive ways. Mauss
stresses this perception as perception (he uses the phrase "in fact" more than

once) and is keenly aware in the final quoted sentence of the fact that men readily ascribe negative magical abilities to women, presumably blaming women when things go wrong. What is significant about Mauss's assertions is that they directly present one way that women come into hiddenness as other specifically through notions of what magic is.

Through Mauss's siphoning off women as a magically supercharged "separate class" in light of devil-associated magical markings, we can begin to consider the specific situation of African American women as another group within the already marginalized group of African Americans generally. Not only are such individuals black, they are women—as Spivak suggests, they are not only women but more so since "if you are poor, black and female you get it in three ways" (90). Evelynn M. Hammonds uses language almost identical to Irigaray's but applies it to black women specifically, writing that their

> sexuality is often described in metaphors of speechlessness, space, or vision, as a "void" or empty space that is simultaneously ever-visible (exposed) and invisible, where black women's bodies are always already colonized. In addition, this always already colonized black female body has so much sexual potential it has none at all. Historically, black women have reacted to the repressive force of the hegemonic discourses on race and sex that constructed this image with silence, secrecy, and a particularly self-chosen invisibility. (171)

Black women can thus represent the visible invisible, a situation imposed upon them but also one that can be appropriated, subverted, signified on. The positive role of being objectified by a male gaze can itself be turned into an active role. Where, as Audre Lorde writes, "within this country where racial difference creates a constant, if unspoken, distortion of vision, Black women have on one hand always been highly visible, and so, on the other hand, have been rendered invisible through the depersonalization of racism," it is also the case that this "visibility which makes [them] most vulnerable is also the source of [their] greatest strength" (41). In other words, black women act and react within this external-internal interpolation in secrecy— something that Joice Heth may have been trying to do, although with little or no resulting liberation.

Even more than white women, black women have both signified and performed as magical figures. Pinn notes that "women made up the bulk of voodoo practitioners" (39), and Chireau, exploring black women's involvement with "alternative spiritual beliefs," writes that women "were at the center of the world of conjure" (75). Zora Neale Hurston offers the following anecdote in *Tell My Horse: Voodoo and Life in Haiti and Jamaica:*

> "What is the truth?" Dr. Holly asked me, and knowing that I could not answer him he answered himself through a Voodoo ceremony in which the Mambo, that is the priestess, richly dressed is asked this question ritualistically. She replies by throwing back her veil and revealing her sex organs. The ceremony means that this is the infinite, the ultimate truth. There is no mystery beyond the mysterious source of life. The ceremony continues on another phase after this. It is a dance analogous to the nuptial flight of the queen bee. The Mambo discards six veils in this dance and falls at last naked, and spiritually intoxicated, to the ground. It is considered the highest honor for all males participating to kiss her organ of creation, for Damballa, the god of gods, has permitted them to come face to face with truth. (113–14)

This passage is particularly significant because it combines Du Bois's notion of the Veil, the *chora,* and the secrecy of the black female body. The female organ serves as the ultimate secret-as-fetish.

Houston Baker is especially keen to link black female spatiality with magic in *Workings of the Spirit: The Poetics of Afro-American Women's Writing.* Drawing on Bachelard's discussion of imagistic fields as phenomenological definers of space for readers of literature, Baker considers black female spaces that are defined by "spirit." He argues "that a poetics of Afro-American women's writing is, in many ways, a phenomenology of conjure" (66). Speaking to one of the prime ways of maintaining secrets, Baker ventures the observation that if "one seeks the classical in Afro-American expressive culture, one discovers without great difficulty a mode of discourse or performance that I call 'mythomania.' . . . Mythomania is most aptly defined as: 'a compulsion to embroider the truth, to exaggerate, or to tell lies'" (74). Baker pays particular attention to the theatricality of black female spaces of conjure, offering the following striking account, discussing the theatrics of voodoo

> captured in a report from the New Orleans Times-Democrat of 24 June 1896. Describing a voodoo festival it reads as follows; "The rites consisted in building a large fire, in a dance on the part of the central personage, the destruction of a black cat and its devouring raw. The scene concluded with an orgie, in which the savage actors ended by tearing off their garments" . . .. The participants in the festival were doubtless "actors" who must have been delighted with the newspaper's "savage" accounting since it probably increased the white patronage of future occasions. (79–80)[22]

This black female exceptionalness was accompanied by and was the result of a unique spatiality. Patricia Hill Collins particularly explores the spatiality of black women, writing that "African-American women's social location as a collectivity has fostered distinctive albeit heterogeneous Black feminist intellectual traditions" (*Black Feminist Thought* 17). She discusses two spatial-economic factors that established spaces which influenced black women's subjectivity. The first is that "prior to World War II, racial segregation in urban housing became so entrenched that the majority of African-American women lived in self-contained Black neighborhoods where their children attended overwhelmingly Black schools, and where they themselves belonged to all-Black churches and similar community organizations" (9). The second was the set of "common experiences [black women] gained from their jobs. Prior to World War II, U.S. Black women worked primarily in two occupations—agriculture and domestic work" (10). While these spaces were not exclusively black or female, both contributed to the generation of a uniquely black female perspective, and Collins goes on to note regarding the second factor that black women's "ghettoization in domestic work sparked an important contradiction. Domestic work fostered U.S. Black women's economic exploitation, yet it simultaneously created the conditions for distinctively Black and female forms of resistance" (10). These forms of resistance resulted from the fact that these women were able to be in the otherwise inscrutable (to them) space of white public-life secrecy. As Collins explains, domestic work

> allowed African-American women to see White elites, both actual and aspiring, from perspectives largely obscured from Black men and from these groups themselves. On one level this insider relationship was satisfying to all concerned. Accounts of Black domestic workers stress the sense of self-affirmation the women experienced at seeing racist ideology demystified. But on another level these Black women knew that they could never belong to their White "families." They were economically exploited workers and thus would remain outsiders. The result was being placed in a curious outsider-within social location . . . a peculiar marginality that stimulated a distinctive Black women's perspective on a variety of themes. . . . (10–11)[23]

Bonner, Burrill, Duncan, Graham, Hurston, Johnson, Miller, and Spence were not domestic workers (they were well-educated representatives of the Talented Tenth), but they nevertheless understood the nature of the constrictions of space that the majority of black women faced, and certainly they themselves were not untouched by it. They, too, faced the "peculiar marginality that stimulated a distinctive Black Women's perspective"; accomplished as they were, they faced limitations of options for publication and/or production of their works. As Gloria T. Hull notes, "[D]espite what appears to be full participation of women in the Harlem Renaissance, one can discern broad social factors and patterns of exclusion" (*Color, Sex, and Poetry* 7). Noting Locke's misogyny as well as that of other leaders in the Harlem Renaissance, Hull observes that the "personality-patronnage [*sic*] issue broadens into general revelations about the customary male circles of power and friendship, which during the period crossed racial lines" (9). It is hardly surprising that black women writers formed their own groups, however loosely constituted; in such black-female communities as Georgia Douglas Johnson's S-Street Salon (the sobriquet given to the informal meetings at her house in Washington, D.C.), there was freedom to exchange ideas under the protection of secrecy.[24]

What must be noted about such black-women's spaces, however, is that they were not exclusive but, like secrecy itself, characterized by multiple interpolation—a fact that carries implications for strategies of both concealment and revelation. It would be inaccurate to suggest that Johnson's S-Street Salon was a sort of black woman's secret society simply because numerous men are known to have been present at the meetings. It is actually the permeability of these black women–controlled spaces that makes them sites of secrecy-discourse—places where concealment and revelation could be controlled by black women. In their lives as well as in their work, one can see similar suggestions of alternate oppression by various foes, whether they be dangerous white men, unsympathetic or well-meaning but ineffective white women, or powerful black men. The first two groups seem obvious enough external enemies (although George Hutchinson documents the role of white people in enabling Harlem Renaissance artists and writers), but it is also the case that while there were certainly black women in visible leadership roles, "the increasingly masculinist bias within the African American literary community [created] . . . an environment in which . . . [the] daily [lives] of Black women [were] no longer perceived as viable sites of meaningful resistance" (Mance 19–20). This principle transfers to black women's writing, in which they articulated their perspectives as black women and clearly counted black women in their imagined audiences but also realized that black or white men as well as white women could and would encounter the work. What these black women could do in their writing was to reveal as well as conceal while controlling that revealing. These spaces, whether "real" groupings of black women or fictional ones or simply the spaces of a written text to be performed, operated within and/or created secrecy-discourse game situations in which secrecy-moves could be used to mobilize enemies, educate potential friends, and consolidate members of the in-group. Theater was one of these secrecy-discourse situations, and these writers' one-act plays exhibit multilayered approaches to their dealings with individuals or groups who were to varying degrees outsiders.

Consider, for example, Eulalie Spence. In her biographical sketch of Spence in her anthology *Black Female Playwrights: An Anthology of Plays before 1950*, Kathy A. Perkins offers an interesting and revealing anecdote:

> A member of Du Bois's Krigwa Players from 1926 until the group's demise two years later, Spence respected the activist, but the two had major disagreements. Du Bois attempted on many occasions to persuade her to use her excellent writing skills for propaganda. Spence emphasized that her rationale for avoiding propaganda issues was that she knew nothing about lynchings, rapes, nor the blatant racial injustices in this country. As a West Indian, she claimed, these issues were not part of her background. Spence was also adamant in her belief that a play could not depend on propaganda for success. She was a "folk dramatist," who wrote for fun and entertainment. (106)

It seems evident that Spence was playing Du Bois. Undoubtedly Spence really did write "for fun and entertainment," and some of her plays bear a marked light-heartedness and foregrounding of "play." But when one reads *Undertow*, which examines the turgid life of a dysfunctional family in Harlem in which a black man's black wife is jealous of his lighter-skinned ex-lover, the conflict of which ends in his murdering his wife, one might wonder if "fun and entertainment" were Spence's *only* reasons for writing. Likewise, her play *Fool's Errand* partly critiques the potential for injustice in a patriarchally inscribed black religion. However much "fun" Spence may have had writing, her plays could also cut deep, much deeper than her alleged purposes suggest. What emerges from Perkins's account of the interaction between Du Bois and Spence is not so much that Spence was politically unaware or unconcerned, but that she did not care to have her voice colonized by Du Bois's propagandistic designs. She sought the visibility he offered her, but she also wanted to reserve her own rights and control of her writing self. Indeed, Yvonne Shafer points out that when Spence's play *Fool's Errand* won $200 in New York's 1927 National Little Theatre Tournament, "a dispute [arose] about the prize which Du Bois accepted to pay for production expenses, so it did not go to Spence. . . . This exacerbated the differences between them and may have led to the disintegration of the Krigwa players shortly thereafter" (275).

Spence may have been interacting with James V. Hatch in a similar manner some five decades later when he would ask for a copy of her play *The Hunch*. In a letter dated May 28, 1970, she informs Hatch, "I am sorry that I have no copy of *Foreign Mail* or *The Hunch*" (SCRBC). Yet her niece was in possession of a copy of the *Carolina Quarterly* (now in the Schomburg Center) that included the full text of her play, and it is not beyond reason to think that Spence may have in fact had at least a copy of the typescript of *Foreign Mail* at that time. Of course, Spence may have misplaced either or both of the texts and found it simpler to say or really believed she no longer had copies (or maybe she had given them away and later recovered them), and it may strain hermeneutics to suggest that this instance represents a conscious secrecy-move. But her recalcitrant streak can be often found intertwined with distinct secrecy-moves. As Perkins has noted, the light-skinned West Indian Spence apparently passed as a teacher at the Eastern District High School in Brooklyn; even her star student, Joseph Papp, claims not to have realized that she was African American (Perkins, email). Another example of a secrecy-move can be found in a letter to Alain Locke dated June 1, 1927:

> I have also taken various cultural courses at the College of the City of New York. (I have no degree.) I could get one with very little effort, but I can't be bothered. After all, those things mean very little, really, as I see them.
>
> Some people wonder that I am teaching in a High School, without a degree. Well, let them. My qualifications were satisfactory to the Board of Education and that is all that matters. (SCRBC)

Spence was passing both in terms of race and education, and as she goes on to acknowledge that her letter has become more than a simple biography, one can discern her jealous preservation of her credentials and space.

Georgia Douglas Johnson apparently employed similar passive-aggressive secrecy-moves in her dealings with powerful black men. Alice Dunbar-Nelson notes in her diary that "Georgia has done the big thing in letting Locke, DuBois [*sic*], and Braithwaite weed out her verses until only the perfect ones remain. What she has left are little gems, characterized by a finish of workmanship that is seldom seen in our people" (88).[25] Like Spence, Johnson displayed a marked tendency to be, as Martha Gilman Bower puts it, "[e]xtremely secretive about her past, her heritage, her parents and her grandparents—even her age—Johnson, like some of her characters, seemed to suffer from a repressed identity, which caused her to be 'ontologically insecure'" (13). Dunbar-Nelson writes that "Georgia showed me the manuscript of her new book, which Braithwaite is offering to the publishers. She does exquisite verses, and these are wonderfully fine—a story, running like a fine golden thread through them all" (88). More specifically, she speculates as to the inspiration of the volume:

> "An Autumn Idyll," it is called, the love story of a woman in the autumn of

life. It makes you blush at times, the baring of inmost secrets of a soul, as it does. I wonder what Link [Johnson's husband] thinks of it? You might call it poetic inspiration, if you will, but it looks suspiciously to me as if Georgia had had an affair, and it had been a source of inspiration to her. Something like my "Dream Book," though I would never give it to the public, only the fragments which I did give—the sonnet "Violets," and the one or two others, for which E. J. S. has never forgiven me. (88)

Turning to "literary" writing, Marita Bonner grapples with secrecy and the complexities of a black woman's subject position in her essay "On Being Young—a Woman—and Colored." Tracing the grave threat that black women's hopes for the future tailspin into despair as they grow older, Bonner notes that in youth black women envision a bright future but "one day you find yourself entangled—enmeshed—pinioned in the seaweed of a Black Ghetto" (FSE 3). In this ghetto people are "shoved aside in a bundle because of color and with no more in common. Unless color is, after all, the real bond" (4). She observes that there "are all the earmarks of a group within a group" and while a black woman might "hear that up at New York this is to be seen; that, to be heard . . . you know that—being a woman—you cannot . . . break away to see or hear anything in a city that is supposed to see and hear too much" (4–5). "That's being a woman," Bonner explains; "A woman of color" (5). Not only are black women restricted spatially, but, Bonner goes on, "Why do they [white people? black men?] see a colored woman only as a gross collection of desires, all controlled, reaching out for their Apollos and the Quasimodoes with arid indiscrimination?" (5). Bonner closes the essay with an important observation about a strategic secrecy-move in a passage that employs secrecy-moves in its form (its ellipses and dashes, as will be explained later).

> So—being a woman—you can wait.
> You must sit quietly without a chirp. Not sodden—and weighted as if your feet were cast in the iron of your soul. Not wasting strength in enervating gestures as if two hundred years of bonds and whips had really tricked you into nervous uncertainty.
> But quiet; quiet. Like Buddha—who brown like I am—sat entirely at ease, entirely sure of himself; motionless and knowing, a thousand years before the white man knew there was so very much difference between feet and hands.
> Motionless on the outside. But on the inside?
> Silent.
> Still . . . "Perhaps Buddha is a woman."

So you too. Still; quiet; with a smile, ever so slight, at the eyes so that Life will flow into and not by you. And you can gather, as it passes, the essences, the overtones, the tints, the shadows; draw understanding to yourself.

And then you can, when Time is ripe, swoop to your feet—at your full height—at a single gesture.

Ready to go where?

Why . . . Wherever God motions. (7–8)

In a similar literary work with autobiographical aspects, Hurston's *Their Eyes Were Watching God* interrogates secrecy and in-group cohesion. Janie refuses to tell her story either to the men lazing on the porches or to the black women who are critical and/or jealous of her. Instead, she talks to her friend Phoeby (an exemplification of the black lesbian poetic Barbara Smith identifies) in a small confined space, right in the vision but not within the hearing of men: she occupies the signifying space of the visible invisible. She and Phoeby together constitute an other group, a secret society, as it were, a room of their own apart but still visible. A space in which they can show black men and the world the female bodies they desire but where they can also keep certain things secret. In the meantime, the black men on the porch of Eatonville are waiting, according to Pheoby, for Judgment Day because that is "de day dat every secret is s'posed to be made known. They wants to be there and hear it *all*" (6). Of course, Hurston's passing into obscurity late in life and her subsequent burial in an unmarked grave in Fort Pierce, Florida, is a sad instance of a black woman's passing into invisibility.

These are merely a few instances of the ways secrecy touched these black women's lives; equally sorrowful has been the hiddenness of them and their works after their deaths. Their one-acts (and in some cases the women themselves) have been enveloped in what Derrida calls "the secret of the archive":

What can a library do with secret letters? We shall define libraries in general as places devoted to keeping the secret but insofar as they give it away. Giving a secret away may mean telling it, revealing it, publishing it, divulging it, as well as keeping it so deeply in the crypt of a memory that we forget it is there or even cease to understand and have access to it. In one sense a secret kept is always a secret lost. (20)

Perkins, Judith L. Stephens, and others have worked to pluck the texts of these black women's works from the archive, sometimes having to save the archive itself as well as jump-starting critical conversation about them.[26] The rediscovery and reclamation of black women's voices that have been ongoing for at least three decades are even now still unearthing their one-acts, and many of them actually remain unpublished and even, in some cases, lost. Although the secret of the archive was not written into these plays, the fact of their being unknown for so long heightens the aura of secrecy surrounding them and is particularly painful because it fulfills the fear of black women's silencing that runs throughout so many of them.

This book seeks to add to the effort to bring these women forth from the archival closet.

The
ONE-ACTS

BY THE 1920S AND 1930S, when Bonner, Burrill, Duncan, Graham, Hurston, Johnson, Miller, and Spence were writing, formal African American theater had itself come into a new era of hiddenness.[1] Black dance had become all the rage on Broadway, with musicals bringing black people (however problematically) into the spotlight of white attention. But Bonner and her peers made their mark in the Black Little Theater Movement as part of the Krigwa Little Theatre, the Howard Players, and other such projects.[2] This sort of theater deliberately sought to access less visible themes, the life-stuff unseen in the commercially driven Broadway pageants and musicals. Locally based, characterized by small casts, audiences, and theaters (when there even were "theaters"—the plays were often performed in churches, schools, and other such peripheral and "secretive" spaces as the basement of the 135th Street Branch of the New York Public Library in Harlem), the movement itself may be read as an exploration of secret spaces and themes carried out in those secret spaces. Faced with external oppression created by segregation, lynching, and racist stereotypes while also plagued by such internal issues as colorism, sexism, and highly contested notions about how best to use theater (most famously, Du Bois's "propaganda" argument versus Locke's "folk play" ideal), multiple secrecy-discourse games stood to be negotiated in this version of Harlem Renaissance drama.

In turning to a discussion of the one-acts themselves, it is important to consider further the ways in which secrecy affects the very form within which these playwrights worked. Discussion might begin with the ways that the writing of literature (or of any kind) is itself inflected with secrecy. While writing a play differs from writing a novel or a poem, certain similarities do exist among these genres, and discussion of secrecy's presence and functions in them is important because the plays to be discussed are hybrids that both employ and cross over into these different forms. First, it should be noted that on a deep level, creative writing can function to articulate the hidden, the secretive. Derrida refers to the places in texts

> where it is impossible for the reader to decide between the fictional, the invented, the dreamt event, the fantasized event (including the phantasm of the event, not to be neglected) and the event presented as "real," there in this situation handed to the reader, but to the librarian and archivist as well, lies the very secret of what one usually designates by the name of literature. . . . Therein lies literature's secret, the infinite power to keep undecidable and thus forever sealed the secret of what it . . . avows and which remains secret, even as in broad daylight she/it avows unveils or claims to unveil it. The secret of literature is thus the secret itself. It is the secret place in which it establishes itself as the very possibility of the secret, or the place of it, as such . . . . (17–18)

Additionally, just as dreams, poetry, or fiction can display repressed anxieties or memories as explored by Freud and the myth critics, such as Rank and Campbell, so can the space of the semiotic (the *chora*) erupt into the symbolic in ways that wrench certain components of the symbolic from their otherwise relatively stable signifying. "In taking the thetic into account," Kristeva writes, "we shall have to represent the semiotic (which is produced recursively on the basis of that break) as a 'second' return of instinctual functioning within the symbolic, as a negativity introduced into the symbolic order, and as the transgression of that order" (*Revolution* 69). She goes on to explain that this "transgression appears as a breach [*effraction*] subsequent to the thetic phase, which makes that phase negative and tends to fuse the layers of signifier/signified/referent into a network of traces, following the facilitation of the drives" (69). Of course, such a breach is always negotiated (made intelligible) by the symbolic for individuals ensconced in the symbolic and past the mirror stage of development, thus rendering pure, unmediated access to the *chora* impossible. But these are linguistic components that can be exploited as secrecy-move devices—things such as the dash and ellipses, as I pointed out regarding Bonner's "On Being Young—a Woman—

and Colored." Kristeva pays particular attention to the ellipses, noting that "[f]ar from being the mark of a lacuna in a clause, the three dots rather point to the *overflowing of the clause* into a higher unit of enunciation" (*Powers of Horror* 198), which marks such a rupture of the semiotic. Installment of the ellipses can constitute a secrecy-move when the three dots mark an "absorption of work, a withholding of effort, a deletion of abstraction, so that thanks to them but without stating them, and through them, an affect bursts out, in sound and outcry, bordering close on drive and abjection as well as fascination. Bordering on the unnameable" (203–4).

Mention of the ellipses brings us more fully into a consideration of the concrete ways secrecy serves as a tool in both form and content for literature. The construction of lyric and narrative employs secrecy-moves of silence, lying, and interpretation-based encoding. Plot construction is particularly conspicuous for making use of secrecy by keeping certain details secret from the reader in order to build suspense. The most extreme form of such use of secrecy in plot appears in mystery/detective fiction, and Peter Hühn particularly delves into the role of secrecy in such writing, noting that

> the basic internal tension in a classic-formula novel can be conceptualized as a contest between . . . *writing* stories and *reading* stories. The criminal devises or *writes* the story of his criminal act, at the same time, however, protecting it against reading, composing it as an unreadable secret story. The detective attempts to decipher its traces and interpret their meaning, and in the end he succeeds in *reading* it. But the *story* of his interpretation and reading process is also hidden from its readers. (40–41)[3]

Implicit in Hühn's observations is that the characters themselves are generating the form, which points to the fact that characters keep secrets just as "real people" do; secrecy, that is, inundates the mimetic realm of fictional worlds in ways that function as they do in the nonfictional world, although there are obvious complexities in the connection between the two, complexities that get at the kinds of epistemological concerns that Plato and Nietszche raised regarding theater.

In engaging these plays individually, it is important to note the overarching structure within which all of them work—the one-act form—and the hybridity of duties these women make it enact. Part of the one-act form's pervasiveness results from the fact that a public forum had been provided for this structure that had not been for others. *Crisis* and *Opportunity* magazines created writing contests that included a prize for the best one-act plays, and it is partly in response to these calls for submissions that women took up the one-act form with such vigor. But it is also the case that these women explored it in noncompetitive settings. Without demanding too much of the form, it seems appropriate to consider what it either represented or came to represent for these women as a metaphorical construct and space. It seems more than coincidental, that is, that the one-act represents the most constricted form of a conventionally formatted play and that these black women saw themselves as occupying a space veiled within the Veil. Very few of the plays feature multiple scenes within the one act, and the action in most of the plays transpires in a single setting, and that setting is often one of domesticity or some other domain predominantly characterized by black women or in which black women play a unique and recognizable part (in the home of a white family for which they work, for example). In short, although this form was an elicited one, it seems to have served for these black women as a metaphor representing the spatial restrictions and silence so often imposed upon them as black women.

In fact, these women exploited this space as that of the visible invisible, a space of secrecy-discourse that could serve game-theatrical purposes. These plays faced tenuous prospects of both publication and production. Even the award-winning plays were often not published in the respective magazines holding the contests, and scores of them were never published at all.[4] A number of them were produced but usually in extremely limited settings to audiences of less than two hundred and apparently rarely consisting of non-African Americans. Again, a situation conspicuously informed by the sorts of oppressive conditions facing black women: winning awards and writing plays increased their visibility, yet that visibility remained limited, often controlled by black men or black male–controlled superstructures. Seemingly in response to this situation, the women accentuated and played within a poetic of the visible invisible. They did so by creating works that were something between closet dramas and performance spectacles, a hybrid form that amounts to a paradoxical game that emerges in various ways in the texts. For one thing, the stage directions for these plays are notoriously impractical. Perkins interprets this fact as a sign of inadequate training in theatrics, writing that although "the Little Theatre Movement was composed of committed individuals, these members for the most part lacked experience in acting and directing. . . . It must be emphasized that blacks during this period were still developing as playwrights and directors. One could only expect so much from these novices" (16). Perkins may be correct, but not only does the observation not hold true in all cases (Eulalie Spence, for example, was an actor as well as playwright), the impracticalities of the text can also be read as subtle attempts on the parts of these writers to exploit dramatic form in both its visible and invisible, theatrical and antitheatrical aspects.

Consider, for example, the matter of dialect in these plays. The topic itself is fraught quite apart from its presence in these plays, as a perusal of any of the issues of *Crisis* or *Opportunity* will yield articles on dialect and its problems, problems that center on performativity. The question, of course, is whether or not there is such a thing as "authentic" black dialect, and if there is how can it be represented without resorting to white-defined minstrelsy stereotypes; this problem articulates the larger issue of accessing and celebrating black folk culture while simultaneously dismantling white-defined markers of that culture. Zora Neale Hurston embodies this paradox of dialect. On the one hand, in her essay, "Characteristics of Negro Expression," Hurston writes that if

> we are to believe the majority of writers of Negro dialect and the burnt-cork artists, Negro speech is a weird thing, full of 'ams' and 'Ises.' Fortunately we don't have to believe them. We may go directly to the Negro and let him speak for himself. Few Negroes, educated or not, use a clear clipped 'I.' It verges more or less upon 'Ah.' I think the lip form is responsible for this to a great extent. By experiment the reader will find a sharp 'I' is very much easier with a thin taut lip than with a full soft lip. (31)

In her fiction, however, Hurston does not seem so sure of this "biological explanation" for dialect. One example should suffice: although the black character Joe Starks pronounces the first person pronoun as "Ah" as do the other black characters in *Their Eyes Were Watching God,* he is also able to pronounce it as "I" when he appropriates the "white" phrase "I god," suggesting that dialect is performative.[5]

Use of dialect in theater foregrounds the thorny issue of performance-perception inherent in the form, and the one-acts of Bonner and the others further aggravate the situation, for they are hybrid texts that perform in two theaters: (1) the written-read and (2) the performed-spectated. This paradoxical and ambivalent intentional play is exemplified in Bonner's *The Pot Maker.* The play's title is accompanied with the dictum "A Play to Be Read" (17), and many of the plays *are* reader-geared and most visibly so in their use of "eye-dialect" that spells, say, "laugh" as "laff"—even if some accents pronounce the "au" differently, distinguishing between "gh" and "ff" would defy the greatest elocutionists. Despite these things, however, it becomes clear that Bonner envisions this play being performed as well as read. Note, for example, her description of Lew in which she carefully explains exactly what the actor portraying him should look like:

Lew stands by the stove facing the two at the table. He must be an over-fat, over-facetious, over-fair, over-bearing, over-pleasant, over-confident creature. If he does not make you long to slap him back into a place approaching normal humility, he is the wrong character for the part.

You must think as you look at him: "A woman would have to be a base fool to love such a man!" (18)

Regarding audience, another large question is that of its imagined makeup. Most of these plays' initial audiences, whether readers or spectators, tended to be black and to contain both men and women, although it is not inconceivable that white readers or spectators would have encountered some of these plays. The large variation of secrecy-moves, spaces, and players in the plays allows for audiences of significant variety, and these writers seem to envision the possibility of white Americans as well as other out-group constituents reading or watching them.[6] Kimmika Williams-Witherspoon suggests that dialect itself may constitute an interpretation-based secrecy-move directed to the audience, as she writes that African American vernacular English "or Ebonics idioms in the dialogue of [African American theater], operate as discourse markers that help to 'mask' the hidden transcript and tap into cultural competencies" (200).[7] Such complicated coding requires careful attention to possible audience reactions, and while this volume is no handbook of staging suggestions, observations about possible staging will be offered at times along the way, particularly ways that secrecy may be accentuated or otherwise exploited or presented in the text-production-reception dynamic; as Sandra Richards notes, one "must write the absent potential into criticism; that is, in addition to analysis of the written text, one must offer informed accounts of the latent intertexts likely to be produced in performance, increasing and complicating meaning" (65).

Ultimately, what Bonner and the other writers open up in writing such invisibility into the space of conspicuous visibility is a space of interpretable possibilities—a secrecy-discourse space in which can be performed and enacted secrecy moves. This space is interpretable because it is a secret, opaque space that demands interpretation if for no other reason than that simple and open interpretation is inaccessible. Even the most performable plays in this canon tend to confound performance deliberately, whether by means of technical difficulties in staging, the paradoxes of dialect, or other secrecy moves. It is through this gamut that these plays effected and explored the proclivities of the studiously concealed and the carefully divulged.

I

Innovative, daring, and dangerous, Marita Bonner's play *The Purple Flower* undertakes a complex and nuanced examination of spatiality, race, and the importance of secrets held and secrets revealed within a multiply interpolated culture. Its scope encompasses the sorts of secrecy-discourse games and moves that are central to so many of the one-acts of Burrill, Duncan, Graham, Hurston, Johnson, Miller, and Spence as well as Bonner. Because of this scope, I am going to use the play as the framework for discussion of the other plays. I will move through Bonner's play, using its dialogue and actions to call up plays that use similar details to address similar scenes. Such an approach might well work severe violence on the texts, but since I am including secrecy-in-plot-construction as part of the interpretive field, my hope is that juxtaposition of the plot-level secrecy strategies these women create will help reveal the peculiar similarity-dissimilarity of their works as a group. I also want to convey the sense of uncanniness that one may encounter in reading the plays—the sense of wondering whether or not the similarities are artificial or intentional, whether these women do or do not consciously encode their plays to ply secrets or if similar secrecy-moves appear because of foundational similarities in black women's spaces and experiences.

So let us begin by considering the set and setting of *The Purple Flower.* Bonner takes especial care in delineating the set, and it exemplifies the sort of fluid interstitial secrecy-discourse space within which these women and their plays operate. She dictates that the stage be

> divided horizontally into two sections, upper and lower, by a thin board. The main action takes place on the upper stage. The light is never quite clear on the lower stage; but it is bright enough for you to perceive that sometimes the action that takes place on the upper stage is duplicated on the lower. Sometimes the actors on the upper stage get too vociferous—too violent—and they crack through the boards and they lie twisted and curled in mounds. There are any number of mounds there, all twisted and broken. You look at them and you are not quite sure whether you see something or nothing; but you see by a curve that there might lie a human body. There is thrust out a white hand—a yellow one—one brown—a black. The Skin-of-Civilization must be very thin. A thought can drop you through it. (FSE 30–31)

On its most essential level, this stage vivifies Du Bois's Veil, but it is the permeability of the line dividing the upper and lower parts that is striking. This permeability manifests the ways the various players are interpolated within the play's overarching secrecy-discourse game-space. The economy of silent gestures that contribute to the realization of the lower stage space suggests that it is the secret nonsymbolic, uninterpretable space of the *chora*. Obviously, the set poses challenges to even the most advanced stage-set technology. What substance can permit characters to "drop" through at any point? Within the metaphorical visible invisible poetics of the play as written rather than performed the answer is simple enough: the substance filling the space of secrecy-discourse. The permeable line is one that can be processed by a reading audience much more readily than it can be constructed for a spectating one.

Bonner extends this Du Boisian structure when she notes that there are two types of characters in the play: the "White Devils" and the "Us." The latter group signifies the oppressed African Americans, who can be "as white as the White Devils, as brown as the earth, as black as the center of a poppy" (30). In this group are all the various shadings of subjectivity. The first group, however, represents an interesting designation. Casting devils as white signifies on a white-defined marker of essentialized blackness. This association of black people with magic and magic and blackness with Satan, demons, and demonology appeared in Christian iconography, which reincarnated the Pan of pagan religion as the Satan of Christianity. With his goat's hooves, tail, goatee, horns, and large phallus, Pan represented the height of earthly sensuality that Christianity abhorred, and Pan and the goat he resembled became transformed into signifiers of blackness, as Jeffrey Burton Russell observes, writing that in the Middle Ages, demons, among other things, "were blacks, who were popularly associated with shadow and the privation of light" (49). These medieval figurations of devil-black-goat transferred to the New World and ultimately informed racist figurations of blackness in America, and though no longer a distinctly visible element in the construction of stereotyped blackness by the twentieth century, the goat/Satan/blackness figuration in part composed the groundwork for the image of the "Black Beast," which registered the threat of a black man's raping a white woman, and in its sexual licentiousness the goat remained in alignment with racist notions of essential blackness.[8] By designating devils as "white," Bonner reverses this marker of essentialized blackness.

In keeping with their "magical" designation, the White Devils are marked by a certain kind of activity. Bonner explains that the "Scene" of the play is an *"open plain. It is bounded distantly on one side by Nowhere and faced by a high hill—Somewhere"* upon which grows *"the purple Flower-of-Life-at-Its-Fullest"* (31).[9] The Purple Flower is a metaphor for a secret, *the* secret of fulfillment and advancement, and it is a secret possessed and guarded by the White Devils and kept (by them) inaccessible to the Us's, for Bonner goes on to explain that the

> *Us's live in the valley that lies between Nowhere and Somewhere and spend*
> *their time trying to devise means of getting up the hill. The White Devils live*
> *all over the side of the hill and try every trick, known and unknown, to keep the*
> *Us's from getting to the hill. For if the Us's get up the hill, the Flower-of-Life-at-*
> *Its-Fullest will shed some of its perfume and then there they will be Somewhere*
> *with the White Devils. The Us's started out by merely asking permission to go*
> *up. They tilled the valley, they cultivated it and made it as beautiful as it is.*
> *They built roads and houses even for the White Devils. They let them build the*
> *houses and then they were knocked back down into the valley. (31)*

The White Devils are magicians who "try every trick" to protect the Purple Flower. Both "known and unknown," these tricks are the secrecy-moves (public-life secrets) that prevent the Us's from attaining the ultimate secret.

The term "white devil" appears with surprising regularity in the plays by the other playwrights in addition to Bonner. Its appearance may in part be due to the fact that Mary P. Burrill, who taught some of the other playwrights who themselves influenced others, used it in her early play *Aftermath* (1919). But even when the term itself is not used, these writers employ various ways of playing on signifiers that address the stereotypes of Satan and blackness (for example, in the image of the goat). This element is significant, for it is one of the surreptitious figurations that connect many of these works. A figure related to conjure, assigning to white the term the "white devil," serves as an interpretation-based secrecy-move, a sort of loose code for subverting white-assigned signifiers of blackness.

The action of *The Purple Flower* consists of the Us's discussion about and attempts at attaining the Purple Flower; their conversation runs the gamut of historical attempts at African American racial betterment and attainment of the secret of Life-at-Its-Fullest. The opening scene introduces Booker T. Washington's concept for lifting the race's political, economic, and cultural status in the United States. The curtain rises upon the White Devils singing a taunting song to the Us's:

> You stay where you are!
> We don't want you up here!
> If you come you'll be on par
> With all we hold dear.
> So stay—stay—stay—
> Yes stay where you are! (32)

The Us's hear this song while they "*are having a siesta beside a brook that runs down the Middle of the valley*" (31), and upon hearing it, one of them remarks, "I ain't studying 'bout them devils. When I get ready to go up that hill—I'm going!" at which point he rolls over and proclaims, "Right now, I'm going to sleep" (32). Then an Us identified as "Old Lady" comments that she will "never live to see the face of that flower! God knows I worked hard to get Somewhere though. I've washed the shirt off of every one of them White Devils' backs. . . . [T]hat's what the Leader told us to do. 'Work,' he said. 'Show them you know how.' As if two hundred years of slavery had not showed them!" (32). Bonner thus juxtaposes a lazy Us with a hard-working Us who has followed Booker T. Washington's creed, and both remain shut out of Somewhere.

These opening lines and the visual scene they punctuate introduce a critique that Mary P. Burrill dramatizes in *They That Sit in Darkness*. Although a much different style of play (a folk play that also blends elements of the propaganda play), Burrill explores the problems of the secret of Life-at-Its-Fullest held by empowered White Devils and enforced even in government measures while also critiquing the Washingtonian plan. Burrill's play is set "in a small country town in the South in our own day" (BFP 67) and focuses on the day before a young girl, Lindy Jasper, leaves to attend Tuskegee. This domestic setting is much more common in these black women's plays than Bonner's set in that it consists of a central room that is the site of labor, being simultaneously a "kitchen, dining room, and living room for the Jasper family" (67) as well as the room in which Lindy and her mother, Malinda (a figure much like the Old Lady in Bonner's play), wash clothes for white people. Yet, like Bonner's set, the world of the white people with its protected secret of Life-at-Its-Fullest is visible through a window in which *"one gets a glimpse of snowy garments waving and glistening in the sun"* (67). The white garments here stand in for whiteness itself, representing the Purple Flower even as they simultaneously represent one of the means by which African American women are kept in their places through low-wage labor. The garments, in fact, function like the Purple Flower itself, which is a secret-as-fetish that signifies as a secret but that serves also to hide the "real" secrets of white privilege. In the Washingtonian plan, the creed of industriousness itself serves as a secret-as-fetish, as it seems to be the secret to success; yet the secret about that secret is that it is no secret at all but rather the same old "work" raised to the level of fetish by being injected with the *aura* of secrecy.

Burrill's play opens with the mother and daughter finishing their washing and the mother sitting down complaining about a pain in her side. Worried, Lindy reminds her that all of the hard work washing is causing her health troubles, but her mother insists that she must keep working in order to feed her already starving children, including her newborn baby. In the meantime, the other five children are outside playing and manage to knock down the clothesline that holds the "snowy garments," possibly getting them dirty and ruining whatever hope the family has of eating. The cruelty of the particular secret-as-fetish of manual labor is that not only does it not offer Life-at-Its-Fullest when successfully executed, but also that when derailed it deprives the Us of any "life" at all. The situation is made even more grim by the fact that as Miles, the oldest son, tells his mother, "Mister Jackson say yuh cain't have no milk [for the baby], an' no nothin' 'tel de bill's paid" (69). Meanwhile, Malinda and Lindy struggle to control the children and keep secret from them the fact that there is nothing to eat, their mother ordering them to bed without supper and telling them they "ain't goin' git no suppah 'tel yuh larns to b'have yo'se'f!" (69). This particular secrecy-move raises the issue of in-group fragmentation, a situation benign enough here but highly destructive in other situations. Here, Malinda and Lindy employ such a natural secret to protect their children, and their doing so is meant to increase in-group morale even as its machinery fragments the group, a fact which at least one of them, Aloysius, knows, as he mutters, "Cain't fool me—Ah heerd Lindy say dey ain't no suppah fo' us!" (69). Although Malinda and Lindy clearly mean to keep a secret from the children for their own good and the control of children does not implicate them as social criminals, it is noteworthy that they should be forced by their economic circumstances into lying: the situation creating this "natural secret" results from White Devil secrets, as soon becomes quite clear when Burrill proceeds to show how a White Devil–entrusted secret affects the domain of the Us's.

Malinda and Lindy are visited by a white character named Elizabeth Shaw, a nurse originally from the North. As soon as she enters the stage, Miss Shaw (as she is referred to in the play) chastises Malinda for overexerting herself, warning her that her activities will precipitate her death, to which Malinda replies, "Lor', Mis' 'Liz'beth, it ain't *dyin'* Ah'm skeer't o,' its *livin'*—wid all dese chillern to look out fo'. We ain't no Elijahs, Mis' 'Lis'beth, dey ain't no ravens flyin' 'roun' heah drappin' us food. All we gits, we has to git by wukin' hard!" (70). Malinda then mentions to Miss Shaw that Lindy will be leaving for Tuskegee, which is news Miss Shaw has not yet heard; Malinda explains that going to Tuskegee has been Lindy's dream ever since she saw Booker T. Washington as a child:

> Ah kin see him now[, Malinda rhapsodizes]—him an' Lindy, jes a teeny slip
> o' gal—after de speakin' wuz oveah down dere at Shady Grove, a-standin'
> under de magnolias wid de sun a-pou'in through de trees on 'em—an' he wid
> his hand on my li'l Lindy's haid lak he wuz givin' huh a blessin', an' a-sayin':
> "When yuh gits big, li'l gal, yuh mus' come to Tuskegee an' learn, so's yuh kin
> come back head an' he'p dese po' folks!" He's daid an' in his grave but Lindy
> ain't nevah fo'git dem words. (70)

Malinda's imagery creates an interesting tableau, especially coming on the heels of her evocation of Old Testament imagery. For her, Washington is a magical figure, one of the Elijahs. His being dead and in the grave perhaps highlights her awareness of him as a secular magician, but he is also a figure out of religious magic, as well. And this magical-religious figure stands in contrast to the science Miss Shaw represents.

After helping feed the baby, Miss Shaw resumes her conversation with Malinda regarding the latter's health; reiterating the fact that Malinda is killing herself by working so hard, Miss Shaw finds herself in a difficult ethical situation. Malinda assures her that in the past she has always gone right back to work after having children; besides, she says, she and her husband have

> allus put ouah tru's in de Lawd, an' we wants tuh raise up dese chillern to be good, hones' men an' women but we has tuh wuk so hard to give 'em de li'l dey gits dat we ain't got no time tuh look at'er dey sperrits. When Jim go out to wuk—chillern's sleepin'; when he comes in late at night—chillern's sleepin'. When Ah git through scrubbin' at dem tubs all Ah kin do is set in dis cheer an' nod—Ah doan wants tuh see no chillern! . . . Ah wonder whut sin we done that Gawd punish me an' Jim lak dis! (71)

To the latter comment, Miss Shaw explains that "God is not punishing you, Malinda, you are punishing yourselves by having children every year" to which Malinda asks, "But whut kin Ah do—de chillern *come!*" to which Miss Shaw replies, "You must be careful!" which prompts Malinda to say, "*Be Keerful!* Dat's what all you nu'ses say! You an' de one whut come when Tom wuz bawn, an' Selena! Ah been keerful all Ah knows how but whut's it got me—ten chillern, eight livin' an' two daid!" (71). At this point, Miss Shaw expresses her problem, which is the problem of the obligations of a public life entrusted secret:

> I wish to God it were lawful for me to do so! My heart goes out to you poor people that sit in darkness, having, year after year, children that you are physically too weak to bring into the world—children that you are unable not only to educate but even to clothe and feed. Malinda, when I took my oath as nurse, I swore to abide by the laws of the State, and the law forbids my telling you what you have a right to know! (71–72)

Thus the Thin-Skin-of-Civilization glares in all of its problematic nature. Published in the *Birth Control Review,* this play offers a bifurcated perspective that shows the ways multiple groups are caught up in and/or participate in the furtherance of a web of secrecy. At the same time that it shows the plight of African American women, it also shows a pragmatically driven half-sympathetic/half-condemning portrait of a figure who is, in a sense, both a White Devil and an Us, a subaltern who cannot speak. Miss Shaw is white, but she is also a woman; she maintains sympathy for her patients, and yet she abides by the laws set forth by the white male–ruled government apparently designed to keep the poor poor and unhealthy. It is tempting to see her as a type of hero ("Ah ain't blamin' you" [72], Malinda tells her, seemingly absolving her of guilt in being complicit with the law), but she merely bends to the southern white patriarchal laws that she knows are not fair and were brought into existence to maintain southern white male power; any doubt that the law is based on racist and sexist ideology is swept away when Malinda tells Miss Shaw about her daughter Pinkie, who was raped and impregnated by a white man, who himself faced no retribution from the law and is keeping the secret of his miscegenation. Memory of the situation prompts Malinda to exclaim, "Lor', Mis' Liz'beth, cullud folks cain't do nothin' to white folks down heah!" (71), and the play ends with Malinda dying and Lindy taking her place instead of going to Tuskegee where she might learn about birth control and other secrets to fulfillment and long life.

Robert E. Regan's discussion of secrecy and medical ethics particularly applies as a text contemporary with Burrill's play. He notes that in the revised 1912 code of the American Medical Association a clause was included "advising the physician that occasions might arise when duty might require him to protect a healthy individual from becoming infected with a communicable disease even to the extent of using confidential professional knowledge" (116). He goes on to discuss the "code of ethics currently sanctioned by the American Medical Association" which includes a section devoted to secrecy which he quotes as follows:

> Patience and delicacy should characterize all the acts of a physician. The confidences concerning individual or domestic life entrusted by a patient to a physician and the defects of disposition or flaws of character observed in patients during medical attendance should never be revealed except when imperatively required by the laws of the state. There are occasions, however, when a physician must determine whether or not his duty to society requires him to take definite action to protect a healthy individual from becoming infected, because the physician has knowledge, obtained through the confidences entrusted to him as a physician, of a communicable disease to which the healthy individual is about to be exposed. In such a case, the physician should act as he would desire another to act toward one of his own family under like circumstances. Before he determines his course, the physician should know the civil law of his commonwealth concerning privileged communications. (117)

The ethics of this secrecy statement present an interesting positionality—a patient should be considered as if he or she is a member of the health-care giver's family, yet nothing trumps civil law. Built into the statement are a number of qualifiers whose politics are invisible. The terms "healthy" and "family" in this historical moment tend to signify "white." Added to these limitations is the extra measure of following the civil law, which is itself generated by the white patriarchy.

Burrill's play is a bitter treatise on the devastating power of the White Devils' secrets as well as an effort in a public forum read presumably by both white and black women and men to show the effects of such secrecy. Burrill wants to heighten the visibility of black women's plight as well as the ethical struggles of a white woman—a singular act of interracial feminism, as if her revelation models the similar revelation of health information she thinks "the state" should enact. This play is brave even as it is pragmatic, for at the same time that Burrill must know that her use of dialect will likely fall upon minstrel-conditioned white ears, she nevertheless employs it as if playing by the rules in order to change them. The minstrelsy apparent in the play is especially intriguing, for the play appeared in a special issue themed "The Negroes' Need for Birth Control, as seen by Themselves." One wonders what editorial thinking led to the inclusion of a dramatic piece in the issue; Burrill apparently wrote plays only, and as this one was performed in various settings around the time of its composition/publication, the editors must have thought that providing readers with a producible piece might help spread it to an audience beyond the *Birth Control Review* readership.

In a similar exploration of the politics of pregnancy, labor, and race, Georgia Douglas Johnson's *Blue Blood* considers a secret empowered by whiteness and yet held within the black community as a commodity for empowerment and gain. Also set in a one-room domestic site within a black community, this play too examines the space of labor. The set consists of a *"kitchen and dining-room combined of frame cottage, showing one door leading into back yard. One other door (right side of room facing stage) leading into hall. One back window, neatly curtained, Steps on right side of room leading upstairs"* (PGDJ 63).[10] This scene is the home of Mrs. Bush and her mulatto daughter, May; it is May's wedding day, and she is to be married to another mulatto, despite the fact that a darker-skinned man, Randolph Strong, is in love with her. Like Burrill's play, the action takes place in the South (Georgia) although just after the Civil War instead of during the Harlem Renaissance.

Of May's two suitors, Mrs. Bush prefers Randolph. She tells him at the outset of the play, when Randolph enters bringing May flowers and wishing her the best despite his own broken heart: "Oh! If she'd a only listened to me, she'd be marrying you to-night, instead of that stuck up John Temple. I never did believe in two 'lights' marrying, nohow, it's onlucky. They're jest exactly the same color . . . hair . . . and eyes alike too. Now you . . . you is jest right for my May. 'Dark should marry light.' You'd be a perfect match" (64). When Randolph leaves to get mayonnaise dressing for the reception, Mrs. Temple appears onstage to meet Mrs. Bush. As the two women talk, Mrs. Temple hints that her son is May's better, telling Mrs. Bush, "You'll have to admit that the girls will envy May marrying my boy John" to which Mrs. Bush replies, "Envy MAY!!! Envy MAY!!! They'd better envy JOHN!!! You don't know who May is, she's got blue blood in her veins" (67). Unfazed, Mrs. Temple admits that May is "sweet and pretty, but she is no match for John," at which point Mrs. Bush informs her that May's father is none other than Captain Winfield McCallister, "the biggest banker in this town, and who's got money 'vested in banks all over Georgia [. . .] 'ristocrat uv 'ristocrats . . . that Peachtree Street blue blood [. . .]" (67). Shocked by this revelation, Mrs. Temple goes on to explain that her son John was *also* born of Captain McCallister, the product of a rape, as she explains that he entered her room one night by bribing the woman who owned the boardinghouse where she lived: "I cried out. There wasn't any one there that cared enough to help me, and you know yourself, Mrs. Bush, what little chance there is for women like us, in the South, to get justice or redress when these things happen!" (69). These comments prompt Mrs. Bush to vociferate in a Bonneresque reversal of historical racial categorizations: "The dirty devil!" (69).

The secret of miscegenation thus operates within a powerful overarching hegemony, and it is the burden of the woman to preserve this secret in order to protect the black community. "Mother knew—there wasn't any use trying to punish [McCallister]," Mrs. Temple explains. "She said I'd be the one . . . that would suffer. . . . I told Paul Temple—the one I was engaged to—the whole story, only I didn't tell him who. I knew he would have tried to kill him, and then they'd have killed him" (69).[11] As they frantically try to decide how to handle this situation, Randolph returns with the mayonnaise dressing and the women call May down and break the news to her and Randolph, who then proclaims that he will take her away and marry her. The play closes with Randolph living up to his last name and telling the two mothers as he whisks May out the door, "Mother Bush—just tell them the bride was stolen by Randolph Strong!" (73). Thus the play ends with a reversal in which the black man symbolically steals back the black woman from the (semi)white man. Where May "may," Randolph "will" in his strength provide resolution both to preserve and to denounce the secret of white power and control over the black female body.

Johnson includes a curious dynamic in the play, however. After the mothers reveal May's and John's parentage in the presence of Randolph, they debate about whether or not to tell John the secret. They finally decide not to share it with him, when Mrs. Bush states that they must keep the secret "from him. It's the black women that have got to protect their men from the white men by not telling on 'em" (73), thus repeating what Mrs. Temple has already affirmed, and indeed the latter assents, "God knows that's the truth" (73). And yet the statement is a strange one, made in the presence of and just after the secret has actually been revealed to Randolph. This paradoxical moment reveals something about the nature of the secret and its uses and the consequences of those uses. Just moments before, both women were bartering on the secret of blue-blooded white heritage as a means of affirming superiority within the black community (miscegenation haunts Johnson's plays, she herself being of interracial heritage). But the secret of miscegenation—one to be celebrated in a perverse way even as it is kept—transforms into a different secret—one of incest, which is itself a taboo that is an extension of the verisimilitude of "light marrying light," which Mrs. Bush finds so distasteful (although part of her motivation has to do with her wanting May to be the superior one in her marriage relationship). Randolph then seizes on this transformed secret to attain what he wants; he never even intimates that he might be saving May from an awkward and impossible situation by some chivalric gesture. Rather, he uses the occasion to secure what he thinks should be his, for early in the play he voices his belief that May really does care for him, despite the fact that May seems torn at best, and she tells Randolph, albeit "shyly," that she does not love him (73). Significantly, she never actually says "Yes, I will go with you, Randolph," suggesting that her eloping with him may not be entirely against her will but that it is certainly ambivalent enough to validate his claim that he is in fact "stealing" the bride.

In fact, May herself seems to hold a secret of her own. Her only true assent to going with Randolph is her comment after Randolph's telling her he wants her, "My coat" (73). Hardly an expression of heartfelt love and emotion. And her final lines in the play are, "Oh God, we can't tell [everyone] the—truth?" (73). The dash suggests a hesitation—betraying the presence of a secret—that in turn suggests that the "truth" may not exactly be for her the same thing it is for everyone else in the room. Perhaps the truth is that she did prefer Randolph all along, however unlikely that may seem, but that she feels bound to John in some other way or for some other reason—perhaps she is pregnant with his child. The text does not intimate as much, but in a play so concerned with the politics of pregnancy and superiority of position and color, the possibility of that suggestion should not be discounted. Her comments upon finding out that John is her half brother are odd: she wrings her hands and says (and note the secrecy-moves of the dialogue construction), "Oh, I'd rather die—I'd rather die than face this . . . " (72), statements not that unusual for a woman in love with her fiancé who has just found out she cannot marry him. But she follows these comments with some rather more cryptic, "Oh, God—I've kept out of their clutches myself, but now it's through you, Ma, that they've got me anyway. Oh, what's the use. . . . The whole world will be pointing at me. . . . Those people in there—they'll be laughing . . . " (72). Whose clutches, exactly, has she been trying to evade? And what exactly is the nature of their clutches? Is she being discriminated against because of her light color? Is she worried about losing John? Are "they" the members of the black community in the next room? Or perhaps white people?

May portrays very little about her own feelings or agency throughout the play, and nothing else in it well informs these comments and this behavior. From the beginning, it is clear that she maintains a secret that grieves her, as she first appears dressed in a negligee rather than her wedding dress, a surprisingly sexually heightened outfit that signifies her presence in the bedroom instead of before the wedding altar. When she sees the flowers Randolph has brought, she says "Randolph is a dear!" and then "*Fondles [the] vase and looks sad*" (65). When her mother asks her if she is happy, she replies, "Why—why—(*dashing something like a tear from her eye*) of course I am" (65). When Mrs. Temple enters, May "*retreats partly up the stairway*" and remains there throughout Mrs. Temple's opening speech, in which she states that despite their moving "in somewhat different social circles. . . . I feel that my place to-night is right back here with you!" (66). At this point she sees May and exclaims, "Why, May, are you not dressed yet! You'll have to do better than that when you are Mrs. John Temple! . . . Better hurry, May; you mustn't keep John waiting," to which May replies "Oh, John will get used to waiting on me" as she walks slowly back up the stairs and off the stage (66). While on one level, Johnson seems to want to paint a picture of May as a spoiled young girl frustrated that she must be married at all, in light of Captain McCallister's brutal ways, it seems possible that the secret of May's life may be that she too has been impregnated by a white man (perhaps McCallister himself?) and realizes that marrying the light-skinned John might deliver her from suspicion about her child's parentage. In such a case, the fact of white men exploiting black female bodies continues into the next generation. In the end she leaves with Randolph for reasons known only to herself, her own secret preserved in silence as the other women watch her leave with her new fiancé.

Secrecy and the politics of pregnancy also appear in Eulalie Spence's *Fool's Errand*. Set in the "*living-room of a cabin in an unprogressive Negro settlement*" (BFP 119), the play focuses on the control of the church over the community's domestic policies. Once again, a young girl has two suitors, and through misunderstanding and deceit one of the two suitors is thought to have impregnated her. Where Johnson's suggestion that May could be pregnant is faint at best, the charge of pregnancy is explicit in Spence's play. But, as was also the case in *Blue Blood, Fool's Errand* features a transformation of a central secret—one just as much encoded on a black female body as the other.

Spence's play starts with the instigator Cassie denouncing her young niece Maza to the parson's wife, Sister Williams. Maza "ain't got no mo' shame left," Cassie complains, having accused her of being pregnant and, Cassie thinks, waiting for the guilty man to come visit her while she stands "by the gate an' a-lookin' down de road jes' lak she's done ev'y night dis week" (120). In fact, by subtle suggestion Cassie convinces Sister Williams to see Maza's alleged activities as part of a larger violation of standards within the black community, prompting Sister Williams to say, "Ef such doin's keeps on, reckon our young people'll be jes' as brazen's white folks" (121), a comment that suggestively casts whites as devils. In order to handle the supposed situation with Maza, Cassie and Sister Williams agree to have a church council meeting held at the house (which is Maza's house) where the proper man can be identified and married to Maza.

When Sister Williams leaves to call the council meeting, Cassie takes it upon herself to tell Maza's father, Doug, about his daughter's situation. "*A tall, powerful man*" (122) who drinks and is prone to ill temper, Doug at first does not believe Cassie. But Cassie explains that Maza's "bin makin' de clothes already. Got 'em pretty near all made. Ah seen 'em mahself, jes' by accident in de bottom drawer," at which point she "*jerks her head toward the chest-of-drawers*" standing in the room (122). She explains: "'Cose Ah ain't natcherly cu'rus, but when Ahs seen dat none uh dem drawers was locked, savin' only dat bottom drawer, Ah knowed sumpth'n was wrong. Well, Ah takes out de drawer above, an' looks, an' ef Ah ain't seen a bran' new set uh baby things, mah name ain't Cassie Lee" (122). The presence of this cabinet represents a borrowing from stage magic, for the "curiosity cabinet" had for over two centuries fascinated spectators and had more than once been used as a means of deception, such instances ranging from Houdini escapes that made use of the cabinet to the famous Automaton Chess Player.[12] In the play, the locked drawer invites the suspicion, and yet the suspicion itself can be easily revealed by removing the drawer above it, once again heightening the presence of the visible invisible. Thus, whoever has created this locked-drawer scenario has replicated a convention of secular stage magic, and when Cassie pulls a rabbit out of the hat, as it were, and produces a baby garment, Doug in his rage tears it to shreds and threatens to "choke [the truth] outer [Maza], by Gawd!" (123).

Cassie pacifies Doug by explaining that the council meeting will reveal the truth of the situation. She convinces him to sit down and wait for the council to arrive. Meanwhile she begins singing a song "*in a quavering voice*" while "*crouching down on the threshold*" of the door leading outside while "*rocking to and fro*":

> Camp meetin' in de wilderness,
> Thar's a meetin' here ter-night.
> Doan' let dat sinner hab no res',
> Thar's a meetin' here ter-night.
> Come along
> Thar's a meetin' here ter-night,
> Git yuh ready,
> Thar's a meetin' here ter-night,
> Ah know yuh by yo' daily walk,
> Thar's a meetin' here ter-night.
> Come alone—(123)

The song (which evokes the "hush harbor" poetics of African American religion implicit in the council meeting itself) represents a kind of incantation, a hybrid form of appeal to an overarching magic that will uncover Maza's secret in the "proper" way, and this technique follows the general pattern of the meeting itself in which religious magic combats secular magic—the mystical power of truth designed to expose the fraud of a secular trick.

When everyone arrives, including Maza and her two suitors (Freddie and Jud) as well as the council, the meeting begins. Parson Williams, an imperious man every bit as intimidating as Doug, calls for Cassie to present her charge against Maza, which she does. Maza immediately denies being pregnant, appealing to Parson Williams, saying, "Reckon yuh's got mo' sense, Parson, dan tuh believe dem lies!" (127). The parson, however, is immoveable in his conviction of her guilt and begins reading from the book of Isaiah in a pattern of incantation punctuated by call-and-response eruptions from the council:

> PARSON WILLIAMS. Wash yuh, make yuh clean; put away de evil
>   of huy doin's from befo' mah eyes; cease tuh do evil.
> THE COUNCIL. Amen! Amen!
> PARSON WILLIAMS. Come now, an' let us reason tergether, saith de Lawd;
>   though yo' sins be as scarlet dey shall be white as snow; though dey be red
>   lak crimson, dey shall be as wool.
> THE COUNCIL. (*Singing*)
>   Have yuh bin tuh Jesus fer de cleansing power?

> Are yuh washed in de blood uv de Lamb?
> Are yuh garments spotless, are dey white as snow?
> Are yuh washed in de blood uv de Lamb?
> PARSON WILLIAMS. If yuh be willin' and obedient, yuh shall eat de good
> uh de land. (128)

This incantation rises in intensity toward a climax of exorcism, as the parson exclaims in a voice "*rising ever higher and shriller in a sort of ecstasy*":

> PARSON WILLIAMS. Then yuh calls some mo' an' yuh begs for help—an' de
> debbil will mock you—de debbil will laugh!
> THE COUNCIL. Lawd! True, Lawd! True!
> PARSON WILLIAMS. On de heels uh de guilty thar treads a terribul ha'nt—
> THE COUNCIL. Save us, Lawd! Save us!
> PARSON WILLIAMS. An' de night is dark—an' thar ain't no moon—
> THE COUNCIL. Thar ain't no moon!
> PARSON WILLIAMS. An' thar ain't no stars—an' yuh looks fer de light—an'
> thar ain't no light!
> THE COUNCIL. Light! Light!
> PARSON WILLIAMS. Yuh calls on de Lawd an' thar ain't no sound—an' yuh
> calls out agin an' de debbil laughs—(128–29)

The "debbil" here of course refers to the biblical figure of Satan, but in light of that entity as a recurring one within the context of these plays, the question arises as to whether or not there is implied a laughing "white devil" who is delighted when the African American community crumbles into fragments.

At this point, with the council having reached a fever pitch, Freddie "*leaps to his feet*" and cries, "Damn yuh! Doan' yuh say no mo' Yuh's a debbil! Lemme outa here!" (129). Believing that God has flushed out the guilty party, Parson Williams proceeds to arrange the marriage of Freddie and Maza. As he does so, Jud says, "Reckon—Ah kin go—Parson. Yuh doan' need me—now," prompting Maza to rush to him, saying, "Jud! Jud! Yuh doan' believe Parson! Yuh doan' believe whut dey's sayin' 'bout me! Say yuh doan', Jud! Say yuh doan!" to which Jud replies, "Oh, curse yuh, Maza! Curse yuh!" and stomps out of the house (129). Witnessing this scene, Freddie says to her, "Maza, it's Jud yuh cares 'bout, ain't it? (*She does not answer.*) Dat's funny! Ah mean it's funny Jud's goin'—lak dat—ef he loves yuh. [. . .] Jud's a fool! He oughta know [the council is] all bug-house! Crazy ez loons!" (129). This line of talk continues unresolved for some time, Freddie confessing his love but also his suspicion that Maza cares more for Jud than himself, while Maza herself remains coy about her own desires while criticizing Freddie for his outburst, which she says the council has misinterpreted.

Just as Parson Williams is about to pronounce Freddie and Maza man and wife, Maza's mother, Mary, returns from her trip away working for white people. Mary's occupation is kept a mystery throughout the play, and her very entry onstage is enigmatic, as may be noted below.

> *The door is opened quietly and a short, stout, pleasant-faced little woman enters with a small bag. Every one turns and stares. With a glad cry Maza runs to the newcomer and throws her arms about the latter's neck. The little bag drops to the floor.* (130)

The arrival is auspicious enough, but the effect is further heightened by a strange procession of events that raises as many questions as it answers. While hugging her mother, Maza tells her, "Oh, Mom, yuh's come jes' in time! Yuh'll believe me! Oh, Mom, make 'em see dat it's all lies!" (130). Upon inquiry, Mary realizes what Cassie has charged her daughter with and then sets the record straight by revealing that it is she herself and not Maza who has made the baby clothes and locked them in the cabinet, "an' whut's mo', Ah's de one whut's gwine tuh have dat baby" (130). When everyone in the room expresses shock and incredulity, Mary admits, "Ah doan' wonder yuh's all s'prised—me wid a daughter old 'nuff tuh git married. Ef yuh stares any harder, Doug, reckon yuh eyes'll pop out yuh head!" (130). Hearing this new information, Parson Williams admonishes Cassie, "[S]eems tuh me yuh's brought us here ter-night on a fool's errand!" (130), and this exploration of the term *fool* continues on to the play's rapid end, as Maza tells her mother that Freddie was willing to marry her when Jud clearly believed the lies about her; her mother replies "Freddie ain't no fool" and then looks at her own husband and says, "Wish Ah could say the same 'bout Doug" (131). Indeed, Doug acknowledges "Ah knows Ah's a fool, Mary! An ole fool!" and it seems that multiple epiphanies have been reached and the family will go on with greater self-awareness when Mary rejoins Doug's confession with the alarming comment, "Well, but whut 'bout me, Doug?" (131). Significantly, the stage directions note that "*Doug does not answer*" (131).

The secrets revealed, transformed, and kept in this series of events are intriguing. It seems plausible that Maza's situation is made even more difficult by the fact that she cannot defend herself by revealing her mother's secret, and yet her comments to her mother seem to suggest that she herself does not know Mary's secret; she specifically appeals to her mother on the grounds that she trusts her mother to believe her. When the secret is transformed into another one revealed (that it is Mary who is having the child), then there is no longer any wrong to be righted, and Parson Williams acknowledges that he has been made a fool of through fraud and deception; Spence thus casts Cassie as a representative of secular magic, and even though the council's incantation fails to produce the "guilty" man, Spence's identifying Freddie as being nevertheless the "right" man for Maza seems to reconfirm the power of religious magic even when it is misinterpreted. In the meantime, Freddie is certainly no "fool" in that he can appreciate Maza's worth while Doug *is* a fool. But why is he a fool? Certainly he is a fool for not believing Maza. But what of his wife's closing words? She has not been a fool in the sense of doubting her daughter, so she might mean that she has been a fool for keeping her pregnancy a secret from the family and causing this trouble.

Or perhaps she has been a fool in a very different sense. The fact is that at the same time that Mary has revealed a secret she seems to hold another. Apparently, no one expects her to have a child at her age, and it does not cross Doug's mind that he might have impregnated his wife. It might be significant, however, that, as Cassie noted earlier, Doug has been a drunken loafer since Mary has "bin off wid dem white folks!" (123). It is very possible that Mary has been impregnated by a white man. What lurks about the text is the same thing that haunts Johnson's play—that the true secret lies in the exploitation of a black female body by the mysterious white "employers" (the laughing "debbils") who keep Mary away from home for as much as a week at a time. Indeed, it may be that the "fool's errand" is not that of the council at all but of Mary herself, her own errand taken into the white world. Otherwise, why even keep her pregnancy a secret at all? And perhaps in Mary's case the term *fool* refers as much to the role of trickster as it does to the one who has been tricked.

Particularly intriguing is that "small bag" Mary brings home with her and which she drops when Maza hugs her; Spence never mentions the bag again. The question arises how Spence means for the bag to be portrayed as a player in the drama as well as how its role might be interpreted and highlighted. It could be a stock device of stage magic, just as the small box accompanying the Automaton Chess Player routine included a similar device (a small box) that had no real function in the illusion except to create suspicion, a red herring meant to add another layer to the mystery. It might also represent Mary's pay for her services, a metaphorical element flexible enough to signify both monetary and physical purchase: the bag may hold money, or it may represent her womb holding a child of mixed race whose very birth is the result of economic exploitation. In any case, the bag remains closed and untouched (one might imagine a spotlight being trained on that bag alone on the floor as the play closes), symbolic of a secret unrevealed and lending particular irony to the play's end in which voices outside the house sing:

Ah met mah sister de odder night
    She call me by mah name.
An jes' as soon's mah back wuz turned
    She scandalized mah name.

Yuh call dat a sister?
    No! No! (*Chant the Council*)
Yuh call dat a sister?
    No! No!

Yuh call dat a sister
    No! No!
Who'd scandalize mah name!

(*The curtain descends slowly on the last No! No!*) (131)

The song speaks to the problems of secrets within the in-group, and the play may be read as a dramatization of the simultaneous necessity and destructiveness of secrecy within overlapping fields of secrecy-discourse. Carol Allen suggests that

Maza's plain deposition carries little weight, which brings up gender concerns and, once again, the manner in which black women's articulations have been muted by modern channels. During the trial the council turns to Maza's father for clarification[;] . . . as patriarch, despite his stated distrust of church people and their proceedings, his word can persuade the judges. . . . In regard to a female voice, the mother's narrative is formidable enough to impact on the deliberations because only it can rival the patriarch's . . . indictment. (78)

Ultimately, however, the men in the play are only marginally empowered, for Mary's testimony overturns not a man's but a woman's accusation. It is true that Parson Williams depends partly on Doug for confirmation, but the true discourse in the play is among the women, and Cassie merely *uses* patriarchal authority for her own design, which obviously points to the power of the patriarchy yet also renders the play as a revelation of the "unofficial" power black women can wield, especially in religious and domestic settings. This power is secret, hidden, plied with skill that leaves the surface of official black (patriarchal) power undisturbed. In other words, the entire council meeting is an errand that fools itself, for black women are fooling the black patriarchy with their secret power.

II

Returning to Bonner's *The Purple Flower,* with the Old Lady Us having denounced pointless work as an avenue by which to discover and possess the secret of Life-at-Its-Fullest as embodied by the metaphorical element of the Purple Flower, her compatriots take up in their conversation another aspect of their situation. Four new Us's arrive upon the scene: "*a middle-aged well-browned man, a lighter-browned middle-aged woman, a medium light brown girl, beautiful as a browned peach, and a slender, tall, bronzy brown youth who walks with his head high. He touches the ground with his feet as if it were a velvet rug and not sunbaked, jagged rocks*" (33). Their names are Average, Cornerstone, Sweet, and Finest Blood, respectively, and they take center stage in the action. The Old Lady Us addresses Average, observing that "we ain't never going to make that hill" to which Average replies, "The Us will if they get the right leaders" (33). Cornerstone breaks in at this point, "Leaders! Leaders! They've had good ones looks like to me" (33). When Average rejoins that "they ain't led us anywhere!" Cornerstone replies, "But that is not their fault! If one of them gets up and says, 'Do this,' one of the Us will sneak up behind him and knock him down and stand up and holler, 'Do that,' and then he himself gets knocked down and we still sit in the valley and knock down and drag out!" (33–34).

Just such a challenging of leaders and dissent within the black body politic finds itself dramatized in May Miller's *Harriet Tubman.* This play is one of four that Miller included in her anthology (coedited with Willis Richardson) *Negro History in Thirteen Plays* that dramatize the experiences of black leaders. Three of these are particularly relevant to black women and the secrecy moves they face as well as those they employ to combat the forms of oppression aimed at them.[13]

Set in a marsh in Maryland, *Harriet Tubman* explores the problematics of secrecy, the nuances of interrelation, and the distinction between religious and secular magic as it explores the topic of leadership. The principal characters of the play are the famous liberator herself, her brother Henry Ross, and his sweetheart, Catherine. Miller infuses the play with multiple sets of divisions, beginning with the two opposing groups of slaves: (1) those of Master John, which include the liberation-minded Harriet and Henry, and (2) those of Master Charlie, which includes Catherine. Implied in this plantation setting is also the division between the political spaces of whiteness and blackness, which is further complicated by the fact that white overseers (who appear at the end of the play) are less empowered than the white plantation owners. Added to these divisions of people are spatial divisions: Canada and the United States represent spaces of freedom and slavery, respectively, and the Chesapeake River marks a tropic figuration in the play that delineates the spaces of incarceration and escape. The stage itself represents a liminal space where the various representatives of the various spaces meet; and given that *"the gray mask of twilight hangs over the swamp"* and *"shadows play among the tall, straggly trees and touch threateningly the young Negro Girl and Fellow seated on a fallen log"* (NHTP 267), this marshy half-land, half-water space of intermingling is also one of illusion, inflected with magic and mystery and tinged with the black arts.

Harriet Tubman herself stands as a colossus throughout the play, a semi-mystical figure at ease with both religious and secular magic. She cannot be contained, being the ultimate trickster figure in the female body, a prime example of the visible invisible. The play opens with Henry and Catherine together talking not only about their plans for the future (Henry plans to run away this night with his sister) but also Harriet's evasive skills. "Come on, Cath'rine, thar ain't no use n' yo' breakin' yo'self up lak that. Ain't Ah tole you Ah'm comin' back to git you?" Henry says, and when Catherine tearfully expresses her doubt that he can get back, he replies, "Ain't Harriet comin' back wid ev'ry slave town 'twixt heah an' Canada off'ring forty thousand dollars foh huh?" prompting her to observe, "But the Lord leads Harriet. She says she talks wid God" (267). Despite Harriet's prodigious and divinely bestowed magical abilities, however, Catherine notes that her Master Charles is extremely upset about losing one of his slaves to Harriet's most recent roundup, and there "ain't no way in the worl' he'd let another slave o' his's git to Canada no time soon. If Ah went now, he'd git out the bloodhounds, cover the roads, an' drag the Ches'peake, too; then he'd catch all o' you" (177). Assuring her that everything will be fine and that he will not only escape but return for her, Henry leaves her alone in the woods and goes to find and leave with his sister.

Upon his exit, another slave named Sandy enters. Sandy wants Catherine for himself and reminds her that Master Charles has promised to marry her to him. Also, in his jealousy (for he has heard of her relationship with Henry), he proclaims that he will be rich soon and will be able to buy his own freedom as well as Catherine's. Laughing at him, Catherine tells him he "mus' be a-thinkin' the angel Gabriel's gonna drap a bag o' gold at yo' feet" (272); Sandy explains that the magic involved here does not originate in heaven but rather from his own ingenuity because he stands to be paid by taking part in a plan to trap Harriet, his role being to lock the boathouse on the eastern branch of the river, thereby preventing the only remaining avenue of escape since various overseers have been placed along the roads to watch for slaves planning to run away. When Sandy leaves the stage self-assured in his plan, the frantic Catherine casts about to see how she might get word to Harriet and in the process runs into Sabena, one of Master John's slaves who is loyal to Harriet. Sabena enters the stage singing the song "Go Down, Moses," a signal troping song of escape and magic.[14] Catherine tries to explain Harriet's dire situation to Sabena, but the latter is suspicious of "one o' Mistah Charley's niggers. . . . Ah ain't trustin' non o' 'em, They ain't no good" (276).[15] Unable to convince Sabena to send word to Harriet, Catherine runs offstage to find the leader herself.

At this point, Harriet and her party of escaping slaves appear onstage. Her followers kneel and kiss her dress, but she admonishes them to get off the ground so they can keep moving. She both deflects and invites worship, for at the same time that she negotiates and even discourages the adoration of her followers, she also presents herself as an emissary of God, saying regarding the danger of their flight:

> Ah ain't scared one jot. Ah always trust the Lawd. Ah says to him, "Ah don' know whar to go, or what to do, but Ah 'spects you to lead me." An' he always do. Now, them what trusts wid me, kin follow; the res' kin stay heah. (278)

When Sabena, who has remained onstage, rushes up to her and warns her that "you got to be careful down heah, an' go kinda slow" (278), Harriet responds with an evocation of the apocalyptic vision in Revelation:

> John saw the city, didn' he? Well, what did he see? Twelve gates—three o' them gates was on the North, three o' 'em was on the East, three o' 'em was on the West; but thar was three o' 'em on the South, too. An Ah' reckon if they kill me down heah, Ah'll git into one o' them gates, don'cha? (278)

Like the apostle himself, Harriet sees things hidden (to echo Malcolm Bull again). When Sabena explains that Catherine has told her that watches are out, Henry confirms that Catherine tells the truth, and Harriet remarks, "Ah trusts the sense o' a man in love, 'cause God speaks in him then" (280).

Presently, Catherine herself reappears on the stage and explains the plan that Sandy has revealed to her. At first, Harriet is unconcerned that the boats are unavailable, observing in her indomitable way that "Jesus walked the watah, an Ah've waded many a stream" (281), a comment that not only evokes Christ but also the Old Testament story of Moses crossing the Red Sea, itself already alluded to in the singing of "Go Down, Moses." When Henry observes that the tide is high and they would "be washed down lak

Pharaoh's army" (281), Catherine tells them that Sandy has the key to the boathouse in his pocket. Harriet devises a plan to secure the key, sending Catherine off to cajole Sandy by means of feminine wiles into coming into the swamp where they might capture him and get the key. When Catherine goes off to practice this deception, Harriet mentions that it would be best to tie Sandy up, and Sabena offers her a rope from her "bundle," or luggage, to "tie one o' Mistah Charley's limbs o' Satan" (282). This reference to Satan initiates a series of uses of the word "devil" that continues to the play's end. Soon, Catherine returns with Sandy, and two of the escaping slaves grab him and tie him up while Henry procures the boathouse key. As Sandy struggles, he yells at Catherine, "You two-faced devil! Ah'll tell Mas'r Charles, an' he'll break ev'ry bone in yo' dirty, lyin' body!" (284). They gag Sandy and head for the river, Harriet exhorting her followers, "Come on, folks, you's boun' foh Canaan" (285).

Left alone to perform a Houdini-esque escape, Sandy finally frees his mouth of the gag and calls out for his master. As he does so, a white overseer, Edward, appears; he peers through the gloom to try and see Sandy, asking, "Where the devil are you?" (285), and when he finds Sandy, he exclaims, "Well, I'll be damned. What the devil are you doin' here?" (286). Sandy explains the situation, and as he does so, another overseer named Thomas comes onstage confirming that the slaves have escaped by way of the river. Edward rebukes Sandy, telling him, "I oughta hang you—lettin' 'em git that key. Mistah Charles is gonna raise the devil" (286). In the uses of the term *devil* in this progression, Sandy is a "limb of Satan" for his deceptive complicity with white people; yet, when captured, he curses Catherine for her own deception, calling her a "devil"; foiled by both sides that he tries to play, Sandy finds himself derided as a "devil" by the white overseers who, themselves, realize that their employer will "raise the devil" because of the events that have transpired. The final lines of the play cast the entire situation within the pragmatic proclivities of magic, when after Sandy leaves the stage, the white overseers speak:

THOMAS. That black witch works like magic.
EDWARD. Yeah, damn it—slippin' out like that, with forty thousand dollars
   on her head. (288)

The two white men thereby reconfirm Harriet's status as simultaneously a religious magician and a secular trickster magician. For these men, she is the voodoo queen whose power hits them where it most hurts them as poor whites—their pocketbooks.

Harriet Tubman features the very dynamic Bonner presents in *The Purple*

Flower of black people attempting to tear down their own leaders. Johnson tellingly uses the word "sneaking" to describe the secrecy-move used to fragment the in-group. Yet, at the same time that Sandy tries to derail Harriet's ride on the Underground Railroad, that effect is almost an incidental one in the game he is actually playing, for the payoff of his game is Catherine. Sandy desires freedom as much as any of the other slaves, but he has concocted another way of obtaining it—by using the money he expects his master to pay him for his part in thwarting the escape of Harriet and her group of runaways. "Ah ain't got nothin' to say foh, nor 'gin" Harriet, Sandy explains, but by helping his master, "[t]his time, tomorrow, I'll hab 'nough money to buy bofe o' us free" (271–72). Sandy mentions that "the folks in the kitchen done tole" the master that Harriet is going to "go by the back road" (274). The folks in the kitchen have revealed a promised secret that contains the thorny fact of touching "a serious obligation in justice" whether from the point of view of the masters or the slaves. Sandy, curiously enough, embodies this doubleness, for he is a mulatto who maintains loyalty both to the concept of maintaining slavery and to obtaining freedom. Yet, like Huizinga's spoil-sport, he seems to be playing in his own game even as he ostensibly remains in the slaves' secrecy-discourse situation. The only secret he makes any effort at all to keep is that of his involvement in the runaways' apprehension plan; this secret he tries to keep from Catherine initially so that he can enact his game of getting her. Although Sandy accuses Catherine of duplicity, Sandy himself emerges as the "two-faced devil," and yet (although it might sound criminal), Sandy can be read as sympathetic: at the same time that he is clearly a sellout, it should also be noted that he has fallen prey to White Devil tricks, for surely a subtext of the play is that Sandy will probably never get the payment he expects for his loyalty to his master. Furthermore, whatever the differences in their situations and their goals, Thomas and Edward are playing the same game for money that Sandy plays, and he takes it on the chin from them as well. Viewed this way, Sandy emerges as the victim of the insidious inroads that the white empowered establishment's ideology has on a black person's consciousness, a victim of the multiply interpolated tapestry of secrecy within which he lives and operates.

Regarding Thomas and Edward, it might be pointed out that this is the first of the plays in this discussion besides *The Purple Flower* to feature white characters on stage. Although Bonner puts the White Devils in full view of the audience, most of the one-acts discussed herein transpire in all-black settings; doing so well dramatizes the invisible, secretive power of the white establishment. But Miller repeatedly includes white characters in her plays, which raises a number of issues. First, regarding *Harriet Tubman*, the presence of poor whites seems to complicate whiteness: they are scrambling for the same prize as a black man and are equally ensnared in White Devil tricks, struggling to increase their economic (and possibly even social) status in a system that seeks to keep them as fixed in their (albeit better) status as much as it keeps the Us's in theirs. Reading *Harriet Tubman* through the lens of *The Purple Flower* might even suggest that such poor whites are one of the Us's, although such a reading strains interpretation of both texts since poor whites are as much the enemy as well-to-do whites. But then, is the audience supposed to read poor whites as having been deceived by the white patriarchy just as Sandy has been? It seems telling that Edward and Thomas speak in dialect just as the black characters do. Are poor whites a product, as a race, of empowered whites' divide-and-conquer strategy, as Theodore Allen argues in *The Invention of the White Race*? Speaking of what the audience is to see, another issue raised by the inclusion of white characters is that of staging. Does Miller expect African Americans to perform whiteness? Knowing that these one-acts would rarely be performed outside of all-black settings, Miller must surely have considered this matter. In light of these material conditions, having white characters may be read as a dramatization of the performance of race that throws into relief the constructedness and performance of dialect and other racist markers of essentialized blackness as well as whiteness.

Tubman's strength, her powerful leadership, her ability to exist within overlapping spheres of magic while successfully negotiating multiple secrecy-discourse game scenarios—these are the things that establish her as a model of a black woman's transcendence of her prescribed roles and constricted space. Miller provides a similar model in Sojourner Truth. Just as the setting of *Harriet Tubman* is a wild liminal space far from the constrictions of domesticity and bathed in an aura of magic, so Miller's play titled *Sojourner Truth* is set outdoors, the stage divided between two spaces, the foreground being a clearing dotted by "*irregular roughly-chopped tree stumps*" and the background being filled with "*straggly trees* [that] *form a thin fringe*" (NHTP 315). The scene is a camp meeting in Northampton, Massachusetts, and Sojourner Truth is present onstage from the very beginning and yet hidden, mysterious, and secretive, sitting on a "*mud-bespattered cart*" in the far left and back corner of the stage. "*It is difficult for one to distinguish clearly the tall, gaunt figure sitting on the wagon, smoking a clay pipe*," the stage directions read. "*A soft humming holds the air and gradually the words the woman is singing become intelligible*" (315).

As Truth sings softly to herself, a camp attendant named Mr. Clarkson appears onstage trying to find the source of the singing. When Truth comes out of "hiding" and presents herself to him, he, suspicious of her, warns that she must leave the campgrounds or he will have her removed. He then leaves the stage, telling her that if she is still there when he returns there will be trouble. She placidly climbs back onto the wagon, going back into hiddenness, at which point a group of young boys enters the stage planning to set fire to the tents in the camp meeting—a violent scheme that they strangely see as being a practical joke. Again, the term *devil* appears in various nuances, beginning with one boy telling another in the group not to talk so loud because if he keeps "raisin' the devil . . . the whole camp will be on us like bloodhounds" (319). Two of the boys, Ralph and Jerry, are the leaders of this band, and they use various coercive measures to get the group to follow them, going to particularly strong-armed extremes to get the holdout, Malcolm, to conform. After exhausting all of their persuasive skills, the boys turn to physical efforts, Ralph shouting, "Mal's a coward. Devil take him. Let's chase him out" (323), at which point Sojourner Truth again comes out of her watchful hiding and stands up for Malcolm and admonishes the boys not to go through with their plan. The boys then turn on her, Ralph saying, "Let's teach her what we do with spies" and Jerry exclaiming, "We'll chase her so fast she won't have breath left to tell what she heard" (323). They chase her off the stage, leaving Malcolm and another boy, Henry, behind.

The boys' game here signals a different inflection of secrecy, for although this game threatens to touch "real life," it is a simulation separate from the sphere of "real life." Huizinga's observations regarding play are especially pertinent, as he writes that the

> exceptional and special position of play is most tellingly illustrated by the fact that it loves to surround itself with an air of secrecy. Even in early childhood the charm of play is enhanced by making a "secret" out of it. This is for *us,* not for the "others." What the "others" do "outside" is no concern of ours at the moment. . . . Even with us a bygone age of robuster private habits than ours, more marked class-privileges and a more complaisant police, recognized the orgies of young men of rank under the name of a "rag." The saturnalian licence of young men still survives, in fact, in the ragging at English universities, which the *Oxford English Dictionary* defines as "an extensive display of noisy and disorderly conduct carried out in defiance of authority and discipline." (31–32)

The dynamic of the boys' game is a definite game of "ragging" aimed at religion and the world of adults "in defiance of authority and discipline" they represent. Malcolm is, of course, the spoilsport (Huizinga actually ventures that "the figure of the spoil-sport is most apparent in boys' games" [30]), and it is he who ultimately provides the hope of an abolishment of the current rules and the formation of a new, positive, more inclusive game.

As Malcolm and Henry talk about the fact that they have for some time been reluctant to follow the group, Mr. Clarkson returns and asks where Sojourner Truth is since he has heard a rumor that someone is planning to set fire to the tents, and he thinks that she is the catalyst behind the scheme. A turncoat, Henry takes Mr. Clarkson off to find Sojourner, leaving Malcolm alone at which point the boys come storming in mistaking him for Sojourner. As it turns out, the boys no longer want to harm but rather want to spend time with her. Now they are fascinated by her, and Sojourner returns to the stage to give the boys a talking to.

> I guess you been wond'rin why I come back. Well after I hid behind that tent an' I heard you pass by, I got to talkin' to myself an' I say, "Shall I run away an' hide from the devil? Have I not faith enough to go out an' quell that mob when I know it is written one shall chase a thousand an' two put ten thousand to flight?" (328)

The comment, evoking divine magic, signals a turn in the trajectory of the play. Heretofore, the play has operated on misdirection and hiding—stock elements of stage magic. Truth has remained in the shadows outside of the ken of the characters and only manifests herself when she chooses. This disappearing act now comes to a close in a moment of revelation, a banishing of her secret persona for an instructive display of another self. The boys ask her to tell them about her experiences, and she replies:

> The speriences, boys, what I've had won't never happen to you. An' God my witness, I wouldn't want 'em to happen to none o' God's creatures. 'Mos' the first thing I kin remember is my Mammy sittin' on her doorstep starin' an' starin' at the stars, then weepin' an' weepin', then starin' some more. An' I say to her, "Mammy, why you look at the stars an' weep?" An' she say to me, "Isabella, I look at the stars; my children look at the stars. I know not where they be; they know not where I be." (329)

Her words express the tense politics of secrecy inherent in slavery. She is lifting the Veil for the boys to see the other side of black experience. Her next comment further shows the violence and pain of slavery, as she explains that "I could tell you 'bout when I was a little girl an' how my master once whipped me 'til the blood streamed from my body an' dyed the floor beneath me. But whippings like that is common. Even now thousands o' my black sisters an' brothers are still barin' their backs to the bitin' lash" (329). But this movement toward revelation only reveals the powerful enforcing of secrecy in the divide-and-conquer mentality that keeps black people from establishing family and community solidarity, for still the slaves' "children are snatched 'way an' sold where they never see nar hear o' 'em again, an' still they toil and pray" (329). Truth demonstrates for the boys the devastating power of the secret, and it is her goal to break up their secret society, which looks alarmingly like a juvenile form of the Ku Klux Klan; indeed, early on, Jerry had explained that their aim was to "fix it so as all the tents will start burnin' at once, an' all the folks'll be thinkin' it's Judgment Day an' the world's on fire" (320). Truth ends her lecture to the boys by both scaring them and appealing to their hearts, saying:

> Whenever I see flames lickin' joyous-like at the heavens I say to myself, that's the devil's work. Who knows, tomorrow heart-broken pappies and mammies may be rakin' them ashes for charred bones that was once happy, laughin' little children. No, lads, fires ain't fun; they's jes' a taste o' hell. (330)

The unmistakable double-entendre of these words—referring not just to the fires of children's pranks but also to the burning of black bodies in lynchings—does the trick in changing the boys' minds. The play ends on a positive note. Clarkson returns with Henry and a sheriff to arrest Truth, but the other boys set the record straight. And Clarkson is so impressed that Truth has changed the boys' minds that he changes his mind and tells her she is allowed to go to the camp meeting and speak.

Where *Harriet Tubman* features white characters, *Sojourner Truth* transpires in a white world, an inversion in which there is only one black character. Where the trajectory of *Harriet Tubman* proceeds with the preservation of hiddenness, *Sojourner Truth* moves toward greater revelation. Where *Harriet Tubman* maintains its multiple secrecy-discourse games, the movement toward openness at the close of *Sojourner Truth* enlists all players in a single game. Truth and Malcolm realign the rules of the game by questioning those rules, with Truth proposing others.[16] Here again the question arises as to what sort of interracial bond has been created. The boys are white; Clarkson is white; the sheriff who appears at the end of the play to restore order that Truth herself has already restored is white. Yet all of these white characters speak in dialect, despite their signifying forces of authenticity that can be disastrously detrimental to black people. Unlike in *Harriet Tubman,* these fractured groups unite, seemingly abjuring White Devil tricks that keep them divided and ineffective. The play ends with hope, as Truth sings again the song that she sings at the beginning of the play, though now it has taken on new significance:

> It was early in the mornin',
> It was early in the mornin'

When he rose—when he rose
An' went to heaven on a cloud. (333)

Regarding this cohesion it might be pointed out that Clarkson does not recognize Truth as different until he "sees" that she is black, and, besides Clarkson's stating "you're a Negro" and that he does not "like tramps nor no trouble 'bout run-away slaves" (316), neither he nor the boys designate her by race, referring to her instead as the "old woman."

Pondering the theatrical aspects of this play, the implications of production and reception loom quite large. Again, Miller seems largely unconcerned about the problems of having white characters onstage in the Black Little Theater Movement, but what is especially noteworthy is the possibility that this story of a single black woman against a man's world articulated her sense of herself as a black woman trying to write for the stage. Both Truth and Miller's playwrighting self negotiate a world that is white and male and in which men provide the women with a stage upon which to perform. Not only must Truth be offered a platform by Clarkson, it is when the boys gather around her as an audience that she can begin to speak to any effect. Of course, she seizes the stage initially to defend Malcolm, and it is possible that Miller's point is to say that gaining such visibility depends upon just such an initial, aggressive act—a rupturing of the maternal body into the space of the ordered symbolic, which is the movement from "humming" to "signing." Now visible and placed on the stage, she will presumably go and interpret the scriptures, bringing forth from the shadows therein secrets of instruction to those gathered, injecting a brush arbor meeting with the poetics of the hush harbor.

An arresting and pregnant image/object in the play is a clay pipe that Truth smokes. At the beginning of the play, Clarkson asks Truth if she believes in the Bible, and when she replies in the affirmative, he asks, "And you smoke that pipe? . . . Well, then what can be more filthy than the breath of a smoker? Doesn't the Bible say no unclean thing shall enter the kingdom of heaven?" (317). To this comment, Truth replies, "Yes, Mister, but when I go to heaven, I 'spect to leave my breath behind me" (317). The construction of her reply alone is memorable in light of theatricality: she "spects" (spectates? envisions?) to leave her breath *behind her,* suggesting that her need for speech and performance will no longer be necessary in heaven. Suggesting, too, that such a stage prop *is* necessary for the here and now— for when Clarkson asks her, "Then while you live, you mean to take that clay pipe an' go 'bout preachin', eh?" she replies, "Yes, sir, while my breath holds out" (317). That the pipe is phallic seems clear enough, but the breath is Truth's, and the evident point is that the physical world's domination by men requires her to use the tools at hand (themselves unclean) in order to speak in it; in short, she must use the corrupt medium of the stage to state her own position, to "hold out" both keeping and "outing" her secrets. Curiously enough, however, Truth no longer has her pipe by the end of the play; she apparently loses it in her flight from the boys, for it is just as conspicuously absent when she returns to the stage as it was present before she left (earlier in the play). Has Miller simply lost track of the pipe, a sign of the amateurishness that Perkins sees in these one-acts? Possibly. But its absence may signal Truth's having reached a type of heaven of interracial cooperation, or, less positively, that now in possession of the masculine stage itself she no longer needs the pipe. In either case, the pipe has gone into hiding by the play's end, has apparently dropped through the thin skin of civilization and into invisibility in exact relation with Truth's becoming more visible, implying that the female body grows more incarnate physically, where it was "breath" and shadow before. Of course this visible physicality also has a problematic history, for Truth runs the risk of becoming Joice Heth, a black woman "possessed" by whites, but Miller does not seem to pursue that unpleasant underside of such increase of visibility.

From these interracial plays, Miller turns in *Christophe's Daughters* to an all-black context to address the last day in the life of King Henry Christophe of Haiti as experienced by his daughters Améthiste and Athénaire. The dialect that often marks various types of racial performance in these plays is absent in this play, as Améthiste, Athénaire, and most of the other characters speak the King's English (an especially problematic linguistic situation, given that their historical counterparts would have been speaking primarily in French). Once again, Miller engages the issue of biological versus performed "blackness" in dialect as raised by Hurston, for here an all-black cast must perform white dialect; here again the white power is both omnipresent yet absent, a visible invisible that underpins these black people's performance of an empowered self.

The play opens with a long dialogue between Améthiste and Athénaire in their father's throne room in Sans Souci Palace, which Miller describes as "*very pretentious, . . . done in the ornate style of Louis XIV*" (NHTP 243). In their conversation, the two daughters fill in for the reader/audience certain confirmed and necessary historical details while in the background a drumbeat grows steadily louder (a nod to Eugene O'Neill's play *The Emperor Jones*). Améthiste reminds her sister (in an unfortunately clunky bit of dialogue) that during their father's reign

> Haiti has grown rich. A merchant marine floats in the harbor. We export now, besides sugar more coffee, cocoa, and cotton than the people ever dreamed of. . . . They ought to look to the chateaux throughout the kingdom, to this palace and the citadel, La Ferriere, and see that their king's dreams are not idle. (244)

Yet, as Améthiste goes on to explain to her sister, their father faces deposition because "the politicians are corrupt and stir up rebellion. The mulattoes hate a black king. They call work slavery. The landlords hate justice, and the people, who themselves benefit by labor, are lazy. There is no hope for anything different. Our father, the King, works alone" (245).

Here Cornerstone's complaint that the masses tear down the Us's leader seems to be played out, and yet in a sense it does not. Christophe *has* successfully achieved power, and members of his own in-group are trying to tear him down. But Christophe has merely replicated the power structures of the White Devils. Moreover, the usurpers are *not*, precisely speaking, part of his in-group, for despite the fact that the historical Christophe himself was likely of mixed heritage, he championed the black-dominated northern kingdom of Haiti that opposed the mulatto-led and -inhabited south and was cruel to mulattoes and other mixed-race groups in his own domain.[17] The splendor of his kingdom is the splendor of the white West, and at the heart of the play stand all the problems of postcolonial subjectivity and power that theorists from Fanon to Thiong'o address: namely, that adopting the language and trappings of the center empowers but simultaneously and paradoxically removes one from the periphery in a way that makes one unable to speak for the periphery. This debilitating situation inscribes itself on Christophe's body in stark visibility: Christophe has grasped the Purple Flower; yet his very attainment of power and sophistication has coincided with a simultaneous disfigurement. Améthiste notes that her father "says that to be great is to be lonely; to be magnificent is to have men hate you," but Athénaire quickly notes that

> he was not magnificent this morning and still they hate him. When he came down from the balcony, dragging his poor paralyzed legs to mount his horse before the army, it was pathetic. They should have loved him for his courage, but when he fell in the mud, I heard someone jeer. I didn't wait to see them carry him. I fled from the balcony into my chamber and wept. (245)

Christophe's visible weakness has led his followers to abandon him, and as the drums of revolt grow increasingly louder with the usurpers' approach to the palace, Améthiste and Athénaire anxiously discuss what they should do. Athénaire observes, "King's daughters matter little. I don't understand why we can't flee with our father to safety up to the citadel. We could take the secret passage and reach there before nightfall," but Améthiste says, "We can't do that because out father is still the king and kings don't run away" (250). Such a secret passage is one of many such secrecy-moves Christophe has made to preserve his own power: according to legend, he also promoted the myth that he could be killed only by a silver bullet, and O'Neill's play well illustrates the way such a myth could increase one's power. As for the two girls, Améthiste remains invested in the empowered position and its public-life secrets where Athénaire seems to have accepted already that she has now entered the ranks of the unempowered and so must use secrecy-moves for protection rather than control and oppression.

It is also the case, however, that Athénaire is involved in another secrecy-discourse game that threatens to divide her loyalty, for it emerges that she is actually in love with one of the enemy. This information comes to light when the servant Marie (one of the few nonfamily members to remain at the palace) refuses to bring the girls tea when they request it. Marie explains that her lover, Claude, has gone away with the others and has instructed her to leave the palace herself before nightfall, when, as she explains, "Duke Richard comes [. . .] with men to burn the castle and take the King" (248). Although Améthiste berates Marie, Athénaire allows her to leave, observing that it "brings no comfort to have her stay when her heart goes" (250), a statement that actually describes her own situation for her lover, Jean, the nephew of Duke Richard, the usurper himself.

When Améthiste leaves the room to speak to their father, Jean himself arrives onstage to speak to Athénaire. He tells her that he has a plan to prevent the rebellion and save King Christophe, explaining that there

> are still men in the army who love your father, and there are those, of course, who follow my uncle. They are marching now over the road from Cap Henry. In a little while they will be in the courtyard below. You shall stand with me at the palace gate and I shall cry aloud to the men as they march in, "Look! the happy union of King Christophe's daughter and Duke Richard's nephew. The rebellion is over." All groups will be satisfied. The men want peace and we shall bring it. The King and the Duke will be reconciled. (256)

Although at first suspicious, Athénaire finally acquiesces to Jean's plan for reconciliation. "I shall restore peace," she says to herself in a tone that Miller writes should seem "as if dreaming of a great accomplishment"; "I shall save my father," she says, "I shall make the people happy" (258). Then, just as she turns to go with Jean to enact the plan, "a loud report shatters the quiet of the room" (258), bringing one of Duke Richard's soldiers to make sure that Jean has not been harmed (173). The soldier lets it slip that "Duke Richard's orders were to see [Jean] back safely" (258), and Athénaire, realizing that Jean's plan was not only not motivated by love for her but was not even his plan in the first place, refuses to cooperate any longer and sends Jean away, exclaiming, "I could weep for my own stupidity. To think I believed you!" (259).

Miller invites comparison of Marie and Athénaire by juxtaposing their similar situations in this moment of civil crisis. The two women represent two different roles of black women—one, to accept the mantle of work bestowed upon them by black men and thus acquiescing to the role of "mule of the world," and, second, to protect black men as well as white men from themselves. Marie keeps secret her own convictions regarding the insurrection, submitting instead to her lover's beliefs. Athénaire, on the other hand, nearly falls prey to a deception created to promote a secret plan, a trick that seems to achieve one goal while actually effecting another, for Athénaire observes that Duke Richard "hoped the union of the King's daughter and his nephew could ease the guilty conscience of the men who still nurse some little respect for their majesty. I see through his dirty little scheme now," to which Jean in his pragmatic thinking replies, "It's not a dirty little scheme. It was a good idea. He said our union would end the rebellion," to which the girl rejoins, "Certainly, end the rebellion and bring him undivided support. For that end he used you, and you would use me" (259).

When Jean leaves, Améthiste reappears on stage and informs Athénaire that the shot she heard was that of their father's committing suicide. The play closes with the girls preparing a stretcher to bear their father's body away to prevent it from being mutilated. As they do so, the insurrectionists draw nearer and Jean returns, this time to save Athénaire from the mob. Athénaire refuses his offer of rescue; instead, and at her sister's behest, she gives him "jewels and coins" to scatter "among the rioters . . . to hold them off a while" (263). Jean takes the valuables and leaves, and the sisters and the rest of the royal family leave with Christophe's body, heading for the secret passage while in the background the mob can be heard yelling "Down with the King! Long live independence!" (264).

Where there can be found in *Sojourner Truth* the implication that black women must be enabled by black men in order to perform, *Christophe's Daughters* makes the point clear. The particular cruelty of Jean's treatment of Athénaire lies in his making her think she actually can affect the outcome of the situation when she simply cannot. This woman's futility clashes, nevertheless, with Miller's signal act of female empowerment in placing Améthiste and Athénaire at the center of the story/stage. Miller also commits her own revisionist act of violence by changing the metal of Christophe's fatal bullet, for Améthiste informs her sister that "he sent the *golden* bullet through his brain" (260; emphasis mine). Like Sojourner Truth's pipe, this little bit of material looms large in Miller's text, for by it she seizes the myth that Christophe uses to create his power. Read this way, the play is not so much one on the failings and fallings of black leaders as it is about men as the enemies of women and a woman's retroactive attempt to subvert masculine power and authority. Yet, even that attempt is limited by the control of black men over the Little Theater, and Miller shows that the women characters' power is limited for Améthiste and Athénaire just as it is for Miller herself, for the girls have no authority beyond the throne room, from which Christophe himself is notably absent.

Particularly fascinating is Miller's insertion of magic in the middle of the play. Marie invokes two forms of religious magic in her conversation with the princesses. When Améthiste scolds her for being more loyal to Claude than to Christophe and demands that she stay at the palace, Athénaire defends the woman, prompting Marie to exclaim in gratitude, "Oh, Princess Athénaire, may the Mother Mary protect you" (249). Athénaire responds that "Mother Mary always protects those who are faithful to their trusts," but Marie produces a voodoo charm from her bosom and observes that it "protects the hill girls when the Mother no longer will" (249). At this point, Améthiste breaks in, denouncing the woman as a heretic, vituperating, "How many times have I told you that those charms of the witch doctors are evil? You don't love your God. You still worship snakes," to which Marie replies, "No, no, Princess, I believe in all of them. I love God, but I fear the snakes" (249). Marie's function in the play is intriguing. On one hand, her subjection illuminates the power of the ruling class of which Améthiste and Athénaire are a part, and Marie's folk religion aligns her with the black women typically depicted in the one-acts. At the same time, though, Damballa (the voodoo god represented by the snake) tends to unite groups, often male and female, suggesting that as she is joined with Claude, so Athénaire should go with Jean, who stands for a better order than her father's. In this sense, Marie accentuates the chiaroscuro of Athénaire's situation, and the audience must grapple with seeing Christophe as the hero and the revolters the villains or Christophe as the tyrant and the revolters the champions of the oppressed. How far does family and group loyalty extend? If translated to a white-black dichotomy, the question seems much more easily answered, but to do so would do violence to the play. It is provocative to think that the audience must wonder whether to laugh or cry at Miller's changing the silver bullet to gold or to celebrate or mourn Athénaire's decision to remain loyal to her father and refuse Jean's hand, however unethical and pragmatic the young man may be. Ultimately, the tricks of the White Devils can be discerned still wreaking their havoc even after the White Devils themselves have departed from the political scene, for their effects are what put Athénaire in her hopeless position and cause people to despise her father.

III

Having considered the shortcomings of work and the failure of leadership among their number, the Us's in *The Purple Flower* turn to another matter that they see as having thwarted their progress toward the attainment of Life-at-Its-Fullest. Even as the leaders have been criticized, Old Lady observes that "they [the leaders of the Us's are] going to meet this evening to talk about what we ought to do" (34). Her comment prompts a number of responses. First, Average asks, "What is the need of so much talking?" to which Cornerstone replies, "Better than not talking! Somebody might say something after while" (34). To these comments, Sweet says, "I want to talk too!" When Average asks her, "What can you talk about?" she exclaims, "Things! Something, father!" which leads Finest Blood to say, "I'll speak too" (34). Exasperated, Average shouts, "Oh you all make me tired! Talk—talk—talk—talk! And the flower is still up on the hillside!" to which Old Lady immediately retorts, "Yes and the White Devils are still talking about keeping the Us away from it, too" (34).

Where Average finds talking an ineffective approach to dealing with the Us's crisis, the women around him recognize the importance of talking, and the young Sweet struggles to assert herself through speech. Although Finest Blood takes his cue from the women (and as the play proceeds he emerges as the foremost of the Us's willing to try any and all modes of improvement and empowerment), the realm of talk and discourse seems to be a feminine one among the Us's. This privileging of discourse reflects the fact that Bonner and the other women writers contemporary with her realize that discourse was often the only effective means of agency open to them in creating group solidarity in the face of enemy moves in the games of secrecy-discourse they play. The Old Lady Us well understands the importance of communication, for it is what enables the White Devils to mobilize against the Us's effectively.

Black women trying to speak from within their confined spaces even as men decry their speech clearly informs many of the one-acts written by these women, but certain plays particularly dramatize the struggle of African American women's speech. Eulalie Spence offers three plays that present distinct ways in which women speaking out of their own spaces work within the medium of secrecy to articulate their perspectives and thereby empower themselves.[18] The first of these is *Her.* Another play with a domestic setting, this one-act contrasts two different women: one whose speech is indiscernible and the other whose speech is uncontrollable. Set in a Harlem apartment house, *Her* transpires in the living room of a black couple, Martha and Pete. Spence introduces

MARTHA—*old, black who takes in washing for some "very old families," who is, herself, always immaculate in her grey dress and white apron. Martha, who takes care of Pete, her husband—crippled and an idler for more than fifteen years—Martha, who irons in the living room—eats there for the accommodation of Pete, and spreads her clothes horse there on rainy days. Martha, who is the oldest tenant in the house—who rents the rooms for John Kinney, and collects the rentals, as well.* (BFP 132)

The set itself is as "typical" as Spence's description of Martha makes her; Spence explains that all "*we really need to know about the construction of the room is that a door at back, left, opens upon the hallways*" (132).

The play opens with Martha and Pete in the room talking as Martha does her washing. Martha rules this roost: Pete sits in his "*invalid chair—his steel rimmed spectacles and his Bible lying open on his knees*" (132) throughout the play. Incapable of working and observing that his wife is agitated, Pete laments that he cannot provide for them himself, and speaking from his space of emasculation, he says that "[i]n them magazines yuh brung home last week there was a piece 'bout some cripple fellers—how they's learned ter make money—plenty money. Ah ain't read nuthin' so mirac'lus in a long time, Martha, an' Ah got ter thinkin'—Ah might er bin helpin' yuh all these years, ef Ah'd knowed how" (133). His comments get at the persistent conflict between religion and science that appears in *They That Sit in Darkness*: with the Bible sitting on his knees, he nevertheless reads and takes to heart medical science's promise of miracles in what Martha calls "no 'count books" full of "trash" (133). It turns out that Martha *is* agitated, but not because of her work; rather, she is upset because her landlord Kinney plans to rent out the rooms upstairs. His doing so is a problem for Martha because it places her in an ethical dilemma—whether to reveal or keep secret vital information for the potential tenants. The information is that the upstairs rooms are haunted by a ghost, the ghost of Kinney's wife, whom Martha refers to as "Her." She does not want to show the people the rooms, but she needs money and so has agreed to do so. And it is this impending task that has heightened her agitation.

As it turns out, though, she does not have to carry out the job because Kinney himself shows up just before time for the potential tenants to arrive, planning to show them the rooms himself. Kinney is an interesting character: most readers have understood him to be a white man, and it is true that he does not speak in dialect.[19] But Spence, who gives great attention to color in this play, writes that Kinney's "*yellow face is seamed and somewhat haggard*" (134), making it possible that he is himself an African American man who might even be passing as he works to negotiate a white-controlled business world. Ostensibly, Kinney denies that his wife's ghost exists and is running his tenants out of the apartment. Yet, even though he suspects that Martha is responsible for their fleeing, it also seems to be true what Martha says, that "he bin worryin' plenty 'bout something" (134). In fact, he tells her,

> Looking back over the years, twenty you say—Twenty! I can see what a fool I've been—what a fool you've helped me to be. . . . You—with your talk of signs and omens—sounds and night alarms. You've filled my mind with superstitious fears. I, who used to laugh at fears! . . . Well, you've frightened away my tenants long enough with your gossip and fancies. I won't say that you've done these things out of malice, but—by God! Some men might! (135)

When Martha asks him whether he has ever believed what she has told him about the haunted apartment, he replies, "I did, once. Now I know they're lies or fancies" (135). Whatever the case, he concludes by observing that "the only way to wipe the incident clean from my mind—except as we have occasion to remember some unfortunate happening—is to go up there tonight and show Mrs. Smith those rooms myself" (136). He then adds that he is going to sell the house, because, as he says, doing so is "my one chance of being a free man and I'm not going to lose it" (136). Dashing a black woman's space (both Martha's and Her's, if Her exists) makes Kinney "a free man."

At this point, however, the young couple desiring to rent the rooms arrives. Again, careful in depicting color in the play, Spence describes them as follows: "ALICE SMITH, *a good-looking brown girl, and her husband* SAM, *somewhat browner. Alice wears a tricky little felt hat and yellow raincoat. Sam wears—well—brown hat, coat, and shoes, a very trying harmony for one of his complexion*" (136). Their interchange with Kinney particularly suggests a level of comfort that would seem to result from being in a purely African American group: when Kinney notes that they are "certainly on time," Sam says, "We's colored through and through, Alice an' me 'sceptin' that we's allus on time. When we says eight, we means eight, not half past nine" to which Kinney replies (as Sam laughs at his own joke), "Well, as a man of business I appreciate that" (136). He then introduces Martha and Pete as Mrs. and Mr. Alexander, again suggesting that he himself is not necessarily a white intruder in this space (as it would seem that the informal Martha and Pete would suffice in the social hierarchy of such a situation). With these formalities completed, Kinney takes the Smiths upstairs, leaving Martha and Pete alone, with Pete expressing some doubt as to the veracity of the existence of Her, which leads Martha to scold, "Yuh' allus bin a disbeliever, Pete, an Ah reckon you'll never change 'lessen yuh's give a sign," to which he replies, "I doan need no sign, Martha," which leads her to point to his Bible and say, "Yuh ain't read that thar Book frum cover to cover 'thout comin' cross signs an' wonders a-plenty" (137), again evoking a religious mode of magic and belief. Still, she insists, it is not Kinney and his well-being that concern her but Alice Smith and her young husband. Alice reminds her so much of Her that she does not want to see her hurt or frightened.

Presently, Kinney and the Smiths return, with the latter agreeing to rent the rooms. However, when Kinney reaches into his pocket to get his receipt book he realizes he has lost his wallet. He worries that he has dropped it, but Spence takes care to note that he has reached for it in his "inner" pocket, suggesting that someone has removed it. After a few words of consternation (the stage directions note that he returned from his trip upstairs looking "pale"), he leaves the room alone in search of the wallet. With Kinney gone, Martha tells the Smiths, "Listen! He'll be back any minute, an' Ah's got some-thin' powerful important to say," at which point she offers them the following information:

> It's nigh on twenty years ago when we first seen Her. She was one of these here Philippine gals. John Kinney met her when he was soljerin' in them parts. He was young then, an' handsome. She was pretty's a picture, with her big, black eyes an' a head uv hair lak we doan never see no more. An' she had plenty money. Well, John Kinney marries her an 'bout a year later they comes ter New York. He quits the army, then, an' goes inter real estate. He tole Her he's goin' buy her a beautiful house—an' he takes her money—she was only a furriner—an' young. She didn't know no better. But he doan buy the pretty house he tole her 'bout. He buys this apartment house. That's when she first commence ter see through him. He uster live then in two little rooms back uv his dingy office. 'Tweren't no place fer the like uv Her. She pined fer the country an' the grass and the flowers. She wanted him ter fix up one uv these floors so's she could have some place ter breathe in. But he figgered on the rent from them apartments, an' he wouldn't let her have one. . . . She uster come here ter collect the rents. Many's the time Ah's seen her big, black eyes a-swimmin' in tears. She jes' took ter me right off—An' Pete an me thought the world uv her. We didn't always understan' what she said. She didn' speak no good English lak Pete an' me, but we could make out she was lonesome an' scared uv New York—scared too, uv that husban' uv hers. She missed her folks back home powerful bad. She was jes' a little wild bird, caught an' put in a cage in a dark room. Well, seems lak John Kinney tole her one time that she could have the next floor that got vacant. She runs up here ter tell me—jes' laughin' an' cryin' all together. She uster come here whenever

she got a chance—an' sit here an' plan how she'd fix them rooms. Such funny ideas she had, too, 'bout fixins—but pretty. Well, 'bout three months later, the folks on the top floor move away an' she tole John Kinney 'bout her plans. She was all ready ter move in. . . . If the ole devil didn' up an' tell her he'd changed his mind. Seems he'd done forgot all about it. He tole her he needed the money real bad ter pay some bills. . . . The next afternoon John Kinney found her up thar hangin' between the parlor an' the bedroom. (139)

Nameless and unable to speak intelligible English, Her is as a woman confined to a restricted space completely controlled by a man. She is clearly marked as other, where John Kinney can pass (at least, and may well even be a true White Devil as well as an "ole devil"). Now dead, she cannot speak at all, but where her voice can never be sounded (and was ineffective even when it could), Martha can talk, talk, talk, and in so doing wrests control of space from Kinney.

Having heard the story of Her, Sam and Alice are sufficiently terrified and no longer want to rent the rooms. But as they prepare to leave the apartment house, a "*loud crash is heard*" from upstairs, at which everyone "*starts violently—Pete, so violently that his Bible falls to the floor*" (140). Martha exclaims that the crash happened upstairs and goes out to see what has happened, only to return quickly, shutting the door behind her and rushing to Pete, saying, "Pete! Pete! yuh wanted a sign! Ah jes seen John Kinney walkin' down the stairs with *Her!* She had him by the hand an' she was laughin!" at which point the "*curtain starts to descend just as Alice's piercing scream rings through the room*" (140) in a final triumphant sounding of a female voice that at once and paradoxically signifies Alice's fear and Her's victory in not only claiming Kinney's living space but his body as well.[20]

As a ghost, Her is for Kinney, of course, the return of the repressed, if not the return of the oppressed. His desire to "wipe" his mind "clean" speaks to the ways his fears of the uncanny well up from "the incident" of the past, and Martha observes regarding Kinney's refusal to go upstairs for so long, "Yuh kin call it conscience, or yuh kin call it HER! 'Tis one and the same thing, Ah reckon" (134). Regardless of how Kinney's guilt and the ghost herself are "kin," however, the ghost constitutes an objective reality perceptible to Martha. At the same time, ironically enough, it is as a ghost that the dead woman finally obtains *sub*jectivity as well as a space of her own, a one-room domestic one that she is able to break out of by the play's end. And her speaking is powerful—Pete's resistance to the "signs" of Her speaks to an epistemological problem connected generally with black women as incarnations of the invisible visible. "It ain't natural—this talk 'bout Her," Pete says. And Martha replies, "'Course it ain't natural, but it's *real*" (134).

Much more comfortable with a Derridean sense of deferral of signs, Martha speaks from the ghostlike position that plagues black women generally, and Her and her unseen theater may be read as a metaphor for the plays and production opportunities for Spence and her sister writers.

In an inversion of the usual place of power, however, Her's domain is off-stage, the space normally reserved in these plays for *white* power. Further-more, it is she who has picked Kinney's pocket, a trick normally associated with White Devils. Still, while Her may seem to have grown more powerful in death, it must be noted that she is, in fact, *dead*—removed from the sphere of effective real-life dealings. Addressing the spatiality of the play and the ways it encodes the ills of the Great Migration, Allen writes,

> Learning from past mistakes is still an option for Spence, whose sanctuary resides in a belief that the dead talk, that the universe is capable of righting itself beyond man's selfish impulses (a corrective Gothicism). Yet, because the play's heroine is a ghost, Spence reveals the fragile plane on which her reformist leanings are based. If dead spirits have more power than live black citizens to challenge and ameliorate social conditions, then the migration is nothing more than a death march where the body has to be ceded to the natural environment for it to effectuate change, a classically Romantic take on suffering and social order. (99–100)

As Gothic mystery, the play's plot employs secrecy-moves that reflect the secrecy Martha herself strives to maintain; it is a point of some moment that Martha has strictly avoided revealing Her's presence to lodgers in the past. Knowing that the preservation of her own space depends on Kinney's success in renting rooms, Martha dutifully protects the terrifying secrets of a black woman's oppression, a move that, again, may speak to her dealings with no less a figure than Du Bois himself.

A somewhat different treatment of a black woman's speaking and asser-tion of empowerment appears in Spence's play *Hot Stuff*. The heroine of this play is in some ways not unlike Spence herself (arguably, Her also resembles Spence as an islander in New York); her name is Fanny King, and although a hustler salesman in the play tells her that a garment he wants to sell her makes her look like a queen, her strength throughout most of the play makes her seem more than once to cross the line into a masculine-like power . . . in-deed, more of a *king*. As in *Her*, the play is set in Harlem, in the "living room of Fanny's flat" (WW 43) with one significant variation/addition to the set—a mirror. The play deals with Fanny's dealing in gambling and stolen goods, and the "hot stuff" of the play refers literally to the stolen items Fanny pedals, but also to Fanny, herself, whom Spence describes in the list of characters as "The 'Red Hot' Mama" and whose "beauty is a kind called 'striking.' Large, flashing black eyes, small mouth, regular features and slick bobbed head. Her skin is golden brown; her figure sensuous to a fault" (43).

The play opens with a propitious scene that vividly outlines the nuances of the kinds of secrecy-moves that hide, reveal, and preserve this black woman in her space. Fanny is sitting at a table, working with slips of paper she has sold to various people in Harlem as they play numbers. With her is her friend Mary Green, who herself deals in various underground means of making money—the scene actually culminates in Fanny's selling Mary stolen stockings, which Mary herself in turn plans to sell. As the two converse, Fanny comments that "there's easy money in this game . . . talk 'bout suckers! Believe me, it's here you find them" (44). When Mary laments that she has no luck in the same endeavor and asks how Fanny manages to succeed, Fanny strikingly replies, "Secrets of the trade. You gotta be on the inside!" (44). Her statement carries implications for the entire play, for she proceeds to display those very secrets.

After Mary pays for the stockings and the two discuss the flings and affairs they have with various men (Fanny is married and Mary is not—both may be prostitutes), Mary leaves Fanny to her business. After Mary exits the stage, a woman calls on the phone to play numbers. After this conversation, the phone rings again, this time a man who wants to take her out on the town, which she agrees to do, noting that her husband, Walter, "won't mind! I'll tell him Mary and me have gone to the theater. Naw . . . Walter don't snoop! If he did I wouldn't live with him five minutes" (45). When she hangs up, she hears a knock and finds John Cole at the door; Cole is a customer, a numbers player whom she has scammed by collecting the money on his ticket but then claiming that she lost it and forgot to play it on the right combination of numbers, thereby cheating him out of $250. Fanny refuses to give him his money and he finally retreats, leaving the room before Fanny's wrath. Just after he leaves, however, his girlfriend Jennie knocks on the door. Where Cole had no luck with Fanny, Jennie gets tough by explaining that she works in the same building with Fanny's husband. When Fanny calls her bluff, Jennie proceeds to name the firm for which she and Walter work and says, "All right. I see it suits you if your daddy takes a long rest in the cooler. But lemme tell yuh somethin' kid: he won't go alone. You're his accomplice an' yuh'll get yours same ez him!" (47). What is significant about Fanny's arrangement (she does not deny Jennie's claims) is that Fanny plays both with and against her husband much in the same manner that Spence was apparently playing both with and against Du Bois in regard to her playwriting. Both the author and her created character play men by means of controlling secrets in order to preserve their own independent female spaces. It should be noted, too, that although Jennie is fighting for her boyfriend's money, she is also invested in preserving the secrets that she realizes must persist in order for business to get done and people to survive in their environment. She has known for some time about Fanny's business, working with Walter and also knowing two women who have bought clothing from Fanny. Her only reason for threatening to blow the whistle now is to protect her own space. When Fanny says, "I can't afford to have you squeal. How do I know you won't tell no how?" Jennie replies, "I ain't got no love fer Saltzberg and Olinsky [the firm], an' I ain't got none fer you. But just the same, I ain't one fer doin' my own people like some folks I know. . . . This is a losin' game anyhow, but it could be played on the level" (47).

"Dirty little shine!" Fanny mutters when Jennie leaves, but she has little time to ponder what has transpired because yet another knock comes at the door, and this time the visitor is Isadore Goldstein, "a Jewish peddler of questionable reputation. He is good-looking, sleek, possessing an ingratiating smile and a familiar manner" (47). Goldstein carries a briefcase in his hand, making his appearance startling and unexpected, as it seems strange for Spence to insert such a stereotyped figure in her play: he seems to represent the other's other, as it were, in the play's racial and ethnic economy. Goldstein produces from his briefcase "a beautiful ermine wrap" (48) for her, and she agrees to accept it in exchange for sexual favors. Just as they go into her bedroom to settle the payment, however, Walter arrives (returning from a trip in Brooklyn), finds the two of them, and literally kicks Goldstein out the door.[21] Walter then returns to the bedroom where Fanny "*utters a loud scream. There is a sound of scuffling and other loud screams, sobs and moans. There is never a word from KING,*" at which point Fanny screams "Yuh's killin' me! Gawd! Oh! Murder! Murder!" at which time Walter emerges from the room and leaves the apartment altogether (48).

This closing sequence is especially interesting because it makes extensive use of the mirror. When Goldstein first places the ermine wrap on Fanny's shoulders, she "*glides up to the mirror and preens herself, like a bird . . . unable to tear her eyes away from her image in the mirror*" (48). The Lacanian and Ellisonian overtones here are inescapable, and the presence of Goldstein recalls Emily Miller Budick's comment that "black and Jewish writers, intellectuals, and academics tended to keep each other in mind, as if, indeed, there were a revelation for each of them in the existence of the other" (1). Also significant is the mirror's implication of a patriarchally defined essentialized notion of female duplicity (much like Millwood's mirror speech in George Lillo's *The London Merchant*). Spence uses the mirror further when Walter has finished beating Fanny; when he emerges from the bedroom, he "*walks up to the mirror and adjusts his tie and collar. He flicks a bit of thread from his coat and puts it on. He takes up his hat and puts that on. He listens for a moment to the loud sobs and moans in the adjoining room. Then he walks to the hall door, opens it and goes out, banging the door behind him*" (49). Along with adjusting his tie and collar, he is tidying up and confirming his image as the true "king" in his domain. When he leaves, Fanny herself reemerges, "*in a most disheveled condition. Dangling from one hand is the beloved ermine wrap. She places the wrap close to her face, stroking it with her cheek. She braces up suddenly. She slips the coat about her shoulders. She walks across the floor, painfully, and then as she reaches the mirror, a little sob breaks from her*" (49–50). The play closes with her gazing at herself and saying the following:

FANNY: The dirty brute! Glad he didn't scratch my face none. (*She smooths her hair. She turns around and around.*) Some bargain! (*She walks to the telephone.*) Bradhurst 2400. Hello! Jim? Jim, this is Fanny. Yes, I'm home. Can't make it tonight, kid. Of course, it's Walter. Tomorrow night, same time. OK. Say, honey, I just bought some coat. It's a peach! You'll see me strut tomorrow night, all right. I don't mean maybe. Goodbye, honey. Goodnight. (*She hangs up the receiver with a sigh.*) (50)

Like *Her,* the play provides a progression of delineating black female spaces. Initially, Mary and Fanny together installed in Fanny's parlor constitute a representation of the larger group of black women, and when Fanny observes that "you gotta be on the inside" it is clear that while Mary may not know the secrets, she is on the inside and can learn the secrets from Fanny, herself. Of course, the irony again is that those secrets are compromised by the fact that her words are being uttered to an altogether larger audience that is watching the play and which is not necessarily "on the inside" in its makeup, and in fact is likely or at least potentially just the opposite. But then, Fanny does indeed keep the secrets secret, so that the audience/ reader knows there are secrets and that one must be on the inside and is looking at the inside from the outside but still does not know them. Spence thus creates a secrecy that she can display even as she intentionally conceals it. But again, the most important aspect of these "secrets" is that they are ostensibly contained within an African American female community. And this black female space is exclusive—one cannot deal with it unless one is one of the girls. Witness the impotence of Cole in his dealings with Fanny in her own space: his assessment of what Fanny has done is correct, but his attempts to appeal to her honesty and honor do not succeed, and she turns him out without a cent. Yet Jennie arrives and muscles her way into getting her boyfriend's money. Having succeeded in her mission, however, she too keeps the secrets within the female community (her friends, who are Fanny's customers, are apparently women), so that Jennie too dwells within the secret society of black women in the play; she does not even seek to disrupt Fanny's business except to claim and defend that which is her own. These black women's secrets are, in this secrecy-discourse game, natural secrets with all of the weighty obligations of guarding belonging thereunto.

Fanny's space changes slightly once she is alone, for now she has no representative of her own community to give her secrets away to. Spence's ordering of events in the play is thus significant in unapologetically exposing the techniques that Fanny employs in her negotiations with her surroundings. Fanny is no victim, even when it seems that she is being fully manipulated or mistreated—everything she does is carefully calculated and fully effective. And by opening the play in a purely black female context, Spence seems to initiate the audience into that space, at least on a limited basis, so that when the sympathetic Mary leaves the stage, the audience sits in for the black female community, and it is the audience that sees the behind-the-scenes secrets of Fanny's occupations. Within this private, personal space she must negotiate the image of the other in a way that differs from her other experiences, and she does so by positing the image of the other in the mirror. Not knowing that she has a semi-initiated community (the audience) just beyond the pale of her ken, she must look to another black female, and the other in the mirror serves her purposes, as she has a silent conversation with herself while wearing the ermine wrap, for she has indeed worked quite a bargain, not even having to pay for the wrap at all and suffering no more from Walter than a beating. She is just as in business as before, and in fact has made a killing on this particular evening.

Fanny is one of the strongest women characters in these plays—completely indomitable, she is the female trickster, the secretive black woman who realizes that her body is always on display and uses her "striking" good looks to manipulate a range of men. Viewed from the standpoint of her direct encounters with three different men, the one-act actually emerges as a sort of morality play in which she withstands three tests, or perhaps a fairy tale in which three different Big Bad Wolves comes to blow her house down. Cole, the first figure who might influence her to give in and relinquish her independence to patriarchal control, assays her honor, her honesty, and her morality, but she holds to a course beneficial to her own interests. Goldstein does not try the "good guy" approach at all, but rather attempts to beguile her through craftiness; yet he comes away empty-handed and would have done so even if he had consummated his encounter with Fanny, for she was giving nothing up beyond her control and was in fact seeing herself as coming out on the upper end of the deal. When she offers him herself with the observation, "You said yourself, I was a million dollar kid," he replies, "You win, you little brown devil" (49)—Fanny herself arguably has seized the power of secrets usually held by White Devils. The final test Fanny encounters is the brutal Walter who simply responds to her with violence. Yet even in her encounter with him, she emerges as the victor, for his violence does not impair her visibility in the least, and she can continue to ply her trade with just as much vigor as before.

Not so Hattie, the heroine of *Undertow*. This black woman finds herself pitted against the world—or at least those who inhabit *her* world. Also set in a Harlem flat, the play details the last day of her life. The apparent back-story is that shortly after her marriage, her friend Clem became involved in an affair with her husband (Dan) that resulted in a pregnancy and the birth of a child. Neither Dan nor Hattie knows about the child, because Clem disappeared immediately after the affair was discovered and before she knew she was pregnant. Since that time, Dan and Hattie have themselves had a child, Charley, and Hattie has maintained absolute control over Dan; another powerful woman, she regulates every move her husband makes while he, in the absence of the woman he really loves, acquiesces. Indeed, Hattie has so broken Dan that another lodger in the house, Mrs. Wilkes, observes: "Thar's a man with reg'lar habits. Ah often tells Mr. Wilkes dat Ah wish tuh goodness he was a home lovin' man lak Mr. Peters" (BFP 111). But Hattie's seeming control is not as secure as it might seem or as she might think.

At the outset of the play, Hattie sits at the dinner table alone, when Charley bursts into the room and notices that his father has not yet come home from work. A wild child, a young man who plays the numbers, he is his mother's son, strong-willed, independent, and the exact opposite of his father. In fact, he tells his mother, at one point, "If yu'd bossed me lak yuh's bossed Dad, Ah'd runned away long 'fo now" (108). Later, when he asks her for five dollars to further his gambling enterprise and she refuses to give it to him, asking why he is "allus comin' ter me 'bout money fer?" he replies, "[E]f dat ain't lak a woman! It takes money ter make money!" and when she tells him he must quit gambling and that she will not give him any more money, he retorts, "Yuh think Ah'm Dad, doan' yuh? Well, Ah ain't! Ah wish ter Gawd Ah knew whut yuh's got over on him. No free man would er stood yuh naggin' all dese years" (108). Charley's comments are interesting for two reasons. First, his description of his father as *not* being a free man and, moreover, being "enslaved" to her represents a significant role-reversal from Hurston's "mule of the world" thesis. Even as Hattie takes on the patriarchy, her own son accuses her of operating within similar, albeit reverse, forms of oppression. That she might be doing so out of pain and fear does not occur to Charley. Furthermore, his observations, while submitting to her matriarchal ascendancy, are a bit backhanded, serving as much to highlight the tenuousness of her position as it does the position itself, for the implication is that only Dan is subject to her reign.

The other significant thing about Charley's comments is that they convey his notion that his mother employs some dark secret of the past to control his father. Charley himself uses a secret to empower himself: changing tactics in his pursuit to get money from Hattie, Charley observes that he would not be surprised if his father has left home for good; when she asks why he thinks so, he replies, "Reckon yu'd like tuh know, wouldn't yuh?" (109). After some negotiating (all moves designed to conquer his initial silence-based secrecy-move), she agrees to give him the five dollars if he will tell her what he saw his father "doin' one night las' week up on Lenox Avenue" (109). He explains that he saw his father "walkin' long, slow ez usual wid his head bent, not seein' nobuddy" when

> All uv a sudden, a woman comin' down de Avenue, went up tuh him an' stops him. He looked up kinda dazed like an' stared at her lak he'd seen a ghost. She jes' shook him by de arm an' laughed. By dat time, we come along side an' Ah got a good look at her. She warn't young an' she warn't old. But she looked—well—Ah jes' doan know how she did look—all laughin' an' happy an' tears in her eyes. Ah' didn't look at her much fer starin' at Dad. He looked—all shaken up—an' scared like—Not scared like neither fer Ah seen him smile at her, after a minute. He ain't never smiled lak that befo'—not's Ah kin remember. Nat [Charley's friend] said—"Reckin yuh Dad's met an' ole gal 'er his"—But Ah only laughed—Struck me kinda funny—that! Dad meetin' an 'ole flame uh his—Ah meant tuh ask Dad 'bout her but it went clean outa mah head. (109)

Once again, a female ghost has arisen out of the past to speak, but unlike the ghost of Her this one comes not to confirm the veracity of another female voice but rather to reveal a secret that will cause division.

From this point onward in the play, in fact, the audience witnesses a fragmentation of black female community that is nothing less than chilling. After revealing this information about his father, Charley *"reaches once more for the money. This time he takes it easily, enough. Hattie has forgotten it"* (109), and he leaves. His departure is followed by the arrival of Dan himself, whom Hattie berates for getting home so late and at whom she hurls vague accusations. He is very hungry, he asks for something to eat, but Hattie has thrown out his supper and forbids his going into the kitchen to make something for himself, and so he too leaves the house in search of food. At this point, Mrs. Wilkes appears onstage to inform Hattie that she has a visitor—a tall, light-skinned, pretty visitor whose description matches the one that Charley offered of the woman whom Dan met on the street. Here there emerges a divergence between Hattie's and Mrs. Wilkse's attitudes toward and relationships with their husbands. Mrs. Wilkes comments that

> [Mr. Wilkes] seen her on de stoop. She was jes' gwine tuh ring de bell when
> Mr. Wilkes comes up wid his key. She ask tuh see Mis' Peters an' he tole her
> tuh set in de parlor. Ef thar's ever a stupid man it sure is mah husban'. 'Stead
> uh goin' down an tellin' yuh, 'er hollerin' tuh yuh, 'er sendin' her on down,
> he comes up-stairs an' tells *me* ter go down an' tell yuh. He'd oughta sent her
> down de basement do' fust place. (111)

Mr. Wilkes runs things in his family the way that Hattie does in hers. He
tells his wife what to do, no matter how outlandish or impractical, and, even
more significantly, she does it. However much she may squawk about her
husband, she does his bidding, and although her comments seem to contribute to her finding common ground with Hattie against husbandom, the
two women differ from one another dramatically.

Where Mrs. Wilkes makes some effort to ally herself with Hattie, Clem
emerges as her antagonist, bringing demands that, despite being diplomatic,
further disintegrate whatever in the way of a unified female community
exists in the play. The two women immediately begin to exchange harsh
words regarding the past as well as Clem's current connection with Dan.
Clem's initial tactic is to note that neither Hattie nor Dan is happy, and so
she, Clem, has come to take Dan with her. "Dan ain't knowed a day's happiness sence Ah went away," Clem says. "Ah kin fergive yuh fer takin' him 'way
frum me—an' de way yuh done it—but it ain't easy fergivin' yuh fer makin'
him suffer. . . . Dan's dyin' here, right under yo' eyes, an' yo' doan see it. He's
dying fer kindness—He's dyin' frum hard wuk. He's dyin' frum de want uv
love" (112–13). Not only that, Clem also ventures the observation that Hattie
has always sided with Charley, turning the boy against his father, noting that
"[e]f yuh had brought Charley up diff'rent yuh mighta held on tuh Dan.
'Stead uh dat, yuh's brought him up tuh look down on him" (113). Clem thus
has Hattie not only reversing traditional roles within her marriage but also
enlisting her son in opposing and undermining Dan (although, ironically,
her encouraging dominance in Charley serves to reinforce the traditional
patriarchal attitude in him).

Clem explains that she does not merely want Dan to leave Hattie and
come with her, but also she wants Hattie to grant him a divorce. Hattie
refuses to do so, so Clem proceeds to tell her "de real reason why Ah wants
dat di'voce" (114). Just as she begins to talk, Dan returns and stands in the
room watching the two women. Clem explains,

> Ef 'twas only me—but it ain't. It's fer mah Lucy,—Dan's chile. . . . Ah didn' tell
> yuh, Hattie, an' Ah didn' tell Dan. Whut woulda bin de use? She's a woman

now an' good—an' pretty. She thinks her dad died when she was a baby an' she thinks—she thinks—Ah'm a good woman. She's proud uh me. . . . Ah's wuked hard tuh git her de chances Ah didn' have. She's bin tuh school—she's got an' eddication. An' now she's goin' tuh git married tuh a fine feller whut'll be able tuh take care uv her. Now yuh see dat Ah kain't jes go off wid Dan. It's got tuh be proper—a divo'ce an' all. Yuh see, doan' yuh, Hattie? (115)

For Clem, the secret of her past is a burden, something she wants to maintain even as she tries to arrange things the way she wants them in her life. Her appeal is striking—even as she has worked to make situations different for her daughter, her daughter is still an extension of herself. And Hattie realizes this fact, as she replies sardonically, "Mother an' daughter—double weddin'" (115).

Tension quickly escalates as Hattie refuses to permit Dan to leave or to grant him a divorce. She even begins to taunt Clem, threatening to expose her secret, at which point Dan tells her to shut up, which causes Hattie to taunt *him*, saying, "Yuh'd shut mah mouf' wouldn' yuh? How? . . . How yuh's thinkin' 'er shuttin' mah mouf, Dan Peters?" (116). Dan then proceeds to demonstrate his method of quieting her by choking her until Clem finally intervenes, tearing at the death grip he has on his wife's throat until finally "*with a violent movement of disgust he thrusts Hattie from him*" at which point she "*falls heavily from the chair, her head striking the marble base of the mantle—an ugly sound. She lies very still*" (116). Before long, Clem and Dan realize that Hattie is actually dead, at which point Dan, still raging with adrenaline, assumes the dominant patriarchal role and orders Clem to return to Lucy while he faces his fate alone, certainly years in prison which he will spend "dreamin' 'bout yuh, Clem, an'—an' Lucy! Yuh musn' grieve, Honey. Go now, fer Gawd's sake! Ah hears sombuddy comin' down! (117–18). He watches Clem leave and listens as the gate outside clicks, at which point he seems to deflate again, looking down upon Hattie's corpse and saying, "Ah'm sorry, Hattie! 'Fore Gawd, Ah didn' mean tuh do it!" (118). Spence's choice of title, of course, speaks to the heart of the play. The secrets in the one-act create an unseen but powerful current that overpowers people caught up in its wash. The only thing that quells this destructive force is Dan's refusal to take part in the secrecy games in which he has lived for so long (he, in a sense, plays to lose). On the other hand, Dan arguably has no control of his actions—the undertow of secrecy has arisen in a deadly eruption of the *chora,* shutting the mouth of the symbolic and vanquishing it with a different, primal, bodily language.

Especially noteworthy is the way this play potentially enlists the audience in its secrecy discourse. The drama seeks to play with and upon audience loyalty, for here are two strong black women, both of whom are haunted by secrets but are at odds, with no in-group reconciliation in the end. Whose secret counts more in terms of rendering the characters sympathetic? Brown-Guillory affirms that "*Undertow* is decidedly a feminist play. . . . Hattie is an indomitable, explosive woman who stands up for her rights as wife. The only way a woman of this type can be silenced is by death" (*Their Place on the Stage* 19). The point is well taken, but what of Clem? She is no less "indomitable" and "explosive," and the play rather than marginalizing her establishes a contest between her and her rival, Hattie. Spence masterfully leaves "the truth" secret: the audience has no way of knowing if Clem is correct in saying that Hattie took Dan from her or if Hattie is correct in saying that Clem invaded her peaceful life. Meanwhile, the seemingly weak Dan, who appears to be tossed about by the rages of these women, would have done well to choose whom he wants to spend his life with, for his vacillating between both has contributed greatly to the creation of this mess in the first place. Their secrecy tactics result from their efforts to negotiate the ways Dan has hurt them, and in the end his weakness and indecisiveness prove just as potently destructive as his son Charley's bullheaded and irreverent independence. Dan, in fact, stands as both the initiator and terminator of the secrecy-discourse game that dominates these women's lives, and where he does not possess the stereotypical unapologetic masculinity his son does, his actions are just as devastating. In the end, these women's fortunes are overwhelmingly dictated by a larger "undertow" of a black male–controlled social superstructure that leaves one silenced in death and the other banished from the stage in sorrow.

IV

Having discoursed on discourse, the Us's in *The Purple Flower* find themselves confronted with an inducement to change their pace. Bonner explains,

> *Drum begins to beat in the distance. All the Us stand up and shake off their sleep. The drummer, a short, black, determined-looking Us, appears around the bushes beating the drum with strong, vigorous jabs that make the whole valley echo and re-echo with rhythm. Some of the Us begin to dance in time to the music.* (35)

Two of the Us's comment on those who are dancing, offering two different ways of thinking about such activity. First, Average says, "Look at that! Dancing!! The Us will never learn to be sensible!" (35). But Cornerstone observes, "They dance well! Well!!" (35). These opposing comments speak to the two forms of African American dance being staged during the Harlem Renaissance, what Anthea Kraut calls "black musical theatre and black concert dance" (25). The first includes such Broadway productions as *Shuffle Along,* which arguably promoted stereotypes of blacks as being "by nature" excellent dancers. The second form veered away from popular "neo-minstrelsy" to traditional African-originated dances and, "like the nascent modern dance movement, in general, was concerned with bringing dignity to dance as an expressive art form" (28). In two plays that focus on dancing, Zora Neale Hurston and Thelma Duncan seek to prod deeper, below these two forms of dance to their source material—African American folk and African dance. These were the forms that had become hidden by the musical and concert forms that were coming into hiddenness; Hurston and Duncan were thus resurrecting now-secret forms of the past, the formulations of the forms contemporary with themselves.

Hurston's *Color Struck* moves through more complex spatial constructs than most of the plays written by her female peers. The first of four scenes opens around 1900 in a train that is about to leave Jacksonville, Florida, en route to St. Augustine, where there is to be a cakewalk in which representatives from various locations in the state will compete. As people board the train, one woman emerges as a special target of attention—a mulatto named Effie. The men find her especially attractive because of her light skin, and one man pays particular attention to her once he realizes that she has broken up with her boyfriend ("lemme scorch you to a seat" [BFP 90], he offers in a line rife with implications about "darkening"). Effie is considered to be among the top dancers of the group, but the very best of the dancers are John and Emmaline (Emma), a couple who also boards the train just before it pulls out of the station.

John and Emma arrive fighting over skin color. Emma accuses John of having in the past made eyes at Effie, and it quickly becomes clear that even as she accuses her boyfriend of being "color struck," it is she who is bothered by the color of Effie's skin. Apparently, Emma was refusing to get aboard because Effie was on the train. Once the train leaves the station, the other passengers want the well-known dancers to give them a taste of what they will do for the big cakewalk. First, John and Emma dance to the song "Goo Goo Eyes," Emma *"holding up her skirt, showing the lace on her petticoats"* (92). Then Effie *"swings into the pas-me-la"* to the tune of "I'm gointer live anyhow till I die" (92). Her dance comes off as more sexually charged even than Emma's, for as the accordion player who provides the music exclaims, "Hot stuff I reckon!" Effie *"hurls herself into a modified Hoochy Koochy, and finishes up with an ecstatic yell"* (92). When John applauds and observes, "If dat Effie can't step nobody can," Emma retorts, "Course you'd say so cause it's her. Everything she do is pretty to you" (92). John's reply is "Dancing is dancing no matter who is doing it" (92).

John and Emma reverse the gender positions regarding dancing that Average and Cornerstone maintain in Bonner's play, and Hurston further inculcates this gender conflict with a racial element, for not only is dance linked to African Americans in *Color Struck,* it is also the mode of performance to which issues of miscegenation and skin color—signs inflected with secrecy—within a group of black people is attached. Emma's problem with Effie is not that Effie is *darker* but that she is *lighter.* Even though John assures Emma that "nobody can hold a candle to you in nothing" (92), Effie's skill in dancing turns out to be the final straw, for when they arrive at St. Augustine and the time comes for the "Great Cake Walk" Emma suddenly does not want to dance because she "just can't go in there and see all them girls—Effie hanging after you" (96). When John leaves her to go dance anyway (and does indeed pair up with Effie, to win the competition), she exclaims in a soliloquy,

> Ah, mah God! He's in there with her—Oh, them half whites, they gets everthing, they gets everything everybody else wants! The men, the jobs—everything! The whole world is got a sign on it. Wanted: Light colored. Us blacks was made for cobble stones. (96–97)

It is Effie's whiteness that violates a mode of performance so intricately linked to blackness, which is itself ironic since dancing was one of the things attached to essentialized blackness that Hurston presumably would have sought to dismantle as a marker of blackness.[22]

The final scene of the play presents a radical shift in time and place, for it is set in the present in Emma's *"one room shack in the alley"* (98). The spatial realignment is significant—the fluidity of transportation and Emma's ability to pass through and operate within multiple places (the train is the classic Foucauldian heterotopia) has ceased, and now she is confined to the single-room domestic space so often presented in these one-act plays. The structure of the play resembles the telescoping structure of the plot, for even as Emma occupies several places, in the end she finds herself reduced to the one-room space. Temporally, the scene represents an advance of some twenty to thirty years, and Hurston deftly injects the opening of the scene with secrecy that effects a break in continuity in characterization; after all these years she has aged, and the script makes it clear that Emma is no longer recognizable to the audience, as it refers to her not as "Emma" but as a "Woman" (a move to shroud her body in secrecy much as Sojourner Truth's is at the beginning of Miller's earlier discussed play). Emma/the Woman sits in a rocking chair while another person lies sick in the bed. It turns out that this person is her daughter, and Emma is caring for her, telling her that "[y]ou got right much fever—I better go git the doctor agin" (98). Clearly much has happened in the intervening years since the dance in St. Augustine, for the play has shifted from the bright opening scene that "*discovers a happy lot of Negroes boarding the train dressed in the gaudy, tawdry best of 1900*" (89) to this hidden, dark, dingy shack full of sickness and loneliness.

Presently there comes a knock at the door, and the visitor turns out to be John, who has come back to Jacksonville after years of living in Philadelphia. He hopes to marry Emma. Married for seventeen years, his wife has passed away, and so he has returned "as soon as it was decent to find" Emma because, as he says, "I wants to marry you. I couldn't die happy if I didn't. Couldn't get over you—couldn't forget" (99). Emma gets in a dig regarding his marriage, saying, "Bet you' wife wuz some high-yaller dickty-doo," to which John replies, "Naw she wasn't neither. She was jus' as much like you as Ah could get her" (99). Emma then shows John her daughter, who looks at her and realizes that she is, in an ironic twist, herself a mulatto. "Talking 'bout *me* liking high-yallers," John says, "*yo* husband musta been pretty near white" (100). Emma returns by replying that she was never married at all, and this comment followed by her subsequent observation that "[n]obody don't git rich in no white-folks' kitchen, nor in de washtub" (100) implies that she was been yet another victim of white male cruelty, and that the child is a product of rape. John, however, does not seem bothered by the situation, saying simply "It's all right, Emma" (100) and actually continues to refer to the girl as "our daughter" just as he has from the moment he has been apprised of her existence. Furthermore, he immediately begins to take measures to cure her, telling Emma to go get a doctor to help the child, even giving her money (which she herself does not have). Emma tells *him* to go find a doctor, but he reminds her that "[w]hilst Ah'm blunderin' round tryin' to find one, she'll be gettin' worse" (101), so Emma finally goes to find a doctor.

At this point, yet another twist irrupts in the plot. When Emma leaves, the following events happen:

John sits in the chair beside the table. Looks about him—shakes his head. The girl on the bed groans, "water," "so hot." John looks about him excitedly. Gives her a drink. Feels her forehead. Takes a clean handkerchief from his pocket and wets it and places it upon her forehead. She raises her hand to the cool object. Enter Emma running. When she sees John at the bed she is full of fury. She rushes over and jerks his shoulder around. They face each other.)

EMMA. I knowed it! (*She strikes him.*) A half white skin. (*She rushes at him again. John staggers back and catches her hands.*)

JOHN. Emma!

EMMA. (*struggles to free her hands*) Let me go so I can kill you. Come sneaking in here like a pole cat!

JOHN. (*slowly, after a long pause*) So this is the woman I've been wearing over my heart like a rose for twenty years! She so despises her own skin that she can't believe any one else could love it!

(*Emma writhes to free herself.*)

JOHN. Twenty years! Twenty years of adoration, of hunger, of worship! (*On the verge of tears he crosses to door and exits quietly, closing the door after him.*) (101–2)

This climactic scene is a difficult one to read. The play seems to cast John in a sympathetic light (the very specific stage directions ostensibly provide little room for ambiguity in John's actions regarding Emma's daughter) while Emma comes off as irrational in her jealousy. At the same time, though, John *did* abandon her—not only at the dance in St. Augustine but also afterwards when he left to go to Philadelphia. Moreover, he *did* dance with Effie all those years ago, abandoning Emma in a moment of crisis. There is, then, plenty of room to read Emma as a sympathetic victim, herself "struck" by color not only in her bitter jealousy of lighter-skinned black women but also perhaps in the implied rape by an unnamed white man.

Scholars have discussed the social cohesion and its breakdown in *Color Struck*.[23] Secrecy-moves connected with varying secrecy-discourse situations contribute to this cohesion and fracture. Kraut writes that "by positioning the dances within an enclosed black space, Hurston calls attention to their particularized importance to the southern folk community" (30), and Shafer suggests that the "mood of the play is mirrored in the changing settings" (405). What tortures Emma is that light-skinned African Americans are admired by not only those of their own race but also of the white race. Passing is a secrecy-move that depends on spatiality, spatial traversing: where one is known to be black in one space, one is not known to be so in another. Emma has no access to this openness within the black community (openness symbolized in the ultra-visibility of dancing), so that when Effie "outmaneuvers" her (at least in Emma's mind) in that space, Effie does not know what to do except to retreat into increasingly hidden spaces. Scene 2's mise-en-scène features a Bonneresque stage division, as a curtain stretches from left to right across the stage, obscuring the dance hall beyond from the visible "anteroom." In this less visible space (to the characters in the play), she possesses John and even herself, but when he passes beyond the veil (and out of her and the audience's visibility), she remains alone in a space grown even more secretive. While there, she transforms into the visible invisible, for when she snatches the curtain aside in scene 3 to see the dance, she has been forgotten by the characters as John and Effie dance—indeed, Emma "creeps over to a seat along the wall and shrinks into the Spanish Moss, motionless" (97). Scene 4, of course, shows her installed in the most secret space of all. This relegation of Emma into an envelope of secrecy inundates the play's form and content, from its use of ellipses to its silencing of Emma.

Perhaps the most arresting observation regarding secrecy appears in Emma's enigmatic final words. In answer to the white doctor's asking her why she waited so long to fetch him, she says, "Couldn't see" (102). Krasner ventures a few explanations for these lines:

> With guarded certainty it might be said that she delayed in responding to the child's turn for the worse because she had to "see" John's sincerity. Or, perhaps it is also the fact that she "couldn't see" her own hatred for the child because it reminded her of John's desires, about whom and which she may have thought angrily about while conceiving it, given John's skin tone preferences. Or, it may in fact be Hurston's use of melancholia raised to a symbolic level. (128)[24]

An actor's delivery of this line can go far in either opening up these words or assigning them a specific meaning. From the perspective of the role of secrecy in the play, however, its referring to the ocular sense immediately calls up questions about secrecy-discourse. There are multiple games present in the play: Emma "competes" with Effie for John; there is a dance competition; John enacts a strategy to attain Emma when he returns to her; Emma's daughter's life must be saved, and moves must be made to achieve such a payoff. Arguably, Emma's comment applies to all of these situations, and not all of them are connected with her seeing or failure to see. John cannot "see" how his actions truly affect Emma; Effie cannot "see" past her own goals; dance judges and spectators cannot see how they privilege lighter-skinned blacks; the doctor cannot see the true deep tragedy of her situation. The unkindest cut of all comes when the dance is over and people are celebrating John and Effie's victory: a man "*seeing Emma*" exclaims "You're from Jacksonville, ain't you? Ain't you happy? Whoopee" as he "*whirls her around and around*" (98); while he sees her, he does not *see* her pain at that pain-full moment.

Arguably, dance itself might be read as coded, an interpretation-based secrecy-move with identificatory messages for the in-group. Lawrence W. Levine suggests as much, and, as Kraut has noted, Hurston saw "authentic"

African American dances as having qualities recognizably commensurate with the folk.[25] Such a move, especially when enacted by a black woman, also evokes the *chora*; there is little vocabulary to describe the semiotic expression in bodily movements, although they might be performed within the symbolic. This sort of direction naturally puts us on touchy ground that borders on African American essentialism, but then, as has been noted, Hurston was apparently comfortable with such essentialism-versus-performance paradox. What must be particularly horrifying for Emma, when considered from this standpoint, is that a mulatto can wield such a secrecy-move and thereby solidify her or his presence in the in-group, a presence that ultimately drives Emma herself out, for Krasner notes that "Emma is Hurston's creation taken to the level of symbolic representation; by dint of the fact that she is black, poor, disenfranchised, and rural, she epitomizes the outsider in every way" (114).

The failures of dance and its connections with spatiality and secrecy occur in an African context in Thelma Duncan's *Death Dance*. Set in "a Vai village, West Coast" (PNL 322), this play posits dance as both a conjuring performance and a tool of barter to negotiate levels of secrecy. It opens with the village in an uproar because its inhabitants believe one of their men, Kamo, to have stolen gold from "old Nanda, and mocked his elders" (324). The arbiter of the village is the Medicine Man, and the villagers summon him; he enters the stage, hears the accusations against Kamo, and declares that Kamo will be made to drink the "Red Water," a potion which makes the innocent sick but has no effect on the guilty. Before administering this test, however, Asumana, whom Duncan describes as "a comely dancer" (325), begs to have a word with the Medicine Man in private. A corrupt man impressed with her beauty, he agrees to speak with her alone and sends the villagers away with the accused.

It turns out that Asumana is in love with Kamo, and she now uses her body in the act of dance to try and prevent her lover's punishment. She flatters the Medicine Man, declaring, "You *are* the mighty Medicine Man of Vai, and for your mightiness, I will dance for you" (326). After dancing for a few minutes, arousing his lust and obtaining his favor, Asumana stops, prompting him to command her to dance more. She says she will continue to dance if he will promise to save Kamo from death. Although he has already promised to give her whatever she should want, the Medicine Man balks at her request, explaining that he cannot save a thief and that whether or not Kamo is a thief will depend on his response to the "Red Water." In the face of his hesitance, Asumana asks, "Would you have me dance again,—the dance only the bridegrooms see?" (327). The Medicine Man cannot resist such temptation and so agrees to save Kamo if she will perform this secret dance, which is itself designed to hide her secret reason for pleading for Kamo's life. As she dances, however, the Medicine Man shows that he too has a secret, as he mutters to himself, "It is my mighty medicine that can save him, and it is mighty medicine that can kill him, for I will give him too much, and then Asumana will be mine" (327). Although he thinks these words are unheard, his assistant Alihu hears them. When Asumana finishes her dance, she and the Medicine Man exit the stage to summon the villagers, leaving Alihu alone and in charge of the Medicine Man's supplies, including the "Red Water." At this point, the audience discovers that Alihu is himself in love with Asumana, and because he wants her to be happy, he switches the deadly "Red Water" that the Medicine Man plans to give him with a less potent mixture that will only make Kamo sick and thus prove his innocence.

When Asumana and the Medicine Man return with Kamo and the villagers, the trial (referred to as "the ordeal") begins and is punctuated by the "Death Dance." Asumana leads the other dancers in this performance, which continues as Kamo drinks the "Red Water" and falls down as if dead. Seeing her lover lying there, Asumana stops dancing and runs to him, exclaiming, "The Death Dance, oh, the Death Dance! Have I danced Kamo to his death? . . . Wake, Kamo! You are not guilty. Wake, Kamo! Open your eyes—let me see you smile—I am Asumana, your dancing Asumana—Oh, he is so still, so motionless! He is not—surely he is not dead" (329). Realizing that something is afoot, she turns to the Medicine Man, accusing, "You—you have killed him. And you promised. I believed you, too," to which he replies, "You asked me to save him from being guilty. Have I not done so? See, the medicine took effect. Surely he will waken soon" (329). At this moment, Alihu steps forward, announcing:

> Weep not, Asumana. Kamo is not dead. He is only asleep. He will waken soon. But look friends, look upon the mighty Medicine Man of Vai. Look upon my master (*They look upon him*) He is the guilty one—I, Alihu, know his secrets. He promised to save Kamo—promised Asumana—(*whereupon the* MEDICINE MAN *threatens* ALIHU,—*the natives cower before his outstretched wand.* ALIHU, *in desperation, seizes the wand, holding it high over his head, he snaps it in two: the natives howl and cower, expecting a catastrophe.* ALIHU, *triumphantly holding up the broken staff, as the* MEDICINE MAN *threatens in speechless wrath and fear*)—You think my master the mighty Medicine Man. Look! He is not good, neither is he mighty. He is a cheater, a robber, and a murderer. He boasts of his cures, but he never boasts of how he kills the innocent. For years I have been his servant, and I know his evil doings. Now you know him. I, Alihu, have spoken the truth. (329–30)

Further spurred by Asumana's informing them that he "has looked on the Dance of the Bridegroom" (330), the villagers turn on the Medicine Man and drive him from the stage and the village. Left alone with the two men that form the love triangle with her in the play, Asumana gives Alihu one of her bracelets because he is "so good, so noble," to which he replies, "I will always remember Asumana, the beautiful dancer. But I must go away now. I have no master" (330–31). He leaves her "in a trance" muttering to herself, "Alihu was kind. Why was Alihu so kind?" at which point Kamo awakens, calling her name, and she rushes to his side saying, "Yes, Kamo. I am here" (331).

In a trajectory that differs from that of *Color Struck, The Death Dance* moves from private to public space. Although the opening moments are public, Asumana's efforts to save Kamo transpire in secret, and it is at the end of the play that Alihu whisks away the obfuscating curtain to show the villagers that the figure they saw as empowered with religious magic is in fact a charlatan skilled at sleight of hand. Asumana herself emerges as a kind of Josephine Baker, using the sexually charged display of her body to empower herself. While she obtains her desired result, her dance ultimately fails, for besides the fact that her appealing to the Medicine Man reveals to Alihu her desire to save Kamo, her dance has nothing to do with the outcome of the situation. Alihu acts out of his love for Asumana, and it is he who saves the day in the end. Meanwhile, the "passing" in this play is not racial but ethical, for the Medicine Man passes as a true divine magician when he is in fact merely a secular one, and Alihu's unveiling him in the public sphere deconstructs his passing and dooms him to a very different death dance.

As with some of the other plays, it is tempting to read this one as yet another dramatization of a black woman artist/performer's "doing a dance" to increase her visibility among black men. Here are three black male figures, each of whom bears a unique relation to Asumana. Her love for Kamo becomes a natural secret designed to protect him; like the men in *Blue Blood,* Kamo needs this black woman to save him. The Medicine Man is her outright enemy, and it is against him that she aims dance and silence as secrecy-moves to influence him and deflect his attention from her true motives, respectively. Alihu is neither the lover nor the enemy, but the friend who stands between the two and who helps enable Asumana to achieve her payoff while also saving the community. The lover, the misogynist, and the friend—these three men exert various pressures on Asumana as she works to appease their desires as well as her own. At the same time, Asumana's insistence on dancing for the Medicine Man in private testifies to her desire not to disrupt the community—something that Alihu (who enacts the role of the spoilsport) is willing to do in hopes of changing the rules of the village's magic secrecy-discourse game situation. Where dance as public display ultimately isolates Emma and thereby fragments the black community in *Color*

Struck, here both private and public dance confirms the community and its rules. Asumana's differing uses of dance in private and public spaces illustrates the sort of doubleness of secrecy that can be found in Spence's and Johnson's interactions with Du Bois and Locke—keeping the surface waters smooth and untroubled while working to achieve their own goals behind the scenes.

V

At length, the Us's cease their dancing and "*all congregate at the center front. Almost naturally, the Young Us range on one side, the Old Us on the other*" (35). At this point, an Old Us "*tottering with age and blind*" walks to Cornerstone and asks the question, "What's it this time, chillun? Is it day yet? Can you see the road to that flower?" (35). To his query, Cornerstone responds, "No it's not day! It is still dark. It is night," and the stage directions note that indeed, "*the sun has gone and purple blackness has lain across the Valley. Somehow, though, you can see the shape of the flower on top of Somewhere. Lights twinkle on the hill*" (35). The Old Man then laments that he is "blind from working—building for the White Devils in the heat of the noon-day sun" (35) yet announces, in another reversion to the Washingtonian ethic, "I want to tell you all something! The Us can't get up the road unless we work! We want to hew and dig and toil!" (36). This comment draws the ire of the young Us's, one of whom tells him, "You had better sit down before someone knocks you down! They told us that when your beard was sprouting" (36). When Cornerstone admonishes the youth to "not be so stupid! Speak as if you had respect for that beard!" another young Us says, "We have! But we get tired of hearing 'you must work' when we know the old Us built practically every inch of that hill and yet are Nowhere," while yet another ventures, "Yes, all they got was a rush down the hill—not a chance to take a step up!" to which Cornerstone replies, in a manner that exemplifies the gradualist plan, "It was not time then" (36).

This interchange recalls Shirley Graham's *It's Morning,* which addresses white oppression and black labor within the same rubric of day and night and the fullness of time. The play's action begins on the last day of 1862 in a cabin in the slave quarters on a plantation, opening with a singing sequence that sets the tone for the rest of the play because all of the dialogue (along with the songs in the play) is arranged in poetic lines. This technique of blending Shakespearean form with dialect further complicates the already vexed issue of incorporating eye-dialect into the dialogue. Graham writes in the opening "note" that the dialect in "It's Morning" is not uniform. It is not intended to be. Many African languages express different meanings by changes in pitch and volumn [*sic*]. The most primitive of American Negroes indicate slight changes in meaning by changing vowel sounds. Also, the old type of Negro preachers used a biblical mode of expression which cannot be expressed in dialect. (BFP 211)

This lack of uniformity clashes with the uniformity of the line lengths of the dialogue and their echoes of a distinctly European form—a hybridity that reflects the multiply interpolated secrecy that inflects the play. One especially wonders how actors might perform these lines: if they deliver them with conscious foregrounding of the lines as lines, then a level of irony is introduced into the text that could create an uneasiness that would heighten the uneasiness of the play itself. At the very least, Graham's blending the vernacular and the formal poetic creates a doubling that, if anything, highlights the space in between as one full of rich potential for inserting secrecy—such secrecy as can, in fact, cause uneasiness.

The play focuses on a young black woman named Cissie whose master is threatening to take her children from her, showing especial interest in her daughter, Millie, by whom presumably he might beget children and add to his property. Cissie cannot abide this possibility, and her angst is only increased by the fact that she has herself been broken by a white master in her youth. This latter fact is unknown to most of the other slaves until revealed by Grannie Lou, an old slave woman who is "considered a little crazy" (211). When Grannie Lou suggests that there may be a way to avoid the family's breakup, Aunt Sue (one of the slave women) says:

Let huh talk
We allus calls huh crazy, but who knows?
Maybe da Voodoo wo'k dat way, maybe she
bile up sompin' dat kin help. (215–16)

Thus prompted and speaking from within the womanist-empowered magical currency of voodoo, Grannie Lou tells a story about a woman she remembers in her youth who decapitated her three sons to prevent their being sold by their masters. The slave women are horrified by this story, but its precepts clearly take root in Cissie's mind, and when Mille and her brother Pete appear onstage, she tells them to go play and that there will be a party later that night. The first scene of the play closes with Cissie declaring that her children "ain't gwine, yo' hyear me? DEY . . . ain't gwine . . . NEIDDAH!" (219).

Scene 2 opens at the *"hour just before dawn of the following day"* with the cabin *"still bedecked for the party"* but looking *"like an actress, when the comedy is finished, ghastly beneath her grease paint"* (219). Into this masked scene, Uncle Dave, a black preacher who lives nearby, arrives to comfort Cissie and, when he realizes her aim, to prevent her killing her children. But Cissie will not be stopped, and when *"the sound of a galloping horse"* (222) is heard and the other slaves go to see who approaches, Cissie leaves the stage, knife in hand, to enter the room where her children are sleeping. Instead of someone coming to take the children, however, a white Union soldier appears in the doorway, announcing:

> Look! Look, the day has come!
> The day for which we fought.
> Still for a moment are the guns
> And from the fallow earth do rise
> The souls of those who fell
> That they might see you go forth
> Free to greet this Dawn!
> [. . . . .]
> You're free! No longer slave. (222)

This grand announcement sounds, if anything, more artificial than the "lines" of dialect (an artificiality that, as I will point out shortly, informs the even more tragic subtext of this already tragic text). It is punctuated by a scream, and Cissie emerges from the bedroom with her dead daughter's body in her arms. Appalled, the white man staggers off the stage, and as the other slaves moan at the tragedy before them, *"Cissie looks down into her child's face and speaks quietly"* saying, "Hit's mawnin'!" at which point *"from her throat there comes a cry of anguish as she falls to her knees"* and *"on the door, a single spray of mistletoe sways in the morning breeze and then falls gently on the upturned face of the child"* (224).[26] Indeed, the morning has "hit" Cissie and her compatriots with overwhelming anguish.

The inflections of secrecy in the play are readily detected. Cissie's keeping secret her plans to murder Millie resembles the sort of secrecy-move used by the women in *They That Sit in Darkness;* not only must the children be kept unaware for their "protection," but other members of the in-group must be held at bay by means of silence and coded language (Cissie's exclamation "NEIDDAH" confounds the symbolic in what can be read as an eruption of the *chora*). Cissie finds precedent for her action in the narrative that Grannie Lou told about the woman she knew who killed her sons: a wild woman "straight from the jungles in da far off Af'ica," the woman is part and parcel of an exotic space redolent of magic, for she is a superwoman, "straight lak a tree, an' tall, [s]wift as a lion an' strong as any ox. Da sugah cane went down fo' huh big knife [l]ak cottonstalks under de fierces' hail" (216). Then, when the "news comes dat dey sole huh sons down de ribbah," she replies, cryptically, that "day nebbah go" (216–17). At that point, the "white folks laf

> . . . but niggahs dassent lag—dey see huh face.
> She don' say no'tin' mo', but go away,
> An' early in da mawnin' call huh boys,
> An' when dey come, she tell 'em to stan' close,
> An' watch da sun come up out ob da hills.
> Dey sort ob smile at huh an' look,
> An' den dat 'oman lift huh big cane knife,
> She cry out sompin' in a wild, strange voice,
> An' wid one sweep she cut off all dey heads,
> Dey roll down at huh feet—All tree ob dem. (217)

With the woman's wild unintelligible cry, the unknown erupts into audibility much like Alice Smith's scream at the end of *Her*. That mysterious cry foreshadows but also provides the vocal precedent for the offstage scream that signals Cissie's murder of Millie. Both utterances function for their auditors as semiotic eruptions, sounds outside of the symbolic order that herald an alternate logic. Indeed, the next morning, when the banjo player, Cripple Jake (himself apparently marked by physical otherness), conjectures and then ponders Cissie's plan of action, his own alternate logic appalls the slave women just as much as Cissie's enactment of the plan itself later horrifies the white soldier. Jake says,

> Ah'm tinkin' bout dis ting—
> Hebbin is a high an' a holy place,
> Da chilluns done no wrong,
> Dyin' will bring 'em joy,
> Da good book say, "Lam's
> In his bosom—safe."
> While Cissie know dat
> Livin's jes a slow decay
> Wid worms gnawin' lak nits
> Into dey heart an' soul. (221)

To protect the lambs from the goats/White Devils, death emerges as the only option, but, again, Jake's comments meet with disapprovals that "Cissie

Kain't . . . "; "Dey'll beat huh mos' tuh death!"; "She'll be a mu-dress!"; "She'll bu'n in hell!" to all of which Cissie herself says as she enters the room during the discussion, "when da saints ob God go marchin' home [m]ah gal will sing! Wid all da pure, bright stars, [t]uhgedder wid da mawnin' stars—She'll sing!" (221).

The ultimate irony and secret of the play is that, unknown to the slaves, the morning of freedom is provisional at best, and emancipation will prove as problematic and ultimately artificial as the white soldier's announcement of it. To a black audience of the 1930s, it is painfully clear that the achievement of freedom is far away. Read this way, perhaps Cissie *has* done her daughter a favor by ending her life and saving her from the oppression she would nevertheless have faced in a Jim Crow postbellum/post-Reconstruction South. But the end of the play is ambivalent, raising the question—What really is the result of keeping secrets from and/or silencing the voices of others in one's in-group? When the strong African woman of Granny Lou's past acted, she killed her sons and not herself; when Cissie acts, she takes from the world a black woman, perhaps one who could later speak with the same kind of strength as Granny Lou. On the other hand, the brutality of white rape-minded men will forever remain secret to Millie.[27] The play offers no resolution to the dilemma: Granny Lou simply laughs, the young women moan, and little Pete lives to fight another day.

The opposition between the young and old Us and the hopes of a new dawn also appear in Georgia Douglas Johnson's *Starting Point*. Henry and Martha Robinson have sent their son, Tom, to school in Washington, DC, and Johnson opens the play with Martha setting the table for her husband and slipping an envelope from Tom (although the audience does not yet know this) under his plate. Henry returns from his work at the bank and sits down, while Martha observes that his job is one that keeps him busy "at the beck and call of Tom, Dick and Harry," to which he replies, "You're mighty right—my feet seem like they don't belong to me a'tall they're that tired—let me get my slippers" (PGDJ 118). When Martha asks how things have been at the bank, Henry explains that "there's been a whole lot of howdy do down there today over Jim Boyd's son Toby" who has "been writing numbers for the white folks round the bank, and them federal investigators caught him red-handed" (119). Where Fanny's number running in Spence's *Hot Stuff* is the thing that empowers her in her female space, the Robinsons are horrified by such activity, and Henry observes, "We got a lot to be thankful for, our son's doing so fine up there in the doctor's school in Washington. . . . Thank God he's got a fine profession and won't have to set at no white man's door fetching and carrying all his life like me" (119).

As the two talk about their son and their pride in him, Martha finally cannot delay any longer and so pulls the envelope out from under Henry's plate, which he opens, reading the letter inside aloud: "Dear mother and dad: I'm coming home for a day or two. Will be there almost as soon as this letter. Have a surprise for you. Your loving son, Tom" (119). In their joy over seeing Tom they discuss what the surprise might be and as they do so Tom himself arrives, accompanied by a girl, who Tom announces as "My surprise, Mother, your new daughter Belle—!" (120). The moment is an awkward one, as Belle is apparently not the kind of girl they were expecting their son to marry. They also seem to suspect the worst regarding Tom's schooling, a suspicion soon confirmed as they begin to talk to him. After supper, Tom ebulliently raves about his parents' kindness in taking Belle in, at which point his mother says, "Well son—your happiness is our happiness. Tho, we did think maybe you'd get your license. We thought that was the surprise you had for us" (121). As Tom begins his explanation to them for this situation, "*Belle's voice is heard in a popular blues song off stage*" causing all "*three [to] lift their heads with varying expressions. Father and Mother taken aback look askance at each other because of the type of song and rowdy music*" (121). "That girl's a wow!" Tom says. "She sure can sing. Knocked 'em cold in Washington!" (121). His behavior further confirms his parents' notion that he is not the same wholesome Tom they raised to become one initiated in public life secrecy. After this interruption, he proceeds to explain that he will have to wait another year to get his medical license, at which point Belle comes into the room and interrupts him, saying, "What kind of cock and bull story is that you're pulling on your folks, Tom?" (122). As he continues to try and explain his situation, Belle insists that he is lying and urges him to "make a clean breast of it. . . . For God's sake, be honest. Tell 'em. They've got a right to know"; then, after giving him one more chance to tell his parents himself, she says, "He's in the number racket" (122). This news is followed by a knock on the door and a telegram to Tom informing him, "Your—place raided. Town's hot. Don't come back" (123).

Particularly interesting are the reasons Tom offers for his course of action. He tells his father, "I had to have some money, I couldn't ask you or ma for any more—so—well, I had to get busy. . . . I had to do something" (122). Even though Henry's notion of labor is fully inflected by race—he wants Tom to be free of scraping for white people—Tom himself makes no mention of race as a factor in his decision making. He does say at one point that "[t]hey're as tricky as they can be at these schools—always trying to put stumbling blocks in your path and making you go through a lot of red tape" (122), which points to the tricks of the White Devils in keeping the Us's away from the Purple Flower. Yet he does not make racism explicit as the cause of his problems, nor even later in the play when Tom and Belle fight over his actions does race play into the situation. Still, it is tempting to see Tom's race as an implicit factor in his decision to run numbers—it is, after all, a quick way for black people to make money during the 1920s and 1930s. But Johnson leaves this matter tantalizingly undeveloped and inexplicit in the text, a secret never quite revealed even as Tom's other secrets *are* revealed.

Tom's critical situation finds a remedy by the end of the play. The next morning, he apologizes to his father for his actions and for his behavior the night before, when he had defied his father, yelling at him, "Who in the hell do you think you are? You're only my father, you're not God" (124) when his father told him he is entitled to have a say as his parent. The more contrite Tom, however, gains a different response from his father, who tells him:

> That's all right [about last night] son—we all make mistakes, but it's never too late to start over again. Now I been thinking, and your Ma and me figured that since I'm old and about played out, you could step in and take my place. I feel almost certain my boss would be willing. (125)

In this tearfully triumphant moment, "*Tom looks at Belle who stands with clasped hands . . . looks at Tom imploringly and nods her head approvingly*" (125), and the young man follows his father out the door and to a new career in the bank.

The play cavorts within the Washingtonian and Du Boisian modes of improvement for African American status. On one level, the moment is indeed a triumphant one in which a young man who has taken a destructive path has turned away and entered a more wholesome (read "fully visible") profession where he can make money as an "honest" young man. And the fact that Johnson does not have Tom cite race as a reason why he could not get through medical school serves to heighten this story of moral reorientation. But on a very different level, Tom is at a much more distressing sort of starting point—that of a lifetime of servitude to a system of white empowerment, a system in which he finds himself set in the province of the visible invisible. Because he has failed to get his medical degree when it was in his grasp to do so and because he cannot go back to Washington, he now has to follow in his father's footsteps, a fact that ultimately disappoints the hopes that his parents held for him in the first place. As in *The Purple Flower*, the younger generation does not appreciate the importance of self-employment and professional labor where the older generation does, and the striking message that emerges from the play is that it is a dangerous game that African American young people must play, for if they act up and get in trouble and have to turn from a professional career to a career in a bank, the ramifications are much more severe than they would be for their white counterparts.

Of equal significance in the play is the fact that a woman should be the catalyst of change and both the possessor and the revealer of a secret. Belle's very name, which usually signifies a young aristocratic *white* southern woman, signals a higher level of empowerment than one would expect regarding a young black woman. Then again, she is strong, resembling Fanny of *Hot Stuff,* a blues-singing gal from the fast side of life. Combining these two incarnations of relatively empowered women (white "belle" and black "hot mama"), Belle emerges as the sort of young Us who maybe can negotiate a new day in the effort of black and female empowerment, although it must also be noted that she now finds herself in the old setup of a wife to a man who must bow and scrape to white people—her strength brings about no radical change or improvement in the social standing even if it does get Tom out of trouble. Her reading the promised secret of Tom's lifestyle serves to realign the game for him, however suspect the new game may be.

Johnson also dramatizes the results of young African Americans taking matters into their own hands in *William and Ellen Craft,* crafting out of her source material a treatment of a secrecy-discourse game par excellence. Because of her light skin, Ellen will fetch a high price at the slave trade and so will be sent down the river. Seeking to avoid this fate, William devises a plan for them to escape. However, Johnson adds other elements to the original story as written by the real William Craft. The first of these is the addition of another black female character, one Aunt Mandy, a mother-figure to the two young people.[28] The play opens with Mandy warning William and Ellen that she has heard that the plantation owner's widow has learned the locations of the Underground Railroad's local stations. Ellen asks if "they know 'bout our last secret hidin' place in the woods where Cap'n Smith meets the slaves an' takes um to the boat?" to which Mandy replies, "Yes, honey, dey knows all 'bout ev'ything" (PGDJ 95). When William asks how this information was discovered, Mandy explains that "[d]ey caught Jack and Sophie las night an' whupped em till dey tole all 'bout de secret plans an' meetin' places" (96).

With the Underground Railroad shut off from access, William conceives of a way to escape via the real railroad. Since Ellen so greatly resembles their now-dead master *and* can pass for white, William suggests that she dress as a man and take him onto the northbound train as "his" (Ellen-as-man's) slave. The scheme is a remarkable one in light of the black female spatiality so constantly delineated in these one-act plays: Ellen must pass not only as white but also as male and slaveholder. Keeping her true identity secret, she must traverse and pass in multiple spaces otherwise not available to her (the law at the time when the play is set—the time of the real-life Crafts' actual escape—did not permit a white woman to travel with a slave). Most significantly, despite the fact that this scheme is William's it is the woman who must effect it, so that a black female body keep its secrets not, like Joice Heth, in its visibility as other but in its visibility as the patriarchal self—a reversal of the typical black female visible invisible. However, simple bodily display will not be enough to get them to freedom, for she neither talks like a white person nor can she write. William instructs her to pretend to have a toothache, which will explain her remaining silent, and she must fake rheumatism to avoid writing. This plan of Ellen's not talking is an alteration from William Craft's actual narrative in which Ellen herself devises the scheme of pretending to be deaf, and that only when she fears being recognized on the train leaving Savannah. Moreover, the actual Ellen Craft wore bandages over her face to hide the fact that she had no beard while also wearing sunglasses to hide her eyes—a sort of phaneric mask playing on hypervisibility (she surely cut an odd figure, and one might wonder why Johnson passed up the opportunity for commentary on the blindness of white people). The effect that *does* result from Johnson's alterations is that they make Ellen even more of a performing passing body while also silencing her. Again, the subaltern cannot speak, and while traveling with such an "invalid," William seems to put himself in what might seem the unlikely position of having to explain his "master's" sickness. This move achieves a double-reversal of dependency: added to this Hegelian master's dependence on the slave is a dependency on the black male on the part of the black female. In yet another reversal, the entire scheme is dependent on enacting and appropriating the power of the *white man*—as William explains to Ellen, "All you got to do is walk. You don't have to talk, don't have to do a thing but just walk along bigity like a white man" (99), and he proceeds to show her how to walk such a walk. She imitates this imitation (whiteness twice-removed?), and he commends her, "You doin' fine! You see now you is supposed to be sick, you got a toothache, you goin' to a doctor in Philadelphia, you is nearly deaf, an' yo' nigger slave is takin' you—understand?" (99).

As the older leaders do according to the young Us in Bonner's play, Mandy shies away from the idea of escape. At the beginning of the play, Mandy and Ellen are alone, and after telling the girl that her plans have been found out she observes, "Po' chile! I know it's hard, but you got to ben' to do rod. You got to stan' it. . . . Don't no trouble las' all de time. Evething passes soon or late" (95). When William devises his plan, she tells him, "I think youse plum crazy William runnin' way like white folks, you an' Ellen—if dey ketches you— um-m-mh!" (97). At the same time, though, Mandy sympathizes with their plight, commiserating with Ellen that if she "was black an' ugly you would sho' get along lots better. Dem white debils" (96). And when William starts to leave in order to procure one of Master Charles's suits, Mandy explains that she has the only suits left, for "old Miss din't wunt nothin' lef round here to put her in de mind of dat terrible time when young Masser died. She told me to burn up all his close 'cause you know he had dat ketchin' sickness. . . . After I done washed an' laid out young Marse Charles I took every stitch uv his close an burned sulfer thru em in my hut" (98) and so did not burn but actually preserved the clothes. Now having committed to helping with the escape plan, Mandy goes to get the clothes that she secreted, telling William when he voices his concerns that her activities might be found out, "Don't you worry—I'm er ole fox" (98).[29]

With the plan in place, certain impediments arise. First, William realizes that Ellen's hair will have to be cut in order for her to pass as a man. William also realizes that he will need to dig up the money he has buried in the garden in order to afford the trip northward. The tension builds when Ellen worries that another slave (another of Johnson's additions), that "tale-tellin' Sam's got a way of dropping in here right free lak" (99). Hearing this concern, William decides to hide his cutting her hair by having her sit behind a curtain while he works. Meanwhile, voices begin to sound outside. Soon, Mandy returns with the clothes, and William explains the new plan to cover the original plan while Ellen remains behind the curtain to change into her former master's clothes. When William goes to the garden to dig up the money, Sam actually does appear. Mandy explains that Ellen is sick and acts in ways designed to drive him away, but he is suspicious. He asks where William is and Mandy replies that he is in the garden. "Pretty time o night gardenin'," Sam ventures, and William hears the comment as he comes back in and retorts, "I'm trying out a new secret on my tomatoes this year. Everytime I gits a piece o' iron I buries it under em. Makes em blood red an' big as your fist" (102). Unconvinced by this secrecy-move, Sam acts on his suspicion and peeks behind the curtain to see Ellen's new look. Recognizing the escape plot, Sam threatens to expose it, at which point William attacks him, binds him, and then takes him out back and offstage. Exactly what he does to Sam the spoilsport remains a secret although when he returns he says, "I'm sorry, Aunt Mandy, but I had to do what I done to kiver you cause he saw you here" (104), suggesting that he has taken this metaphorical piece of iron, Sam, and buried it/him under the tomatoes with his fist. Meanwhile, as Ellen is "whimpering" in response to the violence and in her fear about the escape plan's success, Mandy tells her in a statement memorable on several levels, "Buck up, chile, white men don't cry!" (104).

The play closes with William and Ellen successfully escaping, which is signaled by a "*train whistle in the distance*" (104), another eruption of the semiotic. The payoff has been attained. Aunt Mandy, however, remains behind, and her reaction to the train whistle is that she "*drops down on her knees on the floor, while the candle sputters and goes out*" (104). The gesture and the darkness that follow seem strange "in light" of the triumph of the moment. Again, the "new morning" for William and Ellen is undercut by Mandy's remaining in the darkness of bondage. Furthermore, despite his being a spoilsport, Sam may be dead—the possibility is strong enough to cast a shadow over William, who may have added murder to his official "crime" of running away.

Still, a black woman gets the last laugh. Johnson's play is about "craft," the intricacies of a game in which both the in-group and out-group players clash with secrecy-moves themselves designed to negotiate situations rife with secrecy. The layering of empowerment accomplished in this game is head-spinning. Mandy, alone at home and possessing the secret of William and Ellen's escape, herself will be rendered by "history" a secret since she does not appear in William's official narrative. If we are to believe Johnson's version of history, then we must read Williams as having obliterated her voice from the official historical account in much the same way that black feminist thought and culture were for years obliterated. Johnson thus "resurrects" her from her hiddenness. Stated another way, Johnson writes a black female secret into history, a secret lost in the new dawn of "freedom," which will ultimately emerge as being as problematic as slavery.

VI

Having roundly decried the Washingtonian plan for racial uplift, the Us's discuss alternative approaches. First, the Us's consider the plan of W. E. B. Du Bois when an Old Man Us announces,

> Here comes a Young Us who has been reading in the books!
> Here comes a young Us who has been reading in the books!
> He'll tell us what the books say about getting Somewhere. (36)

When the Young Us arrives, he throws his books down, declaring, "I'm through! I do not need these things! They're no good!" (36). When asked why, he replies, "I'm through I tell you! There isn't anything in one of these books that tells Black Us how to get around White Devils. . . . The White Devils wrote the books themselves. You know they aren't going to put anything like that in there!" (37). Discouraged by the limitations of reading and education, an Old Us appeals to God, calling out, "Lord! Why don't you come by here and tell us how to get Somewhere?" (37). A Young Us replies to this supplication by telling him, "Aw, you ought to know by now that isn't the way to talk to God! . . . Three score and ten years you been telling God to tell you what to do. Telling Him! And three score and ten years you been wearing your spine double sitting on the rocks in the valley too" (37).

Suddenly, this discussion is interrupted by an exclamation by Sweet. She says, "There's a White Devil sitting in the bushes in the dark over there! There's a White Devil sitting in the bushes over there in the dark! And when I walked by—he pinched me!" (38). First Blood immediately responds to this infraction, "catching a rock" and starting "toward the bushes" (38). When his mother tells him not to go after the White Devil because he will be killed for hurting him, he replies, "I don't care if they do. Let them. I'd be out of this hole then!" to which Average ventures, "Listen to that young fool! Better stay safe and sound where he is! At least he got somewhere to eat and somewhere to lay his head," to which First Blood replies, "Yes I can lay my head on the rocks of Nowhere" (38).

There appears in the passage a wedding of violence and blues form that ultimately registers a fear of lynching and the absence of loved ones who are its victims in the manner that Adam Gussow describes in *Seems like Murder Here: Southern Violence and the Blues Tradition.* Both the Old Man Us and Sweet utilize AAB blues format when they speak, and both the Young Us and Finest Blood seek to redress the violence perpetrated on the Us's with violence of their own. But although it is not stated explicity, Finest Blood's defending a White Devil's sexual attack on a female Us could well face the retribution of lynching. This horrifying treatment stands out in stark contrast with the desire for and disillusionment with education in the first part of the cited passage. First Blood's bitter statement that he can sleep soundly on the rocks of Nowhere chillingly evokes the debilitating restricted space of secrecy behind the Veil—the invisible space from which the Us of all kinds can only glimpse Life-at-Its-Fullest.

There is no shortage of one-acts that explore this confluence of secrecy and lynching. Georgia Douglas Johnson wrote a particularly large number of these, and we might begin by looking at *Blue-Eyed Black Boy,* which explores the violence of white men against black women and the drastically different effects of that violence compared to the consequences of alleged violence of black men against white women. The play is short and simple; set in the home of Pauline Waters, it opens with Pauline herself "*seated in a large rocker with her left foot bandaged and resting on a low stool*" (PGDJ 162).[30] Thus out of commission, Pauline watches as her daughter, Rebecca, irons her own wedding dress for her upcoming wedding to Dr. Thomas Grey. As she works, the two women talk, Pauline expressing her fear that she might get "lock jaw" (a particularly problematic condition given the vital importance of black women's discourse), and the two of them discuss Rebecca's fiancé. They also mention Rebecca's brother, Jack, who is a singular person because of his blue eyes and his love for and ambitions regarding education and its promise of the empowering possession of public life secrets. As Pauline says, "[J]ust give him a book and he's happy—says he's going to quit running that crane—and learn engineering soons you get married" (163).

At length, Thomas enters the stage to dress Pauline's wound, which he notes has been caused by her stepping on a rusty nail (a detail that suggests crucifixion, an echo that appears often in these lynching plays). While he is there, Pauline's best friend Hester Grant bursts in to tell the family that Jack has been accused of brushing "against a white woman on the street" (164) and is now in the hands of a lynch mob. Thomas suggests that they might appeal to "the Judge," but Pauline quickly notes that "he's a lyncher his own self—Don't put no trust in him" and tells Rebecca to go into her bedroom "and get me that little tin box out of the left hand side of the tray in my trunk" (165). Rebecca does so, and Pauline digs into the box and finds a small ring, which she gives to her future son-in-law, telling him,

> Here, Tom, take this. Run, jump on your horse and buggy and fly over to Governor Tinkham's house and don't let nobody, nobody—stop you. Just give him this ring and say, "Pauline sent this. She says they goin to lynch her son born twenty-one years ago." Mind you, say twenty-one years ago—Then say—listen close—"Look in his eyes and you'll save him." (165)

Tom leaves to perform this fateful errand. In the meantime, tension builds as the women hear and see white people with guns walk by offstage. When the anxiety reaches a critical level, Pauline prays,

> Lord Jesus, I know I've sinned against your holy law, but you did forgive me and let me hold up my head again. Help me again, dear Jesus—help me to save my innocent child—him who never done no wrong—Save him, Lord— Let his father—(*She stops and looks around at the two women, then cautiously speaks.*) You understand all I mean, sweet Jesus—come down and rise with this wild mob tonight—pour your love into their wicked hearts—Lord, Lord, hear my prayer. (167)

As she closes her prayer, the other women cry out that the military is passing by and Tom returns announcing, "He's saved, Miss Waters, saved. Did the Governor send the troops?" (167).

The rest of Johnson's lynching plays conclude with a much more grim vision. Four of these are doubled—two versions of two different plays. The first pair of these is composed of *And Yet They Paused* and *A Bill to Be Passed*. The plots of both plays are essentially the same, composed of four scenes, with scenes 1 and 3 set in a "*small, unpretentious church*" (PDGJ 168) in Mississippi and scenes 2 and 4 set in the National Congress in Washington, DC. Scenes 1 and 3 in both plays are similar, but scenes 2 and 4 differ significantly, including different conclusions.

The Mississippi scenes detail Reverend Timothy Jackson's dealings with his congregation in Mississippi. The action begins with his talking to Deacon Brown about an antilynching bill being debated in Congress and the fact that the congregation has sent a delegate to listen to the proceedings in Washington. The delegate is Henry Williams, and Deacon Brown observes that "we couldn't of picked out no better young feller than Henry Williams. He's got plenty of schoolin'. He'll get the news" (169). Presently other members of the congregation appear and they sing a song about the fall of the walls of Jericho, the Reverend exhorting them to sing "it like you mean it. Because we sure are trying to pull down that wall of hatred that's got us all shut away from our rights" (169). This meeting is interrupted, however, by a sister who arrives later and announces that

> I think it's my duty to report what I just heard. Something that just happened downtown. Since we're here praying for the bill that's gonna stop all this lynchin'. . . . You know that young Joe Daniels that they beat and drove out of town for bootlegging? . . . He oughta knowed they don't 'low no colored folks do no bootleggin' down here. That's white folks' business. . . . Well, it 'pears like de white store keeper on the hill was killed last night and dey took up Joe Daniels on suspect. (179)

This ominous news, of course, exhibits the threat of the very thing the bill in Congress is meant to stop, and the Reverend Jackson, much like the Old Man Us, prays:

> Oh Lawd, you know our hearts, you know our hopes—you know our down-sitting and our uprising. Like stumbling pilgrims trying to make our way through these dark shadows on and up to the precious light of day. You know Lawd, how long we've been in these low vales of sorrow. Dear Father, let the glory of your infinite love shine into the hearts of the men that make the laws and guide them to lift the heavy yoke that bows their brothers to the dust! (171)

The scene then shifts to Congress, where the proceedings are described. Henry Williams shows up at Congress with a reporter and an elder named Jasper Greene. Guards standing outside the door do not permit the three black men in the gallery, ostensibly because it is too full, but they allow the reporter to listen in at the door and report what he hears. The reporter gives much less detail about the proceedings in *And Yet They Paused* than he does in *A Bill to Be Passed*. What quickly emerges from the reporter's reports is that the White Devils are up to their usual tricks. He notes that "they're calling the roll. (*pause*) Now they're saying they ain't got a quorum" to which Williams shrewdly replies, "But you know they have. They've been here day after day and keep on saying they ain't got a quorum. You know they're playing for time" to which Greene adds, "Of course, stallin'—" (171). Williams and Greene then comment that they are tired of waiting for change, with Greene making a pertinent observation in light of secrecy: "I know I get so tired of waiting outside of doors, always outside waiting, but waiting is our part to do now—We musn't forget the good men who long ago fought our battles behind closed doors too—Lincoln and Brown and a host of others fought, bled and died for this very hour" (172). The scene then ends in *And Yet They Paused* with the Congress's calling a recess and Williams saying in bitterness, "They don't want to finish [deliberating and vote on the bill]. They want to keep us on the cross! I just can't see how men with any spark of human feeling, regardless of racial differences, can dilly-dally, while the very life-blood of a people hangs in the balance" (172). Scene two of *A Bill to Be Passed* is much longer, offering much more detail from the discussion in Congress. In this play, the reporter relates the nuances of the discussion, showing the back-and-forth discussion regarding the bill.

Scene 3 returns to Mississippi. After singing more songs with the congregation, Reverend Jackson stops to hear the news of a young boy who appears in the congregation and explains that a mob has indeed formed to lynch Joe Daniels. There then follows a series of offstage events, which as in *Blue-Eyed Black Boy*, is in part related by offstage sounds and in-part by the narration of the characters on stage. The scene is as gruesome as may be expected as the characters comment that the mob blows holes in Daniels's body with a blowtorch, the comments themselves being punctuated by screams and glares of light in the church building's windows. Finally, an "Old Brother" states, "They's through. They's burnin' him up. They's sot fire to him," which leads the reverend to deliver another prayer, "Oh Merciful Lawd, forgive me if I sin in thy sight, but Father, I humbly pray that you sear the heart and conscience of these white people as they have seared the flesh of our brother and help us all to walk humbly and justly before Thee" (175).

The plays then close with very different final scenes. Again, *And Yet They Paused* is much shorter; in it, a telegraph boy comes into Congress with a message that the audience actually hears a congressman read aloud without the mediation of the reporter because the boy leaves the door open. The congressman announces that the telegraph tells of yet another lynching in Mississippi and he declares, "Gentlemen—this sin is upon our heads! This blood upon our hands! We can hesitate no longer. This bill *must be passed!*" (176). At this news, the reporter "*dashes from stage. Williams stands for a moment stunned—breaks down, then covers his face with his hands. Elder puts arm around Williams's shoulder patting him on the back paternally as the two walk slowly off the stage while the curtain descends*" (176). The play thus closes focusing on the tragedy of yet another lynching that has occurred because white people have stalled in creating antilynching laws, and whether or not such a bill will ever be passed remains a disappointing mystery at the play's end. *A Bill to Be Passed* ends in a much different manner; after the congressman reads the telegram and makes his impassioned plea, a guard at the door insists that only one of the three black men may listen in, so Williams and Greene stand aside as the reporter continues to relate the debate inside. After delineating everything from the nature of justice to states' rights (Johnson includes arguments for and against racial discrimination and cruelty), the Congress votes to pass an antilynching law. Jubilant, the reporter shouts, "It's Passed! It's Passed!" as Greene exclaims, "Glory hallelujah" (187). Yet, while this play seems to close on a more positive note, the final lines come from Williams, who announces with excitement, "Thank God . . . let me send that telegram to the church back home. Then ON TO THE SENATE!!!" (187). While the Congress's decision provides hope that Williams seizes upon in his own vision for the future, the audience likely experiences little excitement, knowing that the bill's passage through the senate will be every bit as tempestuous.

Where the two plays *And Yet They Paused* and *A Bill to Be Passed* are very similar in content, the two plays with the same title of *A Sunday Morning in the South* differ somewhat. Designated as the "White Church Version" and the "Black Church Version," the titles effectively align the plays on opposite sides of the color line, with their respective secrets, and together exemplify the sort of double interpolation of both whites and blacks within the tortured dynamics of secrecy.

Both plays focus on Sue Jones and her grandson Tom Griggs. The plot unfolds in the morning with Sue cooking breakfast for both of her grandsons, Tom and Bossie, on Sunday morning. While eating breakfast, a friend of Sue's named Liza visits them and reveals that a white girl has been raped and the white authorities are in search of what they assume to be the black perpetrator of the crime. The police then appear at the house with the white girl who tacitly "recognizes" Tom as the rapist, so they take him into custody. Fearing a lynching, Sue tries to get white Judge Manning to intercede for her son, but before she can do so, she learns that the mob has already lynched Tom.

Certain elements are at work in both plays; one is that Tom is a "good" boy, who currently enacts the Washingtonian plan of industriousness but also intends to fulfill the Du Boisian vision of education. In the White Church Version, it is unclear where Tom works, but he tells his grandmother that "my back feels unjointed like. I ain't never gointer try to lift no more boxes, big and heavy like them was yesterday all by myself" (PGDJ 130), but in the Black Church Version, Johnson links the work to the white world, as Tom tells his grandmother, "Eugh—there's the church bell. I sho meant to git out to meeting this morning but my back still hurts me. Remember I told you last night how I sprained it lifting them heavy boxes for Mr. John?" (PGDJ 140). In both cases, it emerges that Tom was so worn out from his work the night before that he was in bed and asleep long before nine o'clock, which is an hour before the time when the white girl was allegedly raped. Actually, the fact that a rape ever even occurred is in doubt, as Sue and Liza at one point debate the veracity of the charges leveled at African American men by white mobs, with Sue observing in the White Church Version that "I don't believe half of 'em is tellin' the truth. They holler out 'rape' at the drappin' of hat. Half these tales is lies, jest lies" and Liza saying, "Why I knows it fer a fact that they lynched a man in Texas last year and found out most a mont afterwards that a white man done it—he blacked his face and put it on the poor Nigger" (131). When Liza also mentions that "I sho wish I could read and write and talk proper. I'd make folks set up," Tom says, "You know. I gointer get a good schooling some day so as I can help my folks get away from this terrible thing. I wonder sometimes what would I do if it happened to me—" (131). The Black Church Version's discussion differs in that Sue defends the law but Liza argues that even the law can be wrong and lead to the murder of an innocent party. Much like the optimistic trust in the potentialities of law in *A Bill to Be Passed* as opposed to the visceral pessimism of *And Yet They Paused,* the Black Church Version of *A Sunday Morning in the South* presents a belief in the law with healthy suspicion, where concerns about law and its potentials, both good and bad, are absent in the White Church Version. Even Tom's speech differs, as he says, "I been thinking a whole lot about these things and I mean to go to night school and git a little book learning so as I can do something to help—help change the laws . . . make em strong . . . I sometimes get right upset and wonder whut would I do if they ever tried to put something on me" (142). Tom's comments are punctuated by lyrics drifting from the church: "Shine on me, shine on me, / Let the light from the lighthouse shine on me" (143), and it is while Tom is saying, "It takes a sight of learning to understand the law and I'm gointer" (143) that the police enter the scene.

In both versions of the play, Sue's efforts to save Tom take a nonjuridical approach as she tries to appeal to white power; exasperated with the rules and/or the law, she desperately takes what measures she can by whatever means she finds available to her. Nevertheless, the dynamics of the play and Sue's appeals are significantly different. The White Church Version of the play is divided into two scenes, the first being set in Sue's kitchen and the second at a white church. In this version, Liza is on her way to the black church services, and it appears that Sue and her grandsons will be going as well once they have eaten breakfast. When Tom is arrested and taken away, Sue herself rushes with her other grandson, Bossie (who is seven years old), to the white church where an organ sounds and the song "Jesus Savior Pilot Me" can be heard sung by white voices. This song poses a different form from the song that Sue sings to herself at the beginning of the play, which although religious as well follows a blues format: "Oh poor sinner Eughum—Now is the time—Oh poor sinner Eughum—What you gointer do when the lamp burns down?" (130).[31] Standing outside the building, Sue asks the usher to get Judge Manning, urging him to tell the judge that it is Sue Jones (suggesting some relationship with the judge in the past). The usher finally summons the judge who appears, annoyed, assuring Sue that no one will lynch her son on a Sunday morning, to which she replies, "[Y]ou don't know these bad white folks lak I do—You'se good—they'd do anything, anything Jedge, Please sur common!" (135). Nevertheless, he goes back inside to get his hat and while he is gone, two white men walk by talking, and she hears one say, "'Well we strung him up all right.' But when he kept hollering, 'Granny, Granny,' [*sic*] it kinder made me sick in the belly" and these words are punctuated from the choir singing "Going home, going home, yes I'm going home" to the melody of "*Dvorak's World Symphony*" (136). Upon hearing this news from the white man, Sue "*clutches at her heart and reels to the ground*" and the judge "*comes from the church steps, hat in hand, and halts stunned by the tableau of the old woman dead on the ground with the little boy kneeling, crying beside her*" (136).

The Black Church Version transpires entirely within a black setting and offers elements that change the trajectory of the play in various ways. The play has no scene breaks, and appears to take place later in the Sunday morning than the other version, for as Sue and her grandsons are eating breakfast, the church bell from the nearby black congregation rings and Tom says, "Eugh—there's the church bell. I sho meant to git out to meeting this morning but my back still hurts me" and then proceeds to discuss the fact that his working so hard for Mr. John kept him in bed late (140). The effect of this change is to show that the work that Tom must do for the white people cuts him off from his religion and the community of which it is the center. This effect finds further heightening when the police arrive and prevent Sue from going to any church service at all, white or black. The music in this play is different, composed entirely of a cappella renderings of hymns such as "Amazing Grace" and "Alas and Did My Savior Bleed." Jeanne-Marie A. Miller ventures that this "Christian music underscores the brutality of the crime; the innocence of the victim who believes in both Christ and democracy; and the hypocrisy of the murderers, whose behavior conflicts with one of the major tenets of Christianity—brotherhood" (357). When the police take Tom in the Black Church Version, another friend of Sue's shows up: this woman, Matilda, Sue sends out to get a "Miss Vilet" explaining that

> I got to git to Miss Vilet . . . I nused her when she was a baby and she'll do it. . . . Her pa's the Jedge. . . . All right Tildy. Tell Miss Vilet her nuse Sue is callin on her and don't fail me; tell her they done took Tom and he is perfect innercent, and they gointer take him away from the police, and ax her to ax her pa the Jedge to go git Tom and save him fur God's sake. Now hurry, Tildy, fly! (145)[32]

Matilda leaves but soon returns to convey the news that it is too late to save Tom, at which point Sue dies in her chair while the singers at the church services sing, again in a modified AAB form:

> Lord have mercy.
> Lord have mercy.
> Lord have mercy over me. (148)

The final one of Johnson's plays that addresses the problems of black male status and the efforts of a black woman to preserve and protect the black man is *Safe: A Play on Lynching*. Set in a southern town in 1893, all of the action transpires within the domestic space of the African American Pettigrew family, which consists of Liza, who is nine months into her pregnancy, her husband, John, and her mother, Mandy Grimes. Mandy is the sort of matronly black woman who appears often in these plays, and the dramatic action opens with Liza trying to convince her mother to take a break from washing the dishes because Liza herself will likely have to rest soon and her mother's help will be needed. As Mandy relaxes and Liza sews baby clothes, John reads in the newspaper that Sam Hosea, a young black boy, has been in jail because "he and his boss had some sort of dispute about wages—the boss slapped him and Sam up and hit him back they says," to which news Mandy observes, "[T]hat's mighty unhealthy business for this part of the country. Hittin' a white man, he better hadder made tracks far away from here I'm er thinking" (PGDJ 155). At this point, their neighbor Hannah Wiggins pays them a visit to tell them that a lynching mob is forming in town. John decides to step down the street to check on the situation.

When he leaves, the women remain behind discussing the horrors of lynching. Their discussion leads Liza to ask, "What's little Nigger boys born for anyhow? I sho hopes mine will be a girl.—I don't want no boy baby to be hounded down and kicked round—No, I don't want to ever have no boy chile!" (157). Mandy tells her not to say such a thing because it is "a sin—God sends what he wants us to have—we can't pick and choose" and Hannah adds, "No, we sho can't. We got to swaller the bitter with the sweet" (157). No sooner has she spoken than a gunshot sounds, and the noise of the approaching mob increases. The women dim the lights because, as Hannah notes, "[Y]ou can't tell what them devils might git it in they heads to do" (157). As the lynch mob passes (offstage) the house, the women hear Sam calling for his mother, and Liza goes into labor, which prompts Mandy to send Hannah out the back door to fetch the doctor. Meanwhile, Mandy strives to allay Liza's fears, telling her not to think about Sam Hosea at this time but rather her "own little baby—you got him to think about—You got to born him safe!" (159). Liza (much like Cissie in *It's Morning*) responds to these words "*wild-eyed*" asking her to repeat what she has just said, which Mandy does, saying, "Born him safe! Born him safe! That's what you got to do" (again echoing the AAB blues form) to which Liza responds, "*turning her head from side to side as she stands half stooped in the doorway*" repeating, "Born him safe!—safe," at which point she "*hysterically disappears into the next room*" (159). As soon as Liza leaves the stage, John returns followed soon by Dr. Jenkins, who arrives to help with the birth (Hannah does not return). John and Mandy sit in the front room waiting for the birth when they hear a baby's cry followed by muffled sounds. Then Dr. Jenkins appears to tell them that something has happened: they ask him frantically what has happened, and he responds:

> Wait a minute, calm yourselves. I've got something to tell you, and I don't hardly know how— . . . She's all right and the baby was born all right—big and fine—you heard him cry? . . . And she asked me right away, "Is it a girl?" . . . And I said, "No child, it's a fine boy," and then I turned my back a minute to wash my hands in the basin. When I looked around again she had her hands about the baby's throat choking it. I tried to stop her, but its little tongue was already hanging from its mouth—It was dead! Then she began, she kept muttering over and over again: "Now he's safe—safe from the lynchers! Safe!" (161)[33]

May Miller's *Nails and Thorns* offers a plot very similar to that of *Safe*, only in this play it is a *white* mother and child who suffer the dangers of lynching. Set in the house of the white Landers family, the one-act's cast consists of Stewart, his wife, Gladys, and their child, Stewart. He and his wife and child are attended by a hired African American woman named Annabel.

Stewart is the sheriff of the town where the action takes place, a town that Miller describes as "probably South, probably West—a small town ruled by frenzy" (SF 177). Miller follows her description of this semirural space as being one "ruled by frenzy" by actually introducing representatives of the rulers of this town—the sheriff and his wife—in a frenzied state, for Gladys, "a slender woman in her late twenties, is standing before the screen door nervously latching and unlatching the catch" while Stewart "pretends to be reading, but furtively he follows his wife's nervous movements" (177). The screen door that Gladys continually latches and unlatches foreshadows the ambiguous locked-in/locked-out insider/outsider status that she maintains throughout the play, for at the same time that this play deals with lynching it also addresses the cloistering of women, both white and black, and the overpowering finality of their confinement and ultimate silencing of their voices.

The play acts out the typical progression of a lynching. Gladys's nervousness results from the fact that her husband has not contacted the governor to call in the state militia regarding a situation arising from "a Negro's assault on a white woman" (177). Stewart has had a black man whom he calls "simple Lem" arrested because "pretty damaging evidence seemed to point to the half-wit, and we thought we'd better lock him up for safekeeping; that's all" (178). Responding to his wife's concerns that the white people in town will lynch Lem, Stewart notes that no lynchings have ever taken place in the history of the town and that there have been no signs or sounds of a gathering mob. At this point, Annabel arrives for work so frightened from hearing that a mob *is* gathering that Stewart finally does leave to make sure that Lem is safe and to quell any mob action. Left alone, Gladys and Annabel soon hear the roar of a lynching mob passing by the house and by the play's end the mob has its way and lynches Lem because, as Annabel says, "the folks was gonna give Lem a li'l necktie party so as others would 'member that even if they ain't got sense, they gotta know a white woman" (181).

While the play powerfully dramatizes the wrenching experience of a lynching, Miller's true focus rests on the experience of women cloistered and cut off from traumatic events and their struggles to interfere, disrupt, and alter the male-dominated actions that happen on the other side of the wall of their imprisonment. Both of the women in the play are othered by their alternative association with and use of language and narrative. When, at the beginning of the play, Gladys voices her fears that a lynching will occur, Stewart tries to calm her by giving her a comic strip to read named "Desperado Joe" in which, by jarring coincidence, a gang has captured Joe because he "kidnaped [*sic*] Percy's girl" (178). Stewart actually laughs as he points out that "the gang's got him, and he is scared!" and Gladys replies, "The gang's got him. Stewart, how can you laugh," to which he responds, "Gladys, you're losing your sense of humor" (178). The moment seems forced—how can a kidnapper caught by a mob be humorous on any level? "After all, it's only a funny," Stewart observes (178), but it seems a strange subject matter for "a funny," and it suggests that Gladys perceives the serious side of the comics that Stewart cannot see, perhaps a serious subversive element that the author of the comic actually intends. Certainly experience has taught her to read the narrative of lynching deeply and to interpret it in a complex and expansive way that Stewart simply cannot seem to grasp; she explains that

> I lived in a town once where they lynched a man and I can never forget how the town and the people suffered. It wasn't what they did to the unfortunate man alone. He was out of his misery. It was what they did to every soul in that town. They crucified everything that was worthwhile—justice and pride and self-respect. For generations to come the children will be gathering the nails and thorns from the scene of that crucifixion. (180)

Gladys's position seems implicitly inclusive, although her concern is more directed toward the damaging results of the spectacle of lynching on the *white* community's future than the black community's. In fact, she explains to Stewart that "I worry about the kind of world Junior will have to live in. That's the reason I didn't like the comic strip you showed me. I hate the thought that he'll be reading about gangs and mobs and enjoy them" (180), implying that her complaint seems to be with the barbaric actions of a mob more than her concern for the victim.

Nevertheless, Gladys reads the narrative of lynching differently from Stewart, and such alternate involvement with language, as may be expected, also informs Annabel's speech. Where the white sheriff claims to have seen no signs of mob action, Annabel explains:

> Some o' the men uptown done tole their friends an' say foh 'em to git off the streets to keep out o' trouble 'cause they wouldn't like to hafta burn up all the good cullud folks, too. That's why I was so scared. Mah folks at home tried to keep me, but I knowed you all 'ud be lookin' foh moe so I stole out an' kinda bent ovah so as nobody couldn't see mah face an' I sneak on up heah. . . . [When Stewart observes that she has not been harmed on her trip, she replies,] Yes sah, but all along on the streets I seen a li'l bunch o' folks heah an' a li'l bunch there, an' they all was gittin' together talkin'. then they'd go jine up wid the other bunch. One time one o' 'em hollered at me an' I started runnin' an' jes' keep right on 'til I got heah. (179)

When Stewart goes out to try and stop a mob from forming, Annabel reveals that the situation is dire because the Davis girl's cousin holds the key to the jail and will likely allow the mob to take Lem. When the mob passes by the house offstage, Gladys takes her baby and rushes out, crying, "I'll tell that mob how I feel. I'll tell them how you feel. I'll show them my baby—he is this town's tomorrow" (183). Soon some of the sheriff's men show up to protect the house, and when they discover that Gladys has fled to the mob one of them goes to retrieve her. At length, Stewart himself returns, announcing that the mob could not be stopped and asking with increasing alarm where his wife and child are. Soon the sheriff's man returns with Gladys and a doctor, and Gladys tells him the baby is "dead! Didn't they tell you? The mob lynched your son along with crazy Lem. They knocked him down—they stamped on him. Oh, Stewart, they won't listen—they can't even see me—they're killing my baby. . . . He's dead, dead, I tell you, and I'm glad. (*laughing hysterically*) He'll never have to see a lynching" (186). Gladys's final proclamation speaks to the vividly destructive ways people on both sides of the color line are embroiled in the web of secrecy.

The synergy among these plays is, in my opinion, so evident that to draw it out any further with tedious comment would only mar it with harrying. Moreover, much has been written about these plays, especially Johnson's, and the ways that secrecy touches upon the theater of lynching have been mentioned earlier in this volume while the secrecy moves that I have not explicitly pointed out in them have likely by now become familiar to the reader.[34] I seek to linger on these plays only in order to discuss what is perhaps the most conspicuous thing they all have in common—they each and all place the lynching itself offstage. This maneuver is noteworthy, for at the same time that it replicates the Foucauldian removal of punishment from visibility (an ironic move, given that lynching is ostensibly a spectacle), the maneuver itself seems a different kind of deferral. The vivid descriptions as well as the sounds and visual symbols (the flashing of lights, for example, that serve as gestures) all show that the plays seek neither to escape from lynching in denial of its horrors or to render it truly invisible. It would be understandable if these writers did not want to dramatize visibly such a painful scene, although staging it would arguably lessen its power and Johnson and Miller understood that suggestions and descriptions coupled with "the horror of nothing to see" would make the terror-effect even greater. But in considering this secrecy-move (for that is what it is) further, it seems equally possible that this sort of absenting, this kind of Derridean deferral, stands as a technique, a weapon, to write against, write out, and control lynching itself. In these plays, the offstage lynching scene is the lynchpin, the necessary element that is markedly absent. It is ironic that Johnson could get none of these one-acts accepted for publication or production by the NAACP on the grounds that they were too disturbing when, in fact, no one actually gets lynched onstage.

This absence, to get to the point, transforms an ultravisible into an invisible spectacle, and this creation of invisible visible seems very different from the sort of body-presence typically found in African American examples of the visible invisible. If anything, these plays represent a victory even as they articulate a horror, the victory of an angry writing b(1)ack—a white infant boy perishing with a "simple" (childish?) black man, a bill being passed in the House whatever the unlikeliness of its passing the Senate, a potential victim actually being saved. Any time the lynching "victim" takes his final bow, then the lynch-act has been undone. It is through this secrecy-move that such subversion finds realization, or at least the hope of such.

VII

Faced with such helplessness, the Us's consider one last option for advancement when a newcomer walks onstage carrying bags of gold. The new Us puts the bags down and groans, prompting an old man to ask, "'Smatter with you? Ain't them bags full of gold" to which the newcomer replies, "Yes, they are full of gold!" leading the old man to ask, "Well why ain't you smiling then? Them White Devils can't have anything no better!" to which the newcomer replies, "Yes they have! They have Somewhere! I tried to do what they said. I brought them money, but when I brought it to them they would not sell me even a spoonful of dirt from Somewhere! I'm through!" (39). The futility of money is heartbreaking, especially in light of the fact that even after black soldiers had performed heroically in World War I they were not rewarded at home with social advancement or equal pay.

The problems of the Us's struggles to attain riches, the problems accompanying what money they do gain, and that gain's failure to deliver Life-at-Its-Fullest find treatment in a one-act by Spence that deftly plays with secrecy titled *The Starter.* The setting is a bench on a summer day in Harlem where T. J. Kelly sits waiting for his girlfriend, Georgia. As he waits, he reads a newspaper, commenting to himself on the things he reads. The stage directions note that Kelly's *"face is the most important thing that ever happened to him. For the rest,* T. J. *is tall, dapper and in love"* (PNL 207). One of the headlines in the paper reads, "Woman gives Birth To Four Healthy Sons," to which he responds, "Gee! A male quartet! Four! . . . 'Father Overjoyed!' Like hell, he is," at which point he throws the paper down "in disgust," saying, "Gee! Suppose something like that was to happen to me!" (207). With that thought in mind, he *"grabs his coat and hat and prepares for flight,"* but then *"stops short, laughing sheepishly"* and says, "Reckon them things only happen to furriners. Sure!" (207). He then *"whistles a few lines from ''Tain't Gonna Rain No Mo''*

(207). The audience may wonder if he has the same sort of fear that plagues the heroine of *They That Sit in Darkness*—that he may already have initiated the cycle of having children unplanned and against his will, which will lead to a life of poverty and unrealized dreams.

Presently two women walk by, hoping to get a seat on the bench, and when one of them asks Kelly to move over to make room for them, he replies with "*a provoking grin*" that they are reserved and "*spreads both arms along the back of the bench*" (208). One of the women responds to his actions by telling him, "Take yo' arms off dat bench, you loafin' nigger!" to which he replies, "Now, see here Angel face, and you too, Grape Nuts! Ah know you're both dying for a real live hug from an honest tuh goodness he-man. Well, come on an' get it. I won't charge you nothing" (208). Although he speaks in jest, he nevertheless refers to the exchange of currency. When one of the women says in shock, "Ah like yo' gall!" he replies, "They all do! You're not the only one!" (208). Disgusted with Kelly's rudeness, the two women walk on and are passed by Georgia who appears on the scene and approaches Kelly, who "*makes an elaborate bow and sweeps his belongings to one side . . . [and then kisses her] Valentino-fashion*" (209). The two women exclaim to themselves, "Brazen!" and "Hussy!" but Georgia thinks "they was jealous all right!" (209).

The rest of the play features dialogue between Kelly and Georgia as they sit on the bench. Kelly says he does not doubt the women's jealousy at all, and Georgia bristles at his arrogance, saying, "[Y]uh doan' hate yuhself, do you?" to which he replies, "Naw! 'Tain't no use hating the person you have to live with. . . . Meaning me—Thomas Jefferson Kelly—at your service" (209).[35] As they talk, it emerges that Kelly thinks of himself as someone who deserves a higher status in the world than that which he possesses. He is an elevator starter, which is "just one step better'n the man who runs the cage" even though he has had two "full terms in High School, and don't you forget it" (210). Georgia observes, "Yuh's had too much schoolin'—that's whut's the matter with yuh—" (210). Georgia then goes on to say,

> That's funny! . . . Why T. J.—yuh knows Ah does sewin' doan yuh? . . . Well, Ah ain't never tole yuh 'bout mah place 'cause it's so low-down. Eyetalians and Jews and colored—all in tergether. It's a dump. Well, I'm what they calls a Finisher. Finisher on dresses! See? That's whut Ah meant—You bein' a Starter and me a Finisher! (210)

Kelly's response to the revelation of this secret is that the two would make a good team and so why not get married? Georgia's response to his idea is to ask him how much money he has, and he replies that he has fifty-five dollars. Disappointed in this amount, Georgia upbraids him for asking her to marry him when he does not have enough money to support her. He then says, "Reckon you wouldn't say how much *you've* got in your bank," to which she replies two hundred dollars (212). Even though her having more money than himself daunts his pride for a moment, Kelly quickly begins to consider the possibilities offered by her having the money:

> Two hundred dollars! Say, you know what, Georgia? That's enough money to start on. We could get a nice room—Why I've got a peachuva room. An' we could get new fixings—pay down a deposit, you know. I could arrange all that at the store. They know me—Two hundred dollars ain't so bad! Say! Say—many a man's got married on less! (212)

But despite Kelly's efforts to turn Georgia into the starter (she has enough money to "start on"), she continues to be suspicious, criticizing that he will likely try to buy her a cheap ring where her experience "frum 'sociatin' wid them Jews an' Eyetalians" has taught her about diamonds and their worth (213). She also comments that she has been saving that money for rainy weather, which prompts Kelly to whistle "'Tain't Gonna Rain no Mo'" again. But soon she too ponders the advantages of marriage, saying

> Ef we got married yuh would'n' mind mah stayin' home when things was slow, would yuh, T. J. (*T. J. swallows painfully.*) Gee, it would be great tuh be able tuh stay in bed mornin's. Yuh know, T. J. the thought uh hittin' de chillies has driv' plenty into matrimony befo' now. Gee! Tuh lie in bed on a cole winter mornin' when de sleet an' rain er batterin' at de winders! (213)

Kelly quickly grows exasperated at this reverie and says that "all this talk 'bout cold and sleet—an' stayin' in bed—Gee! It's enough to give a man cold feet" (214) and he quickly steers the conversation back away from the topic of marriage, pointing at the city and admiring Harlem's lights. But Georgia turns to him and asks, "Is we engaged" to which he responds in the following manner:

> (*Annoyed*) Lawd! Do we have to go all over that? (*In a kindlier tone*) Keep yuh eyes on them lights, Honey an'—an' forget it. (*The park is very much darker now.* GEORGIA's *head snuggles up against* T. J.'s *shoulder. His arm slips about her waist. The Moon-man hangs his lantern in the heavens, and we do the only kindly thing we can think of. We draw the Curtain.*) (214)

In its playfulness, *The Starter* licenses, well, play. The play's hopefulness—an exuberant hopefulness, even—channels through T. J.'s singing and the possibility that he, too, might beget a "male quartet" to sing with him. His play creates a play; a performing performer, T. J. creates his own theater on the park bench, and there he plays out the role of potent male (although not *too* potent, for he is no Black Beast rapist). Spence exhibits a very light touch, confining such negative elements to fleeting references as she develops the play's joie de vivre. This latter aspect appears in the stage directions' dictating that the "*Moon-man*" hang "*his lantern in the heavens*" in what seems a clear reference to the play that Nick Bottom and his erstwhile comrades perform for the court of Theseus and Hippolyta. Spence's play offers a similar lovers' encounter in summer, a sort of lighthearted New York City park romance. And yet this touching exuberance grows richly tragic by the shadows that flit about its corners. Shallow though T. J. may be, he really is momentarily worried that he either has or will get a woman pregnant, and he is hurt by the fact that he does not have enough money to ask for Georgia's hand. Over-spreading all of the play's action, too, is the reality that neither of these young people face much prospect of getting rich: Washingtonian workers instead of Du Boisian intellectuals, their life is a "low-down" one, and the fact that money is not theirs to be had in sufficient much less great quantity suggests the secret, literally the "dark" side, of the Shakespearean rude mechanicals' performance.

Even if Spence *was* just writing for fun.

Spence particularly develops a sort of metaphoric system embodied in the two young peoples' occupations. T. J.'s role as starter is one in which he literally never gets off the ground even as he moves other people along.[36] Georgia's occupation is that of stitching things up, closing them, finalizing them. The metaphorical overtones can be read in several ways: a starter who never finishes, T. J. fails in truly putting together a life for himself and in that sense may be read as emasculated, whereas Georgia, despite her streak of independence smacking of feminism (despite the fact that she even makes to seize the [in the play] male role of starter), fails to break out of the con-ventional female role of staying at home. While the two lovers might seem to complement each other, the one's inability to move and the other's stitching-together suggest that they will remain with the Us's looking toward but never attaining Somewhere.

VIII

Having tried every way to get Somewhere, the Us's are exasperated in *The Purple Flower*. Suddenly, however, an "Old Lady" declares, "Last night I had a dream" (39). Although a young Us disparages this older Us epistemology, when the Old Lady explains that in it she saw "a White Devil cut in six pieces—head here (*pointing*), body here—one leg here—one there—an arm here—an arm there," an Old Man Us cries, "Thank God! It's time then! . . . Bring me an iron pot!" (39). Again, a young Us complains about the Old Us "conjuring," but the Old Us is unstoppable. The Old Man gets his pot and then calls for a handful of dust and through it calls up the spirits of the Us's who have gone before and are now "*ten million mouths through rock and dust*" (40). The Old Us then starts a fire with the books, throws gold into the pot, and calls for blood to pour into the mixture. The Old Man explains that God "told me to take a handful of dust—dust from which all things came and put it in a hard iron pot. Put it in a hard iron pot. Things shape best in hard molds!!" (43). He tells everyone the ingredients, commanding them to put "in books that Men learn by. Gold that men live by. Blood that lets Men live" (43). From this amalgamation, "God will shape a new man Himself" (43).

Such conjuring and magic appears in several of the plays previously discussed, but it takes center stage in two of Johnson's one-acts: *Frederick Douglass* and *Plumes*. *Frederick Douglass* examines the interstices of secrecy and magic to reveal the central secret of Douglass's own most famous text—the particulars of his escape to freedom. Perhaps one of the most frustrating if not intriguing parts of Frederick Douglass's *Narrative of the Life of Frederick Douglass* is his keeping secret the specifics of his escape on the Underground Railway to the North. He writes that

> I now come to that part of my life during which I planned, and finally suc-
> ceeded in making, my escape from slavery. But before narrating any of the
> particular circumstances, I deem it proper to make known my intention not
> to state all the facts connected with the transaction. My reasons for pursu-
> ing this course may be understood from the following: First, were I to give a
> minute statement of all the facts, it is not only possible, but quite probable,
> that others would thereby be involved in the most embarrassing difficul-
> ties. Secondly, such a statement would most undoubtedly induce greater
> vigilance on the part of slaveholders than has existed heretofore among
> them; which would, of course, be the means of guarding a door whereby
> some dear brother bondman might escape his galling chains. I deeply regret
> the necessity that impels me to suppress any thing of importance connected
> with my experience in slavery. It would afford me great pleasure indeed,
> as well as materially add to the interest of my narrative, were I at liberty to
> gratify a curiosity, which I know exists in the minds of many, by an accu-
> rate statement of all the facts pertaining to my most fortunate escape. But
> I must deprive myself of this pleasure, and the curious of the gratification

which such a statement would afford. I would allow myself to suffer under the greatest imputations which evil-minded men might suggest, rather than exculpate myself, and thereby run the hazard of closing the slightest avenue by which a brother slave might clear himself of the chains and fetters of slavery. (137–38)

Douglas guards his natural secret by acknowledging its status as secret-as-fetish; this passage represents one more in a series of secrecy-moves in the text and in Douglass's life.

Although Douglass would actually provide some detail about his escape in his revised and expanded autobiography, *Life and Times of Frederick Douglass,* Georgia Douglas Johnson explores the space of secrecy Douglass leaves in *Narrative* to craft her own version of the escape (and Douglass's life at the time of the escape) that situates a woman at its center. The play takes place in the house of siblings Ann and Bud in Baltimore.[37] Ann is Douglass's sweetheart, and Douglass enters the stage while she is cooking him ginger-bread, his favorite dessert. Douglass (referred to as "Fred" in the play) pulls a stack of silver coins from his pocket, and announces that he has seventeen "dollars and fifty cents—most enough for me to steal away to freedom an' marry with up North" (86). He goes on to explain the means by which he has made money and kept his hoarding it a secret:

Honey, do you know something funny happened tonight? When I give Marse Tom his ten dollars I worked an' made fur him this week, he was tickled to death an' said, "Here, Fred, take this here quarter an' buy yourself somethin'." He ain't got no idea how much extra money I picks up during the week. You see I'm a-workin' for freedom an' you. (86)[38]

When Ann expresses her concern that someone should find out about his hoard, Fred assures her, "I'm scareful. I hides my money an' just brought it along tonight to show you how I'm a-doin'" (86).

The lovers talk about their plans for the future—Fred's freedom and their marriage—while he prepares to teach mathematics to her and Bud, who is away from home at the moment. At one point, Ann tells Fred, "[Y]ou go on an' tell me how 'twas you got all that book learnin'. Slaves roun' here can't read nothin', even down to free ones don't know nothin'. Look at me and Bud!" (88–89). Fred then proceeds to explain the secrecy-move he has used to educate himself:

Well, you see I used to play with young Marse Tom. We both was around eight an' old Miss would read to us an' teach us, but old Marse got mad when he found out about it an' stopped her. . . . But that didn't stop me; I'd got a start an' I kept right on—picked up scraps of printin' from the streets an' wet gutters, dried 'em, hid 'em an' kept a-learnin.' . . . When I got hold of hard words I couldn't spell, I'd say to some one of the white boys when I'd meet one on the street—"Say, I bet you can't read this here word," an' I'd show it to him. He would always spell it out jest to show off. I played lots of tricks like that to get more learnin'. (89)

In these ingenious maneuvers of sleight of hand taken from Douglass's real-life account, Fred grasps the cultural power of inscription.[39]

At this point, another slave—an old man named Jake—comes calling to inform Fred that he (Fred) is in trouble. "Marse Tom's brother, Marse George, come in on dat las' boat," he explains, "an' he swore at Marse Tom an' said he wus a gonner take you back wid him in de morning down on de Eastern Shore agin. Sed he was gonner put you back in de field an' break yo damn sperrit!" (89). Fred devises a plan to escape right away before the morning comes: he sends Jake with money to rent a sailor's suit because you "get by easy when you're a sailor, the white folks don't bother them a-tall" (90), and in the meantime, Fred and Ann wait for Bud's return because Bud has a train pass that will allow Fred on the North-bound train.[40] Jake leaves to get the suit and shortly returns with one, but Fred and Ann's fears about Bud are confirmed when he comes in drunk, nonconversant, and not wanting to give Fred his pass. Fred's return to the plantation seems imminent.

But Johnson provides a new means for Douglass's escape. The old slave Jake undertakes to perform magic to convince Bud to give Fred the pass. Ann has made Bud a mug of tea to drink, and Jake asks him, "Got any leaves in dat mug, Bud?" When Bud affirms that he does, Jakes asks, "Wamme to talk wid de sperrits in yore leaves"? (92). When Bud confirms that he would if doing so would mean he could speak with his dead mother, Jake listens to the mug and "repeats" the "message" the leaves tell him from his mother:

> Tell Bud I can't res' in my grave tell he quits that drinkin'. I'm miser'ble here twix heben an' earth. Tell him I heered his sister ax him fur his pass tonight an' it hurt my soul when he didn't give it. Tell him to han' it to her quick an' then run down to the sycamoo tree at the corner of de fence in de back yard, an' fall down on his knees an' pray. My sperrit is on de way ther now to bless him whilst he prays. Tell him to do all I said this very minute. (92–93)

This bit of conjuring works, as Bud in a trancelike state reaches into his boot and produces the pass and then runs out to the sycamore tree. With the pass in hand, Fred rushes out to catch the North-bound train, which Ann listens for, and when it goes on and she believes Fred has reached the junction in time, she exclaims, "Thank God!" and "*falls down beside the cot as if in prayer as the curtain falls*" (93).

The magic of the tea leaves recalls a similar element of secrecy and magic in Douglass's *Narrative*. One of the most significant turning points in that text occurs when Douglass fights back against the cruel slave-breaker Edward Covey. After having lived with Hugh Auld in Baltimore, Douglass is brought back to the plantation of Thomas Auld, who is Hugh's brother and who takes Douglass from him as punishment for a disagreement with Hugh. Douglass, however, does not suit Thomas: "city life, he said, had had a very pernicious effect upon" him (99). Thomas thus sends Douglass to live with Covey, who "was a poor man, a farm-renter" who "had acquired a very high reputation for breaking young slaves" which "enabled him to get his farm tilled with much less expense to himself than he could have had it done without such a reputation" (100). Covey too finds Douglass unsuitable for field work—spoiled by his time in the city—and so frequently beats him until Douglass finally escapes to register grievances concerning his treatment to his master Thomas. Unimpressed by Douglass's pleas (despite the fact that the slave is bleeding from head to toe when he arrives at his doorstep), Thomas sends Douglass back to Covey, who is determined to beat him for leaving the premises, but Douglass evades him and finds lodging with Sandy Jenkins, a fellow slave whose wife was free and who lived four miles from Covey's place.

Douglass's staying with Sandy turns out to be fortuitous. Sandy is "an old adviser," who explains to Douglass that he "must go back to Covey" but must take with him "a certain *root*, which," as he writes, "if I would take some of it with me, carrying it *always on my right side*, would render it impossible for Mr. Covey, or any other white man, to whip me" (111). Douglass notes that "I at first rejected the idea, that the simple carrying of a root in my pocket would have any such effect as he had said, and was not disposed to take it" (111). However, in order to "please him, I at length took the root, and, according to his direction, carried it upon my right side" (111). Douglass returns to Covey's place the next morning, which is a Sunday, and Covey is exceedingly nice to him, leading Douglass to "begin to think that there was something in the *root* which Sandy had given me; and had it been on any other day than Sunday, I could have attributed the conduct to no other cause than the influence of that root; and as it was, I was half inclined to think the *root* to be something more than I at first had taken it to be" (111). The next day, however, Covey attacks him (an extremely pious man, Covey is loathe to commit atrocities on a Sunday); when Covey makes his move, instead of giving in to the beating, Douglass takes a stand, writing that "from whence came the spirit I don't know [but] I resolved to fight; and, suiting my action to the resolution, I seized Covey hard by the throat" (112). Douglass soon gets the advantage of Covey, who finally yields and then never attempts to beat Douglass again.

Douglass's comments about Covey's change in behavior are curious in terms of their treatment of magic and their incorporation of secrecy. He writes that it

> was for a long time a matter of surprise to me why Mr. Covey did not imme-diately have me taken by the constable to the whipping-post, and there regularly whipped for the crime of raising my hand against a white man in defence [*sic*] of myself. And the only explanation I can now think of does not entirely satisfy me; but such as it is, I will give it. Mr. Covey enjoyed the most unbounded reputation for being a first-rate overseer and negro-breaker. It was of considerable importance to him. That reputation was at stake; and had he sent me—a boy of sixteen years old—to the public whipping-post, his reputation would have been lost; so, to save his reputation, he suffered me to go unpunished. (113–14)

Douglass does not mention the root again until later when he again men-tions Sandy Jenkins and offers the following footnote:

> This is the same man who gave me the roots to prevent my being whipped by Mr. Covey. He was a "clever soul." We used frequently to talk about the fight with Covey, and as often as we did so, he would claim my success as the result of the roots which he gave me. This superstition is very common among the more ignorant slaves. A slave seldom dies but his death is attrib-uted to trickery. (117)

Douglass's comments about the root are interesting, being revelatory of a tension that runs throughout his narrative. This tension is that which arises from his ambiguous feelings regarding slave folk culture. On one hand, he is sympathetic with slaves, and yet on the other he prizes the scientific and linguistic prowess of white society, for he realizes early on that such knowl-edge is what, as Master Hugh tells his wife when she tries to teach Douglass to read, can "forever unfit him to be a slave" and that it is keeping one "fit" for slavery that, as Douglass realizes, constitutes "the white man's power to enslave the black man" (78). Although not made explicit, the text never-theless subtly displays Douglass's commitment to the intellectual machinery of white empowerment which renders his treatment of an alternative (i.e., "black") ideology and policy problematic. It is arguably one of the more nuanced and torturous tensions in the book.

Consider, for example, Douglass's discussion of slave songs. He describes these songs and their importance and their secret meaning to the slaves, noting that "they would sing, as a chorus, to words which to many would seem unmeaning jargon, but which, nevertheless, were full of meaning to themselves," and noting the evocative power of these songs, he writes that "I have sometimes thought that the mere hearing of those songs would do more to impress some minds with the horrible character of slavery, than the reading of whole volumes of philosophy on the subject would do" (57). The comment is striking, for it assents to the power of slave folk culture over white reason, logic, and linguistic sophistication. Yet Douglass's thinking (and his mode of expressing his thinking) derives from his reading, beginning with "a book entitled 'The Columbian Orator'" which, when young, he reads "over and over again with unabated interest. They gave tongue to interesting thoughts of my own soul, which had frequently flashed through my mind, and died away for want of utterance" and so "enabled me to utter my thoughts, and to meet the arguments brought forward to sustain slavery" (83–84). Having entered into the white linguistic world, Douglass's text displays the difficulties that Spivak observes—that the native informant initiated in the cultural center ceases to be fully peripheral and in this compromise no longer speaks from the perspective of the subaltern. Writing backwards from his life in emancipation, Douglass cannot even equate himself with the other slaves at all, and he writes regarding the slaves' singing:

> I did not, when a slave, understand the deep meaning of those rude and apparently incoherent songs. I was myself within the circle; so that I neither saw nor heard as those without might see and hear. They told a tale of woe which was then altogether beyond my feeble comprehension; they were tones loud, long, and deep; they breathed the prayer and complaint of souls boiling over with the bitterest anguish. Every tone was a testimony against slavery, and a prayer to God for deliverance from chains. The hearing of those wild notes always depressed my spirit, and filled me with ineffable sadness. I have frequently found myself in tears while hearing them. The mere recurrence to those songs, even now, afflicts me; and while I am writing these lines, an expression of feeling has already found its way down my cheek. To those songs I trace my first glimmering conception of the dehumanizing character of slavery. I can never get rid of that conception. Those songs still follow me, to deepen my hatred of slavery, and quicken my sympathies for my brethren in bonds. If any one wishes to be impressed with the soul-killing effects of slavery, let him to Colonel Lloyd's plantation,

and, on allowance-day, place himself in the deep pine woods, and there let him, in silence, analyze the sounds that shall pass through the chambers of his soul,—and if he is not thus impressed, it will only be because "there is no flesh in his obdurate heart." (57–58)

This passage manifests the same ambiguity that Douglass's consideration of the root displays: the magical influence of Sandy's root is everywhere evident, yet Douglass resists the magical "black" explanation, instead turning various intellectual backflips to explain what prevented further beatings from Covey—explanations that he himself admits do not entirely satisfy him. Douglass's tension about his cultural background arises from the sorts of secrecy-moves that inundate that culture, infusing the text with the sort of cryptonomy that Abraham and Torok describe. Johnson recreates the tension in Douglass's text between the magic of black folk culture and the science of white society. She does so by having her plot turn on a trick—a sleight of hand that purports to be real magic—and this tea-leaf trick evokes the similar magical element (the root) that conversely seems to be real magic but which the historical Douglass himself attempts to pass off as sleight of hand by explaining it away logically. Moreover, where Douglass in his ambiguous treatment of the root keeps alive the possibility that true magic really does exist, Johnson reduces all such folk belief to mere legerdemain.

The similarities between this play and *William and Ellen Craft* have surely already been recognized. An extension of Johnson's writing a more significant black woman's role into the source material by accentuating the presence and purpose of Ann involves her actually constricting the role of another black woman, Douglass's mother. Johnson is generally true to Douglass's text, but she has him deprived of his mother even more than Douglass himself claims, as he writes that

> I never saw my mother, to know her as such, more than four or five times in my life; and each of those times was very short in duration, and at night. . . . She would lie down with me, and get me to sleep, but long before I waked she was gone. Very little communication ever took place between us. Death soon ended what little we could have while she lived, and with it her hardships and suffering. (48)

But in Johnson's play Fred tells Ann at the beginning of the play, "[T]his here little bit of kitchen of yours is the nearest I ever been to heaven since I been born," to which she replies, "You forgittin' your own Ma's cook kitchen, ain't you?" to which he in turn replies,

I never saw it—I never saw my own Ma but one time in my whole life. [. . .] 'Twas when I was around six years old. I remember wakin' up long about midnight . . . I never will forget it. She was huggin' and kissin' me an' her tears was fallin' all down in my face like rain. She said "My poor baby . . . my poor baby . . . I'm your ma, honey," an' she went on callin' me sweet names an' cryin'; then all sudden like, she almost throwed me down on the palatte an' darted out through the door like mad! (87)

Ann responds to this tearjerker by saying, "I'm gointer make it all up to you—I'll be yore wife an' ma all rolled into one" (88). Taking on a dual role, Ann becomes both supporter and protector, both of which combine her overarching role of secret-bearer.

Johnson's *Plumes* also explores the magic potion by considering the things that coffee grounds "really do" tell about the future. Unlike *Frederick Douglass*, this play is set in the present. The setting is domestic, the home of Charity Brown and her sick daughter Emmerline, who is lying upon death's doorstep.[41] The play opens with Charity "*heating a poultice over the stove*" for her daughter (PGDJ 74). Presently, her friend Tildy pays her a visit, and the audience learns that in between sessions of nursing her daughter, Charity is sewing a dress that may very well be the one the girl will wear in her coffin. Tildy actually lends a hand to relieve her friend of her work on the dress, and Charity instructs her as to what to do, explaining that she needs to "[w]hip that torshon on and turn down the hem in the skirt"; when Tildy asks her how deeply she should turn down the hem, Charity responds in dialogue riddled with semiotic eruption, "[S]he wears 'em short, but—it might be—" and then Tildy finishes the thought, saying, "I see exzackly. (*sighs*) You'd want it long—over her feet—then" (75).

The two women then enter into a discussion regarding how Charity should act in the event that Emmerline's illness requires surgery. It turns out that Charity's other two children have died already, and because she had to spend so much money on doctors to try and cure the children she was unable to pay for decent funerals for them—the kind she refers to as "a sho nuff fun'ral, everything grand—with plumes!" on the horses in the funeral procession (76). Because of her past experiences with doctors, she explains, "I've got no faith a-tall in 'em. They takes all your money for nothing," to which Tildy adds, "They sho do, and don't leave a thing for putting you away" (76). For these African American women, the authority of science carries no weight. Rather, their faith resides in another medium altogether: magic coffee grounds. Tildy smells coffee boiling and Charity pours them cups of it to drink and lift their spirits. As they sit drinking, Charity looks into her cup and says, "I wish Dinah Morris would drop in now. I'd ask her what these grounds mean" (77). Hearing this comment, Tildy notes that she knows a little bit about how to read the grounds, so Charity passes her cup over to her. Tildy gazes at them and then speaks:

> I ain't seen a cup like this one for many a year. Not since—not since—[...] Not since jest before ma died. I looked in the cup then and saw things and ... I stopped looking. [...] I don't like to tell no bad news—[...] Since, you're bound to know I'll tell you. (*Charity draws nearer*) I sees a big gathering! [...] Yes, a big gathering—people all crowded together. Then I see 'em going one by one and two by two. Long lines stretching out and out and out! [...] Looks like (*hesitates*) a possession. (77–78)

Just as Tildy finishes, the sound of an actual procession does rumble into hearing, and the women go to the window to watch it pass by. They conjecture that it "must be Bell Gibson's funeral coming away from Mt. Zion" and Charity is particularly exultant over the hearse, saying, "My Lord, ain't it grand. Look at them horses—look at their heads—plumes—how they shake 'em! Land O'mighty! Ain't it a fine sight?" (78). Such a procession with plumes costs fifty dollars, Charity confides to Tildy, and Charity has been saving up that amount of money for the eventuality of her remaining child dying.

Once the procession has passed, a white Dr. Scott shows up at the house. While he examines Emmerline in the other room, the two women worry over the possibility of an operation, Charity explaining that it would cost fifty dollars, which is exactly what she has saved for the funeral. Torn between trying to save her daughter and trying to give her a proper funeral, Charity must make a choice regarding what she believes in, and she repeats that she does not believe in doctors while Tildy confirms, "Don't you trust him. Coffee grounds don't lie!" (80). After examining Emmerline, he informs Charity that an operation is necessary but that even then he cannot guarantee that the girl will survive. Tortured by her need to make a decision, Charity explains to the doctor that the coffee grounds are ominous, an observation that this white man of science discounts. When she persists that she cannot afford the operation (even when he has reduced the price to fifty dollars), Dr. Scott says, "I didn't think you'd hesitate about [having the operation]—I imagined your love for your child—" at which point Charity breaks in, "I do love my child. My God, I do love my child. You don't understand ... but ... can't I have a little time to think about it, doctor ... it means so much—to her—and—me!" (81). He tells her he will go back to his office and give her time to make her decision but that "every minute counts" (81). When he leaves, Charity frets over the decision with Tildy, when suddenly "*a strange stran-*

gling noise comes from the inner room" prompting Charity to run inside to check on her daughter (82). After a few minutes, Charity emerges from the room and tells her friend, "Rip the hem out, sister Tildy" (82).

It is practically impossible to ignore Tildy's pronunciation of "procession" as "possession." Charity is fighting for possession of herself and her worldview; her possession of fifty dollars precipitates her necessity to decide what to do with the prize possession that is her daughter. She guards the secret that she possesses, which dictates that in the teleology peculiar to her world she makes decisions that might otherwise seem monstrous. And speaking of monstrous, how is the audience to read/view Dr. Scott? Tildy cannot trust him precisely because he represents and possesses the kinds of public life secrets that keep these women in the dire conditions in which they live. The play offers a sort of secrecy role-reversal in terms of medical ethics. In this case, the white doctor openly explains that he can help the child, but he does not realize the specific situation of these black women—the difficulties of their space and experiences. Unable to reveal the secret of the ethical dynamics of her situation, Charity enacts the poetic of her own name by charitably giving her daughter a respectful funeral rather than trying (and losing) an attempt to save her life. Tapping into this black religious folk magic is a technique not available to the doctor, and the clash between the secrecy-moves of science and those of nonsecular magic exhibit a game in which the players struggle for very different payoffs.

The presence of the horses in the play signals another magical element. Rabotau points out that

> equestrian imagery is commonly used in African and Latin America to describe the relationship between a god and the devotee he mounts and rides in possession. The onset of possession in voodoo rituals in New Orleans was called, according to Castellanos, *monter voudou*. A relic of this imagery can be seen in the term used by blacks in Mississippi for conjurers—"horses." (82)

This passage read with Johnson's play in mind, as well as Raboteau's earlier comment that "[i]mproper or incomplete funeral rites can interfere with or delay the entrance of the deceased into the spiritual world and may cause his soul to linger about" (13), speaks to the possibility that the funeral march itself may indeed be a possession. Undoubtedly, the plumes carry a mystified significance, but perhaps the horses themselves may be read as Charity's children showing their mother the path she should take, doing so in a distinct voodoo code, a secret unintelligible to the white out-group but a natural secret of evocative power for these trouble-beset black women.

IX

As the Old Man Us mixes the magic potion, Finest Blood offers his own blood as part of the requisite ingredients. The Old Man accepts the offer, but specifies a certain way that the blood must be provided: merely pricking one's own skin is not enough. Instead, the Old Man explains, "When God asked a faithful servant once to do sacrifice, even His only child, where did God put the real meat for sacrifice when the servant had the knife upon the son's throat?" (44). To this question, other Old Us's respond in a chorus:

> *In the bushes, Lord!*
> *In the bushes, Lord!*
> *Jehovah put the ram*
> *In the bushes!* (44)

At this point, Cornerstone exclaims, "I understand" and turns to Finest Blood, asking, "Where were you going a little while ago? Where were you going when your sister cried out?" (44). Finest Blood misunderstands, thinking that he must kill the White Devil in the bushes and take *his* blood, but the Old Man exclaims, "No! No! Not that way. The White Devils are full of tricks. You must go differently. Bring him gifts and offer them to him" (44). Finest Blood asks what gift he could offer, and Old Man replies, "There are the pipes of Pan that every Us is born with. Play on that. Soothe him— lure him—make him yearn for the pipe. Even a White Devil will soften at music. He'll come out, and he only comes to try to get the pipe from you" (45). To this speech, Finest Blood declares, "And when he comes out, I'm to kill him in the dark before he sees me? That's a White Devil trick!" to which the Old Man replies:

> An Old Us will never tell you to play White Devil's games! No! Do not kill him in the dark. Get him out of the bushes and say to him: "White Devil, God is using me for His instrument. You think that it is I who play on this pipe! You think that [it] is I who play upon this pipe so that you cannot stay in your bushes. So that you must come out of your bushes. But it is not I who play. It is not I, it is God who plays through me—to you. Will you hear what He says? Will you hear? He says it is almost day, White Devil. The night is far gone. A New Man must be born for the New Day. Blood is needed for birth. Blood is needed for the birth. Come out, White Devil. It may be your blood—it may be mine—but blood must be taken during the night to be given at the birth. It may be my blood—it may be your blood—but every-thing has been given. The Us toiled to give dust for the body, books to guide the body, gold to clothe the body. Now they need blood for birth so the New

Man can live. You have taken blood. You must give blood. Come out! Give
it!" And then fight him! (45)

A number of elements combine in this penultimate scene of the play.
Again, the theme of a new morning appears; again, a modification of blues
format emerges. Particularly significant is Bonner's evocation of the complex trope of sacrifice and the goat, which is rife with religious, cultural,
and magic implications. These implications may be parsed by examining the
function of the goat, sacrifice, deception, and the creation of a "new" body in
Hurston's *The First One* and Miller's *Riding the Goat*. In these plays, Hurston
and Miller subvert the notion of black people as satanic by rupturing the
goat as a signifier of essentialized blackness.

The significance of the goat in white definitions of blackness have already
been noted, but flexibility of the goat as signifier might be lingered on, as it
has been a significant animal throughout the history of Western civilization,
serving as both a positive and a negative emblem. As a pagan figuration, it
carried positive associations. The Greek god of forests and animals, Pan, had
goat's hooves, tail, goatee, horns, and large phallus. Bacchic rites, with their
wine-filled laurel altars of wild and flowing corporeality, were predicated
on the sexual freedom the goat symbolized because in this ancient culture,
the goat carried the favorable connotations of youth, merriment, boundless-
ness, freedom, earthiness, energy, love, involvement, and intercourse. These
Dionysian festivals included dramas—the very word "tragedy" (*tragôidia*)
meant "goat-song."[42] In a Judaic context, the goat represented possibilities
of atonement and thus served as a sacrificial animal. Hebrews depended
on the scapegoat as the creature to bear the sins of a generation and onto
which sins were cast. As a sacrificial animal, the goat was a vessel of salvation. Christian ideology, however, endowed the pagan and Jewish goat with
negative associations. Christianity stressed the goat's sexual licentiousness
and the threat and satanic impulses it registers. Pan was reworked into Satan,
with goat's tail, feet, and horns. Thus, where the goat had originally been a
positive signifier in pagan ideology and to some extent in Jewish thinking, in
Christianity it became a signifier of blackness and all of the things it represented—sexual freedom, merriment, earthiness—and thus registered sexual
and cultural threats to white control.

The goat in fact serves as a malleable enough emblem to permit Hurston
and Miller to equate it with black womanhood, and, most especially, black
women's secrecy-moves. As an animal that finds itself victimized by Western
civilization's whims, the goat mirrors the mule, which Hurston posits as suffering at the hands of both white and male patriarchy and thus representative
of black womanhood. The goat also carries possibilities of female empowerment—perhaps most significantly in the biblical incident of Rebekah and

Jacob's deception of Isaac to steal Esau's blessing. In the story, set forth in the twenty-seventh chapter of Genesis, the patriarch Isaac promises to bless his older and favorite son Esau if Esau will kill a deer, prepare the meat, and bring it to him. Isaac's wife, Rebekah, hears this promise and, as Esau goes off to hunt the desired game, plots a scheme that will help the younger son, Jacob (whom she favors), gain that blessing. Her plan is to have Jacob pretend to be Esau and visit his father. To fool the nearly blind Isaac, she has Jacob dress in Esau's clothes as she prepares venison. To complete the effect, she makes Jacob wear goatskin to approximate Esau's hairiness, a maneuver that successfully deceives Isaac and results in Isaac's mistakenly blessing him instead of Esau. Hurston and Miller saw in this story an example of a woman subverting the authority of the patriarch, using the goat—which the two authors would have recognized as a signifier of blackness—as a vehicle of deception. By constructing plots of Rebekah-like deception, these writers could dramatize usurpation of patriarchal definitions of blackness by reclaiming goats as positive signifiers.

Utilizing this trope of deception-by-goat/goat-as-arbitrary-signifier, Zora Neale Hurston's *The First One* presents a densely packed re-presentation of what the West has posited as the beginning of the black race: Noah's cursing his son Ham with blackness. In this carefully constructed play, "goat" changes from a positive to a negative signifier that becomes arbitrarily connected with blackness. That change is brought about by means of a secrecy-move, a deception wrought by a woman. And whatever possibility of salvation remains at the play's end also lies in the hands of a woman, thus positing matriarchy as a problematized but central aspect of the shift in blackness signifiers.

The play is, like others that have been discussed, set in the morning—emblematic of creation, a new beginning, the new birth (in this case) of blackness. The place is the Valley of Ararat, three years after the Flood. The scenery should be arranged as follows:

> The Mountain is in the near distance. Its lower slopes grassy with grazing herds. The very blue sky beyond that. These together form the background. On the left downstage is a brown tent. A few shrubs are scattered here and there over the stage indicating the temporary camp. A rude altar is built center stage. A Shepherd's crook, a *goat* skin water bottle, a staff and other evidences of nomadic life lie about the entrance to the tent. To the right stretches a plain clad with bright flowers. Several sheep or *goat* skins are spread about on the ground upon which the people kneel or sit whenever necessary. (BFP 80; emphasis added)

The left side of the set is associated with darkness and coldness, with its dingy tent and mountainous landscape, while the right side is low and warm and full of brightness and life and fertility. From the outset, "goat" represents positive order—the goatskin bottle orders the material, water, that when unordered constituted the recent force of destruction, the Flood: goatskin thus designates a space of domesticity and containment, which differs from the pagan figuration of goats representing wild and unrestrained pleasure and animality. Accordingly, the altar on the stage suggests the sacrificial goat, a positive trope of reconciliation. The altar's central position on the stage marks the in-between point of change at which the sacrifice-goat/scapegoat cultural contribution is enacted and where later the goat transforms from positive to negative figuration.

Noah and his family enter the scene for the purpose of commemorating their "delivery from the flood" (81), and a striking visual difference between Ham and the rest of the family appears. Noah emerges from the dingy tent, wearing a "loose fitting dingy robe tied about the waist with a strip of goat hide" (80). Then Noah's wife and Shem and Japheth enter with their families, also "clad in dingy garments" (81). Absent from the scene is Ham and his wife and son, a fact that Shem quickly notes, rebuking Ham for his irresponsibility in a way that immediately betrays his dislike of Ham and Ham's ways. Noah, however, "lifts his hand in a gesture of reproval" to Shem and says, "We shall wait. The sweet singer, the child of my loins after old age had come upon me is warm to my heart" (81). At this point, "There is off-stage, right, the twanging of a rude stringed instrument and laughter" and "Ham, his wife and son come dancing on down stage right [from the area of lightness]. . . . He is dressed in a very white *goat*-skin. . . . They caper and prance to the altar. Ham's wife and son bear flowers. A bird is perched on Ham's shoulder" (81; emphasis added). Ham gives the bird to his father and then plays on his harp, which is "made of the thews of rams" (81).

Hurston thus presents a contrast between Ham and his family—Ham sings, dances, loves life, is free (as symbolized by the bird on his shoulder), and, most important, he is the whitest member of the family, wearing a white goatskin instead of the dingy attire of the rest of the family. His darker brothers and sisters-in-law upbraid him for not working with them in the fields and vineyards; instead he is content to "tend the flock and sing!" (81). Ham emerges as a much more positive and interesting character than his prudish siblings and their wives. His love of life stands in sharp positive contrast to their hard-edged hatefulness and humorless, rigid work ethic. The significance of this contrast lies in the fact that these characteristics of singing, dancing, playing, laughing, laziness, and goatness that later signify blackness here signify the utmost of whiteness and grant Noah's approval. As Kraut notes, Hurston "vexes racist assumptions by proposing that blacks' love of dance antedated their color" (35).

Ham's wife also possesses these and other characteristics that will eventually be associated with blackness. With her "short blue garment with a girdle of shells" and "wreath of scarlet flowers about her head," Mrs. Ham completely differs from all the other characters on stage (81). Whereas Ham is a type of his father and brothers and sisters-in-law, Mrs. Ham represents something totally incongruous, freer, and even more liberated. The greatest difference is that she possesses the only blackness on the entire stage—her black hair. From the outset, Hurston positions Mrs. Ham as a prefiguration of blackness and the potential black matriarch. Hurston later codifies this figuration when she reveals that in fact Mrs. Ham's name is Eve.

Although Ham represents supreme whiteness and enjoys his father's dotage, both he and his wife suffer from the jealousy of his siblings' and their families, particularly his brothers' wives. Mrs. Shem and Mrs. Japheth scorn Ham for not working in the fields, and Mrs. Japheth complains, "Still, thou art beloved of thy father . . . he gives thee all his vineyards for thy singing, but Japheth must work hard for his fields" (81–82). Thus, Ham, who possesses a plethora of what in the twentieth century are black signifiers, here just after the Flood occupies the position of the white-clad plantation youth, who frolics in his father's beaming favor as his darker-clad brothers work in the fields. Mrs. Ham also suffers when she ventures the following comment on the Flood: "[T]here, close beside the Ark, close with her face upturned as if begging for shelter—my *mother!*" to which Mrs. Shem replies, "She would not repent. Thou art as thy mother was—a seeker after beauty of raiment and laughter. God is just. She would not repent" (83). Mrs. Ham responds with the statement, "But the unrepentant are no less loved. And why must Jehovah hate beauty?" (83), highlighting the fact that she, Mrs. Ham, was spared despite her values because of her repentance.

The action of the play moves quickly toward its inevitable and tragic end. Noah, "whom the Lord found worthy; Noah whom He made lord of the Earth," makes a sacrifice to Jehovah and blesses his family and its seed forever (82). The family then begins reveling in their salvation, drinking wine from goatskins. At length, a drunken Noah arises and goes into and collapses in his tent. In the meantime, Ham continually behaves as one who is privileged, including one case in which he grabs apples before his brothers, which prompts Mrs. Shem to comment, "Thus he seizes all else that he desires. Noah would make him lord of the earth because he sings and capers" while Ham laughs and throws fruit skins at her (84).

All this time, Ham sings a song that informs the positive figuration of "goat":

I am as a young ram in the Spring
Or a young male goat
The hills are beneath my feet
And the young grass.
Love rises in me like the flood
And ewes gather round me for food. (83)

In his drunkenness, Ham mixes up the lines so that they repeatedly include the word "goat." He sings, "I am as a young goat in the sp-sp" (84). Ham then goes to "pull [Noah] out of the water, or to drown with him in it" and having checked on his father's condition, announces that "Our Father has stripped himself, showing all his wrinkles. Ha! Ha! He's as no young goat in the spring" (84). Ham then "reels over to the altar and sinks down behind it still laughing . . . [and then] subsides into slumber" (84).

Mrs. Shem then seizes on Ham's impropriety by redefining, for the first time in the play, the word and trope of "goat" from a positive to a negative thing. "Ha! The young goat has fallen into a pit!" she says to her husband. "Shem! Shem! Rise up and become owner of Noah's vineyards as well as his flocks. . . . Shem! Fool! Arise! Thou art thy father's first born. . . . Do stand up and regain thy birthright from . . . that dancer who plays on his harp of ram thews, and decks his brow with bay leaves. Come!" (84). A dull-witted Shem asks how he might get such gain. And Mrs. Shem replies,

Did he not go into the tent and come away laughing at thy father's naked-ness? Oh . . . that I should live to see a father so mocked and shamed by his son to whom he has given all his vineyards! (*She seizes a large skin from the ground.*) Take this and cover him and tell him of the wickedness of thy brother. (84)

Mrs. Shem thus sets into motion whiteness's laying claim to what will later be a black trope, the trickster figure, by reversing the Jacob and Esau scenario in which a woman brings about a return of birthright from the younger to the older, using in this case the goatskin to cover the father's nakedness and to stand as the agent of Noah's deception. To be sure, Ham stands guilty as charged, but he uttered his words out of drunkenness and not from a lack of love or consideration, and Mrs. Shem intends a deceptive representation of Ham's infraction.

Shem and his wife then rouse the still-drunken Noah and inform him of Ham's deed, which leads to Noah's cursing Ham. Noah asks who has mocked him, and Mrs. Shem skillfully replies, "We fear to tell thee, lord, lest thy love for the doer of this iniquity should be so much greater than the shame, that thou should slay us for telling thee" (85). Having thus amplified the significance of Ham's deed and withholding Ham's name, Noah, thus incited to greater anger and "swaying drunkenly," storms, "Say it, woman, shall the lord of the Earth be mocked?" (85). Then, even though receiving no answer to his query, Noah unknowingly curses Ham, saying, "His skin shall be black! Black as the nights, when the waters brooded over the Earth! . . . Black! He and his seed forever. He shall serve his brothers and they shall rule over him . . ." (85).

With blackness now introduced into the world, those things that signify the character of Ham must now signify blackness. Having delivered his curse, Noah falls back into drunken slumber, while Ham emits "a loud burst of drunken laughter from behind the altar" and says "I am as a young ram— Ha! Ha!" (85). Mrs. Noah then asks whom Noah has cursed, and Mrs. Shem replies, "Ham—Ham mocked his age. Ham uncovered his nakedness and Noah grew wrathful and cursed him" (85). Mrs. Shem thus removes herself from taking part in the cursing and places the blame on the patriarch.[43]

Hurston then presents a highly problematic scene that complicates and questions the justness of white patriarchal authority. Ironically, Shem and Japheth use a goatskin bottle of water to sober Noah, whom they inform has cursed his favorite son. Everyone, including Noah, hopes that the curse may be removed. Eve argues that Jehovah should not fulfill a curse uttered in a drunken stupor. Shem blames his wife for having brought this trouble, and she reverses the blame, saying that her actions resulted from his desire for the vineyards. Noah pleads with Jehovah to "record not my curses on my beloved Ham. Show me once again the sign of covenant—the rainbow over the Vale of Ararat" (86). Mrs. Noah delivers a scathing admonishment of Noah, saying, "How rash thou art, to curse unknowing in thy cups the son of thy loins," to which Noah responds with the following:

> Did not Jehovah repent after he had destroyed the world? Did he not make all flesh? Their evils as well as their good? Why did He not with His flood of waters wash out the evil from men's hearts, and spare the creatures He had made, or else destroy us all, *all?* For in sparing one, He has preserved all the wickedness that He creates abundantly, but perishes terribly. No, He destroyed them because vile as they were it was His handiwork, and it shamed and reproached Him night and day. He could not bear to look upon the thing He had done, so He destroyed them. (87)

Noah's enigmatic statement accentuates the problematics of the accepted patriarchal approach to such situations as this one. Eve earlier questioned Jehovah's seemingly arbitrary justice. And now, Jehovah has potentially granted an uninformed request. Noah's unwittingly cursing Ham mirrors Ham's unknowing mocking of Noah. In both cases, they must pay dearly for their deeds. Hurston makes it clear that the men have created all of this trouble, for ultimately even Noah, lord of the Earth, diminishes Mrs. Shem's guilt with the statement, "Shem's wife is but a woman" (86). Hurston also uses this comment to illustrate the ways that men wrest all womanly involvement, both positive and negative, from the course of history.

Jehovah does not offer a rainbow for a covenant but instead grants Noah's drunken curse as Ham awakes and emerges from behind the altar, now a black man. As is always the case with white characters in these plays, the logistics of production here raise an interesting question as to how Hurston envisioned the staging of this scene. Should the actors in this play be white, the one playing Ham spending the time behind the altar smearing black makeup on his face or putting on a mask? Or is the ideal cast one of African Americans wearing white masks or makeup? Here, again, delineating between essence and performance (one might act black but does one become black simply by changing color and not, say, the shape of lips, which Hurston posits as a physical trait that affects black pronunciation of words in "Characteristics of Negro Expression") becomes problematic and threatens to undercut Hurston's attempt in this play to resist white impositions of essentialized blackness.[44]

Because Noah equates the color black with the Flood (death and punishment), blackness already carries a negative connotation, as Mrs. Shem exclaims, "Black! He could not mean *black*. It is enough that he should lose his vineyards" (85). But this signifier is arbitrary—presumably, Noah could have cursed Ham to be as gray as the clouded days of the Flood rather than black as its nights. And when Ham appears newly colored, the family "shrink[s] back terrified" (87). Everything that Noah has cherished about Ham now becomes reversed as Noah says, "Arise, Ham. Thou art black. Arise and go out from among us that we may see thy face no more, lest by lingering the curse of thy blackness come upon all my seed forever" (88). Hurston notes that Noah utters this statement "sternly," showing a distinct change in tone from the conciliatory, regretful, and desperate tone that has just characterized his speech when he thought the curse might be reversed. This tone and this statement are significant in rounding out the goat trope—Ham is becoming the scapegoat upon which the family, particularly the patriarch Noah, will devolve its faults.

At this point, Eve, although not black herself, emerges as the mother of a new race as she finds her son as black as his father. She quickly sees the problematic machinery of the white patriarchy that will exclude and oppress Ham and tells him:

Ham, my husband, Noah is right. Let us go before you awake and learn to despise your father and your God. Come away Ham, beloved, come with me, where thou canst never see these faces again, where never thy soft eyes can harden by looking too oft upon the fruit of their error, where never thy happy voice can learn to weep. Come with me to where the sun shines forever, to the end of the Earth, beloved the sunlight of all my years. (88)

As Eve recognizes, Ham has become the scapegoat who bears the signifying of his family's sins. Eve refers not only to Ham's color when she mentions the "fruit of their error," for she herself remains white; she also refers to the oppression that Ham would face at his family's hands.

Ham then takes his leave of his family and fulfills his role of scapegoat as he takes on the signifiers of blackness. He tells his family, "Oh, remain with your flocks and fields and vineyards, to covet, to sweat, to die and know no peace. I go to the sun" (88). With these parting shots, Ham and his wife and child leave "right across the plain," followed by his "voice happily singing: 'I am as a young ram in the Spring'" (88). Thus Ham becomes the scapegoat sent out of the presence of the sinful, carrying their sins upon his back. At the same time, the audience understands that Ham's goat characteristics now become characteristics of blackness and therefore negative signifiers where they had first been positive signifiers of his whiteness. The devastating and startling point that Hurston makes is that these signifiers (laughter, dance, laziness) that a 1920s and 1930s audience would recognize as portraying an imagined essence of blackness are in fact merely arbitrary personality traits that originate in whiteness, or, more precisely, before whiteness as a racial construct even exists. By presenting Ham's curse as arbitrary rather than full of predetermined and static essentialized racial significance, Hurston deconstructs the very framework of black signifiers. At the same time, she derides the neat concepts of justice allegedly inherent in the white patriarchal framework and exposes its flaws, using a woman's secrecy-move to achieve that exposé.[45]

Whereas Hurston's play deals with a setting in which race ostensibly does not at first exist, Miller's *Riding the Goat* discusses an American and southern setting laden with racist constructs. In the initially monoracial setting of *The First One* the reader/audience witnesses the prefiguration of blackness signifiers; in the time and setting of *Riding the Goat* those signifiers are firmly in place. Even though every character in Miller's play is black, blackness signifiers in Miller's play are packed with meaning even as Miller shows them to be just as arbitrary as the moment they became associated with blackness—the moment shown in Hurston's play. Just as in Hurston's play, deception serves as the play's turn of plot. And this secrecy-move plays out on the goat trope, itself the salvation of the goat as a blackness signifier finds itself facilitated by a woman in a setting dominated by patriarchal hegemony.

In a more typical vein, *Riding the Goat* is set in the "stuffy sitting-room of Ant Hetty's home" in South Baltimore (BFP 153). Like the set of *The First One,* the right side of the stage offers an egress to freedom and brightness, with a door leading to "a white stoop and a few white steps" (153). The door on the left side of the stage leads to the kitchen, a location of work and toil. In the middle of the stage stands an altarlike piece of furniture that represents African American female labor—an ironing board, where Ant Hetty herself stands ironing. Thus, like Hurston's play, the mise-en-scène establishes a triad that posits two points, darkness and brightness, and the transition point in between where, in this case, black male and female may interact and ultimately the location in which, as in Hurston's play, transformation will occur. Unlike Hurston's play, however, the site of labor signifies black womanhood instead of black manhood, and the door leading to brightness and sunlight signifies the freedom of whiteness rather than what Ham declares the freedom of blackness. Miller thus presents the tragic end of Ham's hopefulness and the degradation brought to blackness signifiers by means of racial oppression in the American and southern setting.

The play's action opens by establishing a differentiation between Ant Hetty, "a stout dark woman of about sixty," who represents the strength of black matriarchy and William Carter, "a slender brown fellow of medium height, neatly dressed in a dark suit," who is a physician and has accrued signifiers of whiteness rather than blackness (153–54). Ant Hetty stands as a Mammy figure, wearing a "gingham house dress . . . open at the throat and a pair of well worn bedroom slippers . . . more off her feet than on" and enacting a mode of labor that suggests servitude, as she irons a "stiffly starched white dress" (although it will be worn by an African American on this evening) (153). Steeped in the local African American folklore and tradition, Ant Hetty can forecast weather according to the amount of pain in her feet and she eagerly anticipates and celebrates the local black secret society United Order of Moabites parade which will be held on the day taking place during the play's time (154–55). Carter stands in sharp contrast to Ant Hetty: representative of science and enlightenment and characterized by standard English usage rather than dialect, he represents the newfangled black man, who appropriates whiteness and rejects the blackness signifiers that characterize Ant Hetty. He is a black Dr. Scott, and he hates the United Order of Moabites and its traditional parade, having participated in such an organization only for the pragmatic reason of getting black patients, and he complains that one should not be able to do one's business rather than join what he considers the community's ridiculous customs.

Exacerbating the matter is the fact that Carter is the grand master of the lodge of the United Order of Moabites and so is required to lead the parade.

As he and Ant Hetty discuss his unwillingness to participate, Miller carefully constructs a biblical parallel and system of signification in the day's activities (where Hurston's biblical retelling is explicit), again reinforcing the centrality of the goat. Carter complains that it is too hot to "wear that heavy regalia" of the grand master and see candidates for the lodge in review (155). Ant Hetty is herself excited over the candidates, especially "that reformed scape-goat of a husban' of Rachel Lee's," who now faces reunion with the community from which evidently he had been alienated (155). Given the Christian-informed context that equates goats with blackness and diabolism, the fact that the United Order of Moabites and Ant Hetty resurrect the Judaic tradition that champions the scapegoat subverts the white-defined goat.

Regarding Carter's flaw of appropriated whiteness and the potentiality for black matriarchal intervention in patriarchal failure, Miller offers the following exchange:

> ANT HETTY. Now ain't that jest lak a man atalkin' bout duty an' there's fifty others wantin' your place. A woman ought to have it; she'd know a good thing.
> CARTER. Any woman who'd want it is welcome to the trouble.
> ANT HETTY. Oh, there's plenty. I ustah hear my poor dead Sam talk 'bout a woman who hid in a closet at her husban's lodge meeting an' heard an' saw all the 'nitiation. Nobody knew that she was there; but jes' as they was 'bout to leave, she sneezed an' they opens the closet an' there she was.
> CARTER. (*Laughing.*) What did they do to her?
> ANT HETTY. They give her her choice—she could jine the lodge or die.
> CARTER. Which did she take?
> ANT HETTY. She went aridin' the goat, of course. (155–56)[46]

The introduction of the possibility of a woman's participation in the lodge and parade ushers in the play's heroine, Ruth. Carter has been waiting for Ruth, whom he is courting, but finally must make a call on a patient. As soon as he leaves, Ruth appears, "a tall, well developed brown girl of about eighteen. Her smoothly brushed hair and the pretty checked gingham she wears bespeak personal care" (156). Like Carter, Ruth bears signifiers of whiteness, also speaking in standard English and marked by lighter color and personal care that contrasts with Ant Hetty's slovenly black Mammy-signifying appearance. The foremost marker of Ruth's whiteness is her dislike of the parade: imitating Carter, she thinks it too hot for parading and agrees that being a member of the lodge and the community should not have any bearing on one's business.

Ruth parallels the biblical Ruth, the Moabite woman who pays ultimate obeisance to patriarchal authority even as she manipulates it. The wife of one of the sons of Naomi, Ruth finds herself widowed at an early age. When her mother-in-law returns to Israel, Ruth accompanies her, proclaiming that she will follow her mother-in-law anywhere, Naomi's people now being her own. In Israel, Ruth works on a farm gathering sheaves. The farm's owner, Boaz, sees her, grows attracted to her, and makes special provision for her. Noting his kindness to her, Ruth consults her mother-in-law about what, if anything, she should do in regard to him. Her mother-in-law instructs her to sneak into his home and lie down in secret at his feet and see what promise he makes to her. Boaz awakes in the night to find her there at his feet and then proclaims his desire for her. He cannot, however, marry her for the law says her near kinsman has first rights to her and must release her from the possibility of marriage. Boaz goes to her near-kinsman and arranges to marry Ruth. Her story is one of loss followed by gain resulting from her own initiative from the prescribed passive role of a woman within the patriarchal system.

So Ruth, in Miller's play, finds herself torn between multiple loyalties. As William Carter's sweetheart and an educated woman, Ruth aligns herself with signifiers of whiteness. At the same time, she is a black woman and the niece of Ant Hetty and so owes allegiance to black matriarchy. A third character adds another pull to these extremes: Christopher Columbus Jones, who brings into the mix black patriarchal signifiers. Jones "is a very dark, stockily built fellow of about twenty-three" (158). Confirming his intractable performance of "blackness," Jones himself recalls to Ruth their youthful days when he and she would "race scrubbin' the front stoop" she "always made [hers] whiter'n mine an' got through sooner" (159). Where Ham's laziness has not yet become a black signifier in *The First One,* Jones's blackness is confirmed by the fact that he "never did like to work" (159). Steeped as he is in blackness signifiers and black tradition and community ways, Jones criticizes Carter's uppity ways and blames Ruth for having succumbed to Carter's manner since being connected with him and getting her education. In the Jacob and Esau–type paradigm that Miller constructs, the newcomer Carter has usurped the established Jones's birthright, as Jones complains, "[D]o you think I'm gonna let any fella step in an' take the job that oughta be mine an' my gal to boot an' not raise my hand to stop it?" (160). Although Ruth is part of the "birthright," she is not merely an object, for she has the right of choice as to what set of signifiers she will be loyal.

Faced with the demands of these multiple and conflicting sets of signifiers, Ruth must forge some course of action that will appease them all. Jones leaves the house to take his place in the parade and then Carter returns, at which time Ruth tries to convince him of the wisdom of marching in the parade. But this time Carter resolutely declares that he will not march, and when she continues trying to talk him into doing so, he storms out of the house, leaving his grand master uniform and regalia behind. Hearing the bugle call that announces the parade's beginning, Ruth herself puts on his uniform, which includes a black mask that hides her face, and takes his place in the parade. By doing so, she fulfills the demands of all three sets of signifiers: first, she remains loyal to the pseudo-white patriarchal markers that Carter controls by hiding his failure; second, she conforms to the black patriarchal hegemony by hiding her face in a black mask; third, she maintains her black femininity by hiding her own gender. With this act of deception, Ruth resembles not only her biblical counterpart but also Rebekah, the blessing/birthright thief, examplar of secrecy-discourse game player.

As the parade gets underway, Carter rushes back into the house looking for his uniform, having changed his mind about marching in the parade. Unable to find it and aware of the trouble his failure will cause, he throws himself upon the mercy and enlists the aid of Ant Hetty. She herself offers deception as a means of solving his problem, telling him, "You'll have to tell them you was called on a mattah of life an' death," to which he replies, "All right, Ant Hetty, I guess I shall have to depend on you to help me tell it" (163). At this point, they realize that someone else is riding in his place, and doing so in a way that closely resembles him, as Ant Hetty observes, "If I didn't see you asettin' right there, I'd vow it was you. Even got that sway of yourn" (163). When the parade ends, Carter and Ant Hetty retreat to the site of womanly labor and control, the kitchen, planning to surprise the usurper who they see is headed toward the house.

With black matriarchal forces now completely in control, the deception reaches completion. Ruth enters the midstage transition site, locks the door behind her, and quickly removes her uniform as Christopher Columbus Jones—who has not been fooled by her ploy—begins beating on the door. Ruth tosses the uniform into the kitchen and then lets Jones in. Jones rages at her for "[t]ryin' to save" Carter at which time Carter, who has put on the regalia in the kitchen (and thus not in a transition space, signifying that while he may have changed in this process, his doing so takes place under the thumb of feminine control and does not represent some fundamental transformation), emerges fully dressed to "disprove" Jones's assertions about Ruth. The play ends with Carter's subjecting himself to Ruth, "(*Stooping and placing his helmet on her head.*) Very well, grand master, just as you command. (*As the curtain falls he kneels before Ruth in mock salute.*)" (165). While Carter's "mock salute" illustrates his minimizing of her empowerment, the scene neither confirms his empowerment nor condones or supports his condescension. Instead, he and the patriarchy he represents emerge as impotent pawns in the greater wisdom and control and deceptive means of matriarchal power, control that exists despite the patriarchal view of itself.

That Ruth can manipulate signifiers, including signifiers of blackness, exemplifies their arbitrariness. These differing codes of signification within an at least visibly monoracial framework (at one point Ant Hetty equates Carter's rejection of the community with white doctorship) show that racial signification is arbitrary. Just as Eve establishes a new black matriarchy by accompanying the scapegoat that bears the sins of his community to exile, Ruth takes on the role of scapegoat to atone for Carter's sins even as she (possibly) rides a literal goat, doing so by means of a secrecy-move within a secrecy-discourse game in which black female authority facilitates the salvation of white patriarchal failure.

X

With the nature of the sacrifice that Finest Blood needs to make on behalf and for the future of the Us's defined, the time comes to put this sacrifice into execution. The play ends in the following manner:

Finest Blood
I'll go! And if I kill him?
Old Man
Blood will be given!
Finest Blood
And if he kills me?
Old Man
Blood will be given!
Finest Blood
Can there be no other way—cannot this cup pass? (46)

When the Old Man explains that there is no other way, Finest Blood goes Christ-like into the bushes to meet the White Devil. When he does so, "*All the Us listen. All the valley listens. Nowhere listens. All the White Devils listen. Somewhere listens. Let the curtain close leaving all the Us, the White Devils, Nowhere, Somewhere, listening, listening. Is it time?*" (46).

May Miller addresses this blood sacrifice and the issue of interracial involvement entailed in the giving-taking of blood in her play *Stragglers in the Dust*. The play is set in Arlington Cemetery at the newly created Tomb of the Unknown Soldier. The curtain rises on Nan, a black charwoman, who is sitting on the steps of the (big) house and gazing "*past the columns to the marble sepulcher and beyond that to the mist that rises from the lazy Potomac*" (BFP 145). At the top of the stairway, a mysterious figure darts about, whose face "*is chalky in its paleness and the eyes seem haunted as they stare vacantly about*" (146). Into the scene enters Mac, a watchman who seems to have a Scottish brogue to match his name. He tells her it is about time to lock the gates and leave, observing that he is always glad when the day is over and he can get home to his family, to which she replies that all she has is in the cemetery. When he asks what she means, she explains that it is her son, Jim, who has been buried in the Tomb of the Unknown Soldier. When he asks why she thinks Jim lies in the tomb, she replies, "[A]in't yuh heard dem talkin' 'bout him de uhda day? Dat grand ol' man stand up dere an' tol' how dey call'd an' how Jim lef' me broken hearted tuh go fight for dis country an' den how dem guns got him. An' how dey fin' him finally on dat fiel' in France an' bring back ober heah an put him in dere [in the tomb]" (146). When Mac replies that "they" were not talking about *her* son, that the body in the tomb is "unknown," she says, "Yeah, Ah know some of dem don' know; but Ah knows an' dat man knows. Didn't he say 'Yuh mother dere bow'd in cried.' Ah was hidin' behin' dis very pillow an' Ah heah'd him, but Ah didn' come out cause Ah know'd dere'd be them dere as wouldn't want Jim tuh stay dere cause he's cullud" (147).

Mac continues to try and educate Nan regarding the body in the tomb, but she will have none of it. Evoking Christ imagery similar to that in the closing episode of *The Purple Flower,* Nan mentions that it might have been better had Jim been buried in Europe with a wooden cross to mark his grave under a large blue sky than to be buried here, but then she also appreciates the fact that soldiers keep guard over his body at all times. When Mac asks what the tomb could possibly need protection from, she mentions the strange young ghostly figure of a man who lurks about the cemetery. Mac notes that she is harmless and again urges her to go home, which she does. Before he is able to lock the gates, however, a "distinguished politician" named Lester Bradford appears asking if he can visit the tomb. Bradford mentions that he passed only one person (Nan) on the way in and observes that many people visit the tomb, to which Mac replies that indeed "hundreds visit the unknown's grave. He seems somehow to belong to each one separately" (148). The comment is an interesting one about a secrecy-as-fetish—the tomb that signifies an unknown invites interpretation.[47] It is Derrida's crypt, certainly, but it is also a public life secret, and Bradford proclaims that the unknown "undoubtedly has had an unexplainable effect on the whole of the white race" (148). To this observation, Mac observes, in a manner that describes the multiply interpolated nature of this secret-as-item, "No sir, you needn't make it that narrow. Better say on all races. You'd be surprised at the number of Negroes that visit here" (148). Horrified that a black woman could think that there is a black soldier buried in the tomb, Bradford gasps that if such were the case, "what a terrible joke on America!" (148).

At this point, Mac assures the politician that the soldier cannot possibly be black and that it is natural to see and hear strange things in the cemetery, mentioning for example the mysterious young white man. Upon Mac's mention of the latter character, Bradford explains that he has himself come to see the young man because he thinks that personage may be his son, who has been missing and who he fears may be sick (to the latter possibility, Mac responds, "God knows he was white enough" [149]). At length, the young man appears, and Bradford does recognize him as his son, although Miller skillfully refers to him first as "*the unknown*" (149). The young man at first speaks to Mac as if his father is not there, and when he speaks the play identifies him as "Straggler," suggesting that his true identity is secret, or that perhaps he has himself changed, another self having arisen as the serviceable public one. He explains that a black man *is* in the tomb and he comes out of it all the time. He then relates the story of the black man, explaining that he, Captain Lester Bradford Junior, had been wounded in battle and this man saved his life but in removing him from harm had forgotten his own rifle and so returned to get it and then was killed by "the shell aimed at me. He holds the tomb meant for me! He sleeps there and leaves me to live on a shell of a man, a shadow tagging after him—me Captain Lester Bradford, Jr.—and I can't die" (150). The comment exemplifies Toni Morrison's argument that the shadow of the African exists in US history and literature, only her observation is reversed and the white man becomes the shadow in this Jim and Huck relationship. As a result of this situation, the young man explains that he has been trying for two days to get into the tomb with Jim, again an evocation of Christ, but one that "reverses" the situation so that the white man is hoping to get into the tomb rather than out of it on the third day. Of course, this entering the tomb brings the unknown into its true hybrid nature and suggests the creation of a "new man" such as the one that Bonner imagines in *The Purple Flower*.

Miller's play then moves to its close with the sounding of a foghorn (perhaps the trump sounding an apocalypse and yet another eruption of the semiotic), which Bradford Jr. notes is the signal for Jim's return to his tomb. At this moment, he actually convinces his father to see the world as he sees it, leaving Mac as the only "normal" person left on the stage. The young man points to the Capitol dome and explains that Jim is standing on top of it (although Mac notes that all he sees is the statue [of freedom] that has always been atop the Capitol). Both father and son watch as Jim walks over the city and across the Potomac toward the cemetery. All of this activity is, of course, offstage, and the audience never actually sees Jim, even when the young man breaks and runs to the tomb. The audience sees the young man fall dead before he can reach it, but his father watches as if a body has indeed run inside the tomb.

The political message of Miller's play unravels a string of interracial engagements. Opening with an encounter of two others, the play then details the encounter of an empowered white man and the Scottish American man. Mac's acknowledgment of the tomb as an emblem that can be interpreted by multiple races seems to establish it in a hopeful code of cooperation. The Straggler's respect for the black soldier's ghost gestures toward interracial involvement, and Bradford's seeing the ghost strengthens what seems to be a new dawn for US race relations. But it is not dawn. It is dusk. And just as *It's Morning* ironically refers to the secret that a new order has *not* arrived, so Miller's play is not so naïve as to think that such interracial recognition is meaningful, for in order for this drama of cooperation to occur it must do so among those who are unseen. The regular visiting hours—the hours of licensed visibility—have passed, and Nan, the Straggler, and the ghost are invisible even as Mac is marginalized by his ethnicity. Bradford must merge with this crew as not-himself in order to see things hidden. And even Bradford's insight is short-lived, for when Mac suggests tending to his son's body, Bradford denies that the dead body is his son's, explaining that his son "went with the Nigger" (152). Jim, the unseen (like Spence's Her), may have been a *person* to Bradford's son and possibly even for a moment to Bradford himself, only to be reobjectified as "the Nigger." Most disastrously, both of the young men are dead; the play works out the undesirable but, sadly, not unlikely outcome of Finest Blood's encounter with the White Devil—that they both end up dead and so unable to forge a new future.

At the end of the play, Nan is no longer on the stage, but her words linger. Like Sojourner Truth, Nan begins the play humming, and her humming turns into a tune with words that speak directly of the moves in secrecy-discourse:

> Keep dis in min' an' all'll go right,
> as on yo way you goes,
> Be shore you knows 'bout all you tells,
> But don't tell all you knows.
> (*Refrain*)
> Be shore you knows 'bout all you tells,
> But don't tell all you knows. (145)

It is possible that Bradford himself may have come into this very sort of secrecy-inflected thinking by the play's conclusion. And yet what is for Nan a private-life secrecy issue becomes for the very public Bradford a public-life secrecy-move, for in denying his son's body he disavows the very revolutionary message his son sought to publish. The secret kept has been lost.

· Mary P. Burrill's *Aftermath* too dramatizes Finest Blood's trek into the bushes to meet the White Devil. Set in the home of the African American Thornton family in South Carolina, the play details the dearly held secret of a lynching and its effect on those connected with its victims. The play opens with Mam Sue, an old woman, singing a song about warfare:

O, yes, yonder comes mah Lawd,
  He is comin' dis way
Wid his sword in his han'
  O, yes, yonder comes—(BFP 57)

Mam Sue is sitting in the room with her daughter Millie, who is ironing clothes while Mam Sue is sewing. As they work, a *"burning log falls apart,"* prompting Mam Sue to observe, "See dat log, Millie? De one fallin' tuh de side dah wid de big flame lappin' round hit? Dat means big doin's 'round heah tonight!" (57). Frightened by this portent, Millie responds, "Oh, Mam Sue, don' you go proph'sying no mo'! You see big doin's in dat fired de night befo' them w'ite devuls come in heah an' tuk'n po' dad out and bu'nt him!" which Mam Sue corrects, saying "No, Millie, Ah didn' see no big doin's dat night—Ah see'd *evul* doin's an' Ah tole yo' po' dady to keep erway f'om townd de nex' day wid his cotton. Ah jes knowed dat he wuz gwine to git in a row wid dem w'ite debbils—but he wou'd'n lis'n tuh his ole mammy—De good Lawd sen' me dese warnin's in dis fiah, jes lak He sen' His messiges in de fiah to Moses" (58).

With the stage thus set, the play proceeds to exhibit the secret that lies at its center. It emerges that Millie has two brothers, Lonnie and John, and the latter has been away fighting in World War I, where he has won the War Cross in France. There, he has come to experience Life-at-Its-Fullest, as Millie observes,

[H]e's been to Paris, an' the fines' people stopp't him when they seen his medal, an' shook his han' an' smiled at him—an' he kin go evawhere, an' dey ain't nobody all the time a-lookin' down on him, an' a-sneerin' at him 'cause he's black, but evahwhere they's jes gran' to him! An; he sez it's the firs' time evah in his life he's felt lak a real, sho-nuff man! (59)

At the time of the play's action, the women have learned that John is on his way home, but this otherwise joyous event has caused consternation because Millie has elected to keep the news of their father's lynching a secret from John. Reasoning that he has had enough to worry him, she has continued to write him letters as if their father were still alive. When Lonnie returns from town to break the news that John will actually be home this very day, Millie's anxiety increases even more, and she urges Mam Sue (who has pushed her to tell John the truth all along) to delay a little longer in revealing the secret because John will only be passing through on his way to Camp Reed, where he will be mustered out. Millie thus sets about trying to fix the house as if their father were still alive but has merely stepped out, taking his Bible from the mantel and opening and placing it on the table where he would read it every morning when he was alive. As she undertakes this preparation, her mother again sings:

> O, yes, yonder comes mah Lawd,
>   He's comin' dis way
> Wid his sword in his han'
> [. . . . .]
> He's gwine ter hew dem sinners down
>   Right lebbal to de groun'
> Oh, yes, yonder comes mah Lawd—(61)[48]

Directly, John arrives back at home and everyone greets him, maintaining the artifice that Millie has constructed. John has returned home bearing gifts, including pistols for himself, which, significantly, he places on the mantel "*on the very spot where the Bible has lain*" (62) which move is followed by his glancing at the passage which his father has allegedly been reading: "But I say unto you, love your enemies, bless them that curse you, an' do good to them that hate you," and he comments,

That ain't the dope they been feedin' us soljers on! "Love you enemies!" It's been—git a good aim at 'em, an' let huh go! [When Mam Sue worries that he has forgotten God, he continues] No, Mam Sue, I ain't fu'got God, but I've quit thinkin' that prayers kin do ever'thing. I've seen a whole lot sence I've been erway from here. I've seen some men go into battle with a curse on their lips, and I've seen them same men come back with never a scratch; an' I've seen men whut read their Bible befo' battle, an' prayed to live, left dead on the field. Yes, Mam Sue, I've seen a heap an' I've done a tall lot o' thinkin' sense I've been erway from here. An' I b'lieve it's jes like this—beyon' a certain point prayers ain't no good! The Lawd does jes so much for you, then it's up to you to do the res' fu' yourse'f. The Lawd's done His part when He's done give me strength an' courage; I got tuh do the res' fu' myse'f! (63)

After this discourse, the family continues to talk until interrupted by the visit of a friend, Elen Hawkins, who greets John and, admiring his uniform, sobs, "Ef only yuh po' daddy had a-lived to see dis day!" (64). With this news revealed, John resolves to go out and meet the lynchers head-on. He takes up his pistols and declares:

> I've been helpin' the wi'ite man git his freedom, I reckon I'd bettah try now to get my own! . . . I'm sick o' these w'ite folks doin's—we're 'fine, trus'worthy feller citizuns' when they're handin' us out guns, an' Liberty Bonds, an' chuckin' us off to die, but we ain't a damn thing when it comes to handin' us the rights we done fought an' bled fu'! I'm sick o' this sort o' life—an' I'm goin' to put an' end to it! . . . This ain't no time fu' preachers or prayers! You mean to tell me I mus' let them w'ite devuls send me miles erway to suffer an' be shot up fu' the freedom of the people I ain't nevah seen, while they're burnin' an' killin' my folks here at home! To Hell with 'em! (65–66)

With these words, "*John rushes out of the cabin and disappears in the gathering darkness*" (66). Thus Finest Blood incarnate rushes to sacrifice himself for the future, a grim conclusive attempt to grasp the ultimate secret of Life-at-Its-Fullest to live free for a moment until his swift and certain death.

Exeunt:
AN ILLUSION

THE PURPLE FLOWER closes with a secret. We do not know what will result from Finest Blood's encounter with the White Devil in the bushes, although the conclusions of *Straggler in the Dust* and *Aftermath* embody the likely outcome. Finest Blood is the new leader of the Us's, but, just like John in Burrill's play, he is likely on the path for a lynching. Meanwhile, what of those left behind, especially the women? It is telling that Bonner, Burrill, and Miller in these and other one-acts rarely envision black women succeeding in effecting change. With a few exceptions, the black women in these plays must ultimately depend on (although they sometimes successfully manipulate) men around them for any hope of attaining the pay-offs they desire. The women in *Aftermath* remain at home at the play's end, and Nan has completely vanished from the stage halfway through *Straggler in the Dust* (although a performance might have Nan either remain on the periphery of the stage or actually place her in the audience for the remainder of the play when staging it). Sidelined thus, these women stand in for their creators, who also depend largely on both white and black men for publication and performance.

A most disturbing manhandling of a black woman takes place in Bonner's *Exit: An Illusion*. This fortuitously named play ushers in the end of this book, for through it we can glimpse a disturbing issue to be addressed regarding secrecy and this discussion of these one-acts that returns us to the central issue of this book—the fact that multiple groups are embroiled in secrecy and that a white man's relation to black women and performance is highly fraught and has been, as in the case of Heth and Barnum (and countless others more horrendous and often still secret), exploitative in the extreme. Using conventions of both religious-folk and secular-stage magic, this play presents a chilling enactment of a black woman's dilemma and her final silencing. Set in a cheap flat, the play explores black male fear regarding a black female body and the ways that such fear is inflected by white male power.

As if to accentuate the multiple interpolation at the heart of the play. Bonner takes pains to note that the room in which the play is set is "mixed" in that there "*are ragged chairs with sorry sagging ragged bottoms.—There are lace curtains with sorry ragged holes—but all over the chairs are scattered clothes, mostly lingerie of the creamiest, laciest, richest, pastel-crepe variety*" (FSE 47). Dishes on the table are mixed with newspapers and shoes, one pair in particular being "*red kid pumps . . . on the edge of the table. Your eyes skip from the scarlet omen of their owner's hasty death—omen, if the bottom still holds in superstition*" (47). There is a window on the back wall, and through it the audience can see snow falling, while the one evident "exit" on the set is a "*brownish sort of nondescript door that shuts a cheap flat off from the rest of the world*" and which "*is not stout enough to be an outer door*" (47). The two principal players are Dot and Buddy; Dot is light-skinned and Buddy is dark, and Bonner lingers on Buddy, writing that "*you can see he is blackly brown with the thin high-poised features that mark a 'keen black man.' You can see at a glance that his slender body is cast for high things. High things. High things of the soul if the soul is fully living—high things of the flesh if the soul is fully dead*" (48). Bonner notes that this room is theirs and that they "*are most assuredly not brother and sister. Neither are they man and wife. The room is mixed*" (48).

The play begins with the two people lying asleep, Dot on a fold-out sofa bed with her arm over Buddy, who lies on the floor. "*Dot suddenly leans over the side toward Buddy. You wonder how she awakens so easily*" and she wakes him up, telling him that she has a date and must go. He awakes as well and immediately starts berating her for going out, seeing as she is sick and it is snowing outside. Furthermore, he does not want her out with another man, even though she claims that the man has been a lifelong friend. When Buddy asks the man's name, she replies that it is "Exit," to which he retorts "Exit? Exit! Where'd he get that! off the inside of a theayter door? . . . What's his other name or is that the onliest one he got?" (49). She informs him that the man's name is Exit Mann, and she proceeds to primp for her date, which includes powdering *"heavily with white powder,"* prompting Buddy to ask her, "You ain't fixin' to go out passing are you?" (50). This starts him berating her again, accusing of her wishing she were white and conjecturing that Exit Mann is himself white. Buddy observes that Mann is probably the person with whom she has been reportedly running around:

> Ol' lop-sided lanky white thing! Been hanging around you at all the cafes and dances and on the streets all the time I'm out of the city! I'm out of the city—working to keep you—you hanging around with some no count white trash! So no count he got to come in nigger places, to nigger parties and then when he gets there—can't even speak to none of them. Ain't said a word to nobody the fellers say! Ain't said a word! Just settin' 'round—looking at you—hanging around you—dancin' with you! He better not show hisself 'round here while I'm here! (52)

At length, Dot tells Buddy, "[D]on't take on so! If you love me then he can't come in between your love and come to me!" which drives Buddy to respond in another lengthy diatribe:

> Damn you! Damn you! Trying to throw this "you love" stuff out to cam'flage and hide behind. I tol' you when we were fussing before you went to sleep that I didn't believe you when you said everybody was lying on you! You said everybody was lying and you was tellin' the truth! Say you ain't never been with other men! Naw I don't love you! (53)

At this point, Buddy takes a gun from the drawer and threatens to call both Dot and Exit, yelling, "I'll Exit him when I get through with you!" and, once she has finished getting ready, snarling, "You ain't going 'till your Exit comes!" (54). Presently, Exit himself does appear, standing behind Buddy, *"half in the shadow. All you can see is a dark overcoat, a dark felt hat. You cannot see his face for his back is turned. You wonder how he came there. You wonder if perhaps he has not been there all the while"* (55). Buddy immediately starts yelling at Exit, who neither moves nor speaks in response, which infuriates Buddy even more, so that soon he yells at Dot, "Go on up to your Exit. Go on so you can go off the way I am sending you off. Go off like you lived! lying in some man's arms—then lying to me. (*As if to himself:*) That's the way to die anyhow: jus' like you lived!" (55). Although Dot pleads with Buddy, "Say you love me! I don't want to go! I don't want to go with him!" Buddy screams at her and opens fire with his pistol as she runs and *"crosses the little space and as quickly the man opens his arms and draws her to him without turning around"* and her voice is heard *"crying smothered against the coats as if she were far away"* saying "Buddy—Buddy—Buddy! Do you love me? Say you love me before I go!" as he continues to fire the gun until a *"stray shot strikes the light"* (55–56). Now that it is dark, Buddy finds a matches and lights it and *"you see the man standing in the doorway—about to cross the threshold. His back is still turned but as you look he slowly begins to turn around . . . and you see Dot laid limp—hung limp—silent. Above her, showing in the match light between the overcoat and the felt hat are the hollow eyes and fleshless cheeks of Death"* (56). As soon as this image has been presented, however, *"almost at once the light flares back. You see the room as it was at first"* and Dot struggles awake, calling to Buddy, "Buddy!!! Buddy!!! Aw God, he can't hear me!—Buddy, do you love me? Say you love me 'fore I go! Aw—ah—ah—!" (56). At this point, she *"stretches rigid and still. The room is quiet an instant. You think you hear the rattling, though"* (56). Then Buddy says:

> Exit!! Mann!! Exit! (*He pauses—then cries aloud:*) You lied! Naw I don't love you! (*He cries so loudly that he comes fully awake and sits up swiftly.*) Say Dot—I had a—! Dot! Dot!! Oh my God! (*He touches her.*) My Dot! (*And he leans over her and begins to cry like a small boy.*) O Dot! I love you! I love you! (56)

I would assert that this play dramatizes something very unusual—*a black woman's lynching.* It may be objected that Dot's death is not a ritual and that it takes place not only in the private space of an apartment but actually within the even more secretive space of Buddy's dream. Moreover, not only may "lynching" seem too strong a word for what transpires, but my use of it obviously violates the dynamics of race and gender inherent in the term. Black *men* are lynched by *white men* in order to control black men's bodies and "protect" white women from them. But what happens when a black man is color struck and a light-skinned black woman powders her face even whiter in order to pass in the mask of whiteface in order to couple with a white man? What happens when a woman attempts to empower herself, working (like Hurston) with a white anthropologist or teaching (like Spence) in a white high school or simply writing (like all of these playwrights), assuming the authority of authorship? What happens when she becomes uncontrollable? When she leaves home?

If we read the historical silencing of black women's voices as a violent measure of control, then maybe Bonner's portrayal of Dot's murder *is* an example of a ritual. Dot is violating constructs that are supposed to corral her; her passing beyond the confines of home and as white causes the same sort of frenzy in Buddy that similar although imagined violations of "the order" create in white lynch mobs—perhaps Exit represents the myths of whiteness-as-better, a corresponding imagined construct that can so fracture the black in-group. No mob kills Dot, but Buddy represents scores of misogynistic black men, and then there is the audience: what of its loyalties? Its gaze? Its role?

Most horrifying of all, to me, is the silent figure of Exit Mann, himself. Horrifying because of what is perhaps the biggest problem about this book, which I referred to in the "Induction"—namely that I am myself a white man. A white southern man, in fact, born in Mississippi of long-established white southern families. It is hard to imagine someone more out-group than myself, and the very argument I have tried to develop raises a series of tortured questions. Have I, like Exit Mann, come calling on these black women only to bring about their deaths? Am I carrying their lifeless bodies away from their spaces, their red pumps, other black men and women, and into an overwrought glare of academic exposure? Have I, a White Devil, penetrated (with all the implications of that word) a barrier of secrecy better left alone? Does my possibly having done so mean that protective secrets have been discovered by one of the out-group and thereby sapped of their power? Can my talking about these plays amount to a colonization of them?

At this point, I want to return to the opening anecdote of this book. The final chapter of the Heth-Barnum case is particularly gruesome and alarmingly relevant. What I did not mention earlier is that Heth's actual age was determined by means of a *public autopsy* ordered by Barnum himself. When her true age was then publicly revealed, Barnum committed the final atrocity of blaming *her* for his hoax, claiming that she had misguided him as to the truth of her "claims" about who she was, which in turn led to his misleading the public. Barnum, in effect, stole this black woman's last laugh by resurrecting her body only to dismantle her secret by repositioning it in his own linguistic trickery.

In writing this book I have been continually haunted by the possible accusation if not the actual possibility that, like Barnum, I am resurrecting these black women only to exploit them. However unassailable I have from the beginning believed my intentions to be, there is the nagging question of what career goals are involved in writing such a book and in the shaping of my career generally. Moreover, how does my positionality affect, directly or indirectly, your reading of this book? A number of comments made to me over the past several years raise these specters. To mention a few, I recall once having lunch with a job candidate when I was an MA student. The candidate was a young African American woman. After the meal, as we walked across campus to the building that housed the English Department, she told me how useful my androgynous name might be for me in my career. She had expected me to be a woman when she received the schedule for the day's events, and I was reminded of her words later when I submitted an article on these playwrights to a journal for publication: even though the submission was blind it was evident that one if not both of the readers thought I was a woman, likely a black woman. Meanwhile, more than one white, male, senior colleague has assured me that African American literature is "hot" right now, that I am smart to write about black women writers. Good business. Juxtaposed with these comments has been my reading in black feminist theory and criticism, where the word "we" signifies "black women," making it perpetually clear just where I stand in this "business."

All of these comments signify market concerns directly related to writing a book and developing an academic career, and I would like to close this volume with a brief consideration of how a scholar's positionality (race, gender, class, ethnicity) is itself interpolated within the far-reaching bounds of secrecy. In the politics of interracial interaction and inquiry, how can a white scholar, especially a southern white male scholar, function? Have we reached the time that Martin Luther King Jr. dreamed of when "the sons of former slaves and the sons of former slave owners will be able to sit down together at the table of brotherhood"? Or are we still tortured by secrets on both sides of the color line and even within the Veil itself that leaves us untrusting and beached on the rocks of nowhere?

At stake in such a line of inquiry is what sort of end is being accomplished when worked out in the murky machinery of secrecy. Whether writing a book or teaching a class, a white scholar-teacher's intentions are always suspect; however much that self may lay claim to an honest, forthright discussion of black life and experience, there always resides in that entity the threat of secret, hidden selves whose pragmatic desires could be fueling and tainting that unhidden self's activities. For that matter, how can a white male scholar ever consciously not position himself in some way in regard to the people he writes about? It seems to me impossible to write about these writers the way I write about, say, William Faulkner. If anything, the fact that I was born in Ripley, Mississippi—Faulkner's ancestral home—is something *not* to flaunt when writing on Faulkner because it lays claim to a kind of nonproblematized autochthony that, in the new southern studies as well as Faulkner scholarship, can actually cause me to lose points as a "serious" critic. Indeed, the hard-nosed northern white or black or southern black man or woman scholar is a more valuable commodity than I in these fields that seek to distance themselves from the old southern white patriarchal discourses that so long dominated them.

But in writing about black women, such outsider positioning is a problem. As Michael Awkward observes, "[T]he black experience represents the hermeneutic tie that binds together Afro-American writer, text, and critic and the hermetical seal that protects black texts from penetration both by uninformed and potentially racist white readers and by even the most insightfully appropriated versions of Western critical thinkers" (28). Even good intentions on the part of informed white scholars are doomed, first because such a proprietarial stance can be precisely the kind of exploitation Barnum was doing ("introducing" and "speaking on behalf of" black women) and, second, because, as Awkward also writes in a passage well aware of the problems of secrecy, perception, and identity,

> a male can never possess or be able to tell the whole truth and nothing but the truth about his relationship to feminist discourse and praxis . . . [and] while autobiographical criticism, like the game of autobiography itself, is poised tenuously between the poles of closure and disclosure, between representation and re-presentation, between a lived life and invented one, I believe that even in the recoverable half-truths of my life are some of the materials that have shaped my perceptions, my beliefs, the self or selves that I bring to the interpretive act. . . . I acknowledge that mine is a necessary participation with regard to black feminist criticism in the half-invention, half-perception which . . . represents every scholar's relationship to cultural criticism. (45)

This threat of harmful and maybe even racist secret intentions has cropped up in recent history with Bill Clinton's invective against Barack Obama and black voters generally during the 2008 race for the Democratic Party's presidential candidate. Clinton's comments raised serious doubts about the validity of his intentions, not only present but past. In a particularly interesting article, Sonya Ross wrote in 2008 that even though in his own campaign for the presidency Clinton was popular with black voters and has been referred to as the first black president, with his comments about Obama, "[s]uddenly, he looks so white." Ross goes on to observe in the article that "nobody bothered to tell Clinton that honorary blackness is also temporary. No matter how much he's done on the subject of race, his brother privileges are always up for renewal." As a white southern man (although his being southern does not make him exceptional), there is always the threat that he might simply be acting, pretending to be a white liberal seeking to improve race relations. Worse yet, perhaps he has been acting all the time in order to achieve power, for as Ross writes, if "anybody knows what Obama is doing to seduce black voters, it is Bill Clinton. After all, Clinton pushed the very same buttons to claim the black vote for himself when he first ran for the presidency." Bill Clinton may not be P. T. Barnum, exactly, but he may have been a white person who concealed his racism or who was perhaps not even himself aware of racism latent within his thinking. Clinton has since emerged as a supporter of Obama, but will that brief abandonment of support for an African American taint his record as a white southern man attempting to move beyond the signs of racism his identity contains? Tellingly, Toni Morrison, who first declared Clinton as the first black president, offered the following comments in a May 7, 2008 article: "People misunderstood that phrase. I was deploring the way in which President Clinton was being treated, vis-à-vis the sex scandal that was surrounding him. I said he was being treated like a black man on the street, already guilty, already a perp. I have no idea what his real instincts are, in terms of race" (Sachs).

Not that there are no spaces for white scholars, male and female, to occupy in African American scholarship. Plenty of white scholars of both genders have been cited in the pages of this volume. In fact, raising the question, does "an autobiographical condition of existence and authenticity exclude non-Afro-American (say, 'white') commentators from Afro-American expressive cultural theory?" Houston Baker writes that the "answer is a painful No" (48). "Painful because the incumbency for the non-Afro-American critic is to finger the grains of a brutal experience in which—if he or she is white—he or she is historically implicated" (48). Baker goes on to explain:

> "Autobiographical," in my proposal, means a personal negotiation of meta-levels—one that foregrounds nuances and resonances of *an-other's* story. The white autobiographer who honestly engages his or her autobiographical implication in a brutal past is as likely as an Afro-American to provide such nuances. (48)

Engaging the brutal presence of white secrecy in the interracial involvement of the United States is precisely what I have been trying to do throughout this book, as it is what I understand *The Purple Flower* and the other one-acts to be doing. From the secrets of white men's raping of black women and the forbidding of birth control information to the silent detrimental presence of the White Devils and Exit Mann, what these plays make vividly manifest is the hard and ultimate reality that a white male scholar is simply unsanitizable. However much I may be trying to be a player who denies my prescribed white-outsider role and realign the rules of the game of interracial academic writing, I cannot abolish my persona as dangerous. The white male scholar always must be a threatening magician.

I have structured this book so that I myself have performed an illusion about my race and gender, unless you were already aware of these things. In so doing, I have perhaps made myself a trickster who is untrustworthy. I did so because I believe that if I had chosen to start the book with the discussion I am now having, then my very openness would be suspect, for I might well have been seen as too readily open, too skillful in my scholarly self's positioning, too eager to make a bid for brother status. In fact, as one of the anonymous readers of this manuscript so astutely noted, my "whiteness" shows through throughout this text—not least in my borrowing Shakespearean forms ("Induction" and "Exeunt") in its structure. I am also well aware that my use of Kristeva, Foucault, and other white theorists is highly problematic in discussing black contexts since those theorists are generally positioned as addressing abstractions that are actually "white." Frankly, presenting myself as some unproblematic person—a white scholar who has dealt with these issues and can assure you that he is one of the good guys (and I am aware of the overtones of that sobriquet too)—seems to me a gross oversimplification of all of the vexed problems of secrecy and interracial politics that I have been trying to delineate and thus a more pernicious form of hiding and trickery than what I have done in structuring the book as I have. To do so is, to me, as inaccurate and ultimately harmful as to argue that racism has ceased to exist in the United States altogether. Better not to pretend that the shadows of racism and the legacy of slavery do not still stretch over us all.

And better to remember that, whether I am correct or not, these playwrights were consciously working in a poetics of secrecy. I am still one of the out-group and I am not so powerful as to be able to find out all or even most of the secrets of black women, because they were highly adept magicians themselves whose plays retain their shadows, keeping secrets I have not yet dreamt of in my philosophy. And in addressing my own issues, it is important for me not to be like Barnum and try to steal the stage back from these writers all over again. The rocks of nowhere have been and are piled deep, but these women's voices are heard from beneath the rubble. They have their own secrets, their own goals, and I (and any other scholar, whatever that person's position) do well to remember Nan the charwoman's song:

Be shore you knows 'bout all you tells,
But don't tell all you knows.

Notes

Induction

1. It should be noted, for the record, that Barnum did free Heth after buying her and that his politics were abolitionist.

2. All emphases in quoted material are original unless otherwise noted.

On Secrecy, Magic, and Black Women Playwrights

1. For a reader who may be encountering these names for the first time, see Bernard L. Peterson's *Early Black American Playwrights and Dramatic Writers;* Yvonne Shafer's *American Women Playwrights: 1900–1950;* and Judith L. Stephens's "The Harlem Renaissance and the New Negro Movement," which provide introductions to these writers, including biographical sketches of them as well as synopses of their one-act plays.

2. On passing, see Sterling Lecater Bland Jr.'s *Voices of the Fugitives: Runaway Slave Stories and Their Fictions of Self-Creation;* M. Giulia Fabi's *Passing and the Rise of the African American Novel;* Mar Gallego's *Passing Novels in the Harlem Renaissance: Identity Politics and Textual Strategies;* Brooke Kroeger's *Passing: When People Can't Be Who They Are;* Kathleen Pfeiffer's *Race Passing and American Individualism;* Werner Sollar's *Neither Black nor White and Yet Both: Thematic Explorations of Interracial Literature;* Gayle Wald's *Crossing the Line: Racial Passing in Twentieth-Century U.S. Literature and Culture* and the essays in *Mixing Race, Mixing Culture: Inter-American Literary Dialogues,* edited by Monika Kaup and Debra J. Rosenthal; *Passing and the Fictions of Identity,* edited by Elaine K. Ginsberg; and *Passing: Identity and Interpretation in Sexuality, Race, and Religion,* edited by María Carla Sánchez and Linda Schlossberg.

3. On secret societies, see Arkon Daraul's *Secret Societies: A History;* Norman MacKenzie's *Secret Societies;* Jasper Godwin Ridley's *The Freemasons:*

A History of the World's Most Powerful Secret Society; George Simmel's "The Secret and the Secret Society." See especially on black masonry George Williamson Crawford's *Prince Hall and His Followers; Being a Monograph on the Legitimacy of Negro Masonry.*

4. See Dale Cockrell's *Demons of Disorder: Early Blackface Minstrels and Their World;* Susan Gubar's *Racechanges: White Skin, Black Face in American Culture;* W. T. Lhamon Jr.'s *Raising Cain: Blackface Performance from Jim Crow to Hip Hop;* Eric Lott's *Love and Theft: Blackface, Minstrelsy and the American Working Class;* William J. Mahar's *Behind the Burnt Cork Mask: Early Blackface Minstrelsy and Antebellum American Popular Culture;* Robert C. Toll's *Blacking Up: The Minstrel Show in Nineteenth-Century America;* and the essays in Bean et al., *Inside the Minstrel Mask: Readings in Nineteenth-Century Blackface Minstrelsy.* Behind such masking, Booker T. Washington could enforce his vision for improving the lives of African Americans, although this maneuvering carries a sinister side, as is illustrated in Ellison's *Invisible Man* and argued recently by Gary Totten. Of course, using their own tactics against the enemy could backfire, as is the case with Charles W. Chesnutt and Paul Laurence Dunbar, who so well mimicked Thomas Nelson Page and Joel Chandler Harris that most readers missed the point altogether.

5. Not to say that the cupboard is bare concerning theorizations of secrecy in literary criticism. Sedgwick's *Epistemology of the Closet* and scholarly works by numerous queer theorists examine a community steeped in a poetics of secrecy: Oliver Buckton, for example, explores the Victorian "autobiographical tension between secrecy and disclosure" (4) surrounding discourses of homosexuality. Leslie Fiedler explores the secret fear that the "freak" as Other might in fact dwell within the so-called normal person's "secret self." The summer 2007 issue of *MELUS* takes as its theme "Thresholds, Secrets, and Knowledge," editor Martha J. Cutter observing in "Notes from the Editor: Thresholds, Secrets, and Knowledge" that for "many ethnic writers, the crossing of various thresholds—from one geographic or geopolitical realm to another, from one racial category to another, or from stories of the past to stories of the present/future—is supposed to yield a type of new knowledge. Yet the crossing of thresholds, boundaries, and borders does not always lead to enlightenment. Or, perhaps the knowledge gained is not what one expects, resulting in the production of new secrets—misprisions which conceal as much as they reveal. I think of Booker T. Washington traveling around Europe . . . crossing national boundaries, trying to move his people into a new future, yet deliberately concealing the racist violence that existed in the US in order to instantiate the European serf as the 'farthest man down'" (1). Additionally, D. A. Miller considers secrecy in Dickens, and Sarah Robertson has recently explored secrecy in Jayne Anne Phillips.

6. I use "somatic-psychic" instead of "psychosomatic" in order to avoid privileging the psychological, which is the heritage of the latter term.

7. Miller goes on to discuss the "open secret," which is not what I mean by secret-as-fetish. I mean, rather, the secret as a form that signifies a function rather than content, a concept closer to Derrida's definition of the function of Certes/*certes* in the writing of Cixous. Noting that the name/word is an anagram for "secret," Derrida writes that "Certes is the Secret, the trope or Secret place of the story that you will never reach" (*Geneses* 45).

8. I have been and will be using the term *interpolate* to signify the full scope of individual and group involvement in secrecy. While I will continue to explore the nuances of these various types of involvement, I want to state at this point that while the term,

for my purposes, signifies the situation of people compelled by their placement within certain systems of secrecy to perpetuate victimization as well as people tragically caught within secrecy that victimizes them, the term is not meant to function as an exoneration of individuals or groups whose connections with and performances of secrecy are used to oppressive ends. What I do want the term to do is to work as a neutral one that allows not only for such ways people are "caught up in" and/or use secrecy but also for the fact that the distinctions between conscious and unconscious, intentional and unintentional involvement in secrecy are extremely nebulous.

9. I use the term *discourse* instead of *interaction* or *play* to highlight the economy of visible signs that players manipulate to control the revealing and concealing of information. I will not be developing quantitive formulas and decision trees or applying prefabricated ones (such as the "prisoner's dilemma") to specific games. Doing so lies beyond the scope of this discussion, although I think such a project would be extremely helpful in precisely delineating the paradoxes of strategy for these writers and their characters and considering how such models compare with ones in later historical moments (I am regrettably the least qualified person to attempt such an effort). Still, I will be borrowing terms from game theory, as derived from the texts by Morton D. Davis, Prajit K. Dutta, Larry Samuelson, and Philip D. Straffin. Regarding game theory and its connections with literature, see Huizinga and the essays in *Game, Play, Literature* (edited by Jacques Ehrmann).

10. Michel Beaujour recognizes a similar three-part breakdown of moves and the overlapping among them in his discussion of game theory and poetics. "Given the fact that I become a part of the game as a poet," he writes, "I face several options, which parallel those of any player who has freely entered the game" (59). These three options are (1) to play "according to the rules"; (2) to "pretend to leave the game in disgust and . . . write nothing"; and (3) to "leave the game, saying [that one does not] have to play in order to be a *poet*" (59). Beaujour goes on to assert, "I believe this short list of options contains all the fundamental poetics which are possible within our culture. The actual poetics of any single poet or group of poets must be a variant of one of these, or a cross between two or all of them. Intermediate types are confused or even coherent, which of course, does not prelude [*sic*] their existence. Also these three options may be adopted successively by any one poet or group of poets, usually starting with One and moving on to Two or Three" (59–60).

11. In *The Genesis of Secrecy: On the Interpretation of Narrative*, Frank Kermode explores the centrality of secrecy as coding. He notes that texts "cast shadows important to the perceiving eye" (20) and in order to "divine the true, the latent sense [of a text], you need to be of the elect, the institution" while outsiders "must content themselves with the manifest" (3). Secrecy is thus entwined methodologically and politically with interpretation, because "the history of interpretation may be thought of as a history of exclusions" (20). Kermode examines the biblical book of Mark, prodding its manifold secrets in content and style and arguing that it seems to function in two ways: one "says the stories are obscure on purpose to damn the outsiders; the other . . . says that they are not necessarily impenetrable, but that the outsiders, being what they are, will misunderstand them anyway" (32), and so "the text as we have it appears both to reveal and proclaim, and at the same time to obscure and conceal" (59). Besides the fact that such coding resembles the "cryptonomy" Nicolas Abraham and Maria Torok describe, Kermode's observations speak to the very important psychological, linguistic, social, and literary aspects of secrecy, because interpretation is a central aspect of forming

in-groups/out-groups which either can or cannot interpret given texts/situations. Such coding is part of the phaneric masking Baker identifies, which has a double function: "first, the indigenous comprehend the territory within their own vale/veil more fully than any intruder. . . . Second, the indigenous *sound* appears monstrous and deformed *only* to the intruder" (51–52).

12. Regarding Socrates, see Plato's *Republic.* For an interesting discussion of Cold War–era concepts of secrecy, see Edward A. Shils's *The Torment of Secrecy: The Background and Consequences of American Security Politics.*

13. Regan recognizes two types of natural secrets: a simple one (which is learned "by chance") and an extorted one, which is "learned fraudulently" (5). The entrusted secret "may be either *explicit* or *implicit*" when the pledge of secrecy is asked for or if it is demanded by "the office or function of the person to whom the secret is communicated"—the latter two designations being referred to also as *official* and *professional* secrets, respectively (8).

14. Derrida reads this event as a type of violence. This violence is complex in accord with the complex balancing aspect of secrecy, because Derrida argues that "revealing by effraction the so-called proper name . . . reveals the first nomination which was already an expropriation, but it denudes also that which since then functioned as the proper, the so-called proper, substitute of the deferred proper, *perceived* by the *social* and *moral consciousness* as the proper, the reassuring seal of self-identity, the secret" (*Of Grammatology* 112). Derrida goes on to write that Levi-Strauss "comes to disturb order and natural peace, the complicity which peacefully binds the good society to itself in its play" and "it is the anthropological eruption which breaks the secret of the proper names and the innocent complicity governing the play of young girls" (113). Explaining that "one cannot or rather must not incriminate the innocent young girls," Derrida argues that a "violation" is brought on by the "rusing intrusion of the foreigner who, having seen and heard, is now going to 'excite' the young girls, loosen their tongues, and get them to divulge the precious names" (113–14).

15. Regarding performance as incarnated in both formal theater and *theatrum mundi,* see, in addition to texts already cited, Auslander, Brisset and Edgley, Lynda Christian, Kershaw, Phelan, Roach, Schechner, and the essays in Reinelt and Roach.

16. On the material conditions of performance and reception, see Susan Bennett's *Theatre Audiences;* Marvin A. Carlson's *Places of Performance;* Lee Simonson's *The Stage Is Set;* and the essays in *Theatre Praxis: Teaching Drama through Practice* (edited by Christopher McCullough).

17. On lynching, see also Edward L. Ayres's *Vengeance and Justice: Crime and Punishment in the Nineteenth-Century South;* W. Fitzhugh Brundage's *Under Sentence of Death: Lynching in the South;* James E. Cutler's *Lynch Law: An Investigation into the History of Lynching in the United States;* Philip Dray's *At the Hands of Parties Unknown: The Lynching of Black America;* Sandra Gunning's *Race, Rape, and Lynching: The Red Record of American Literature, 1890–1912;* Adam Gussow's *Seems Like Murder Here: Southern Violence and the Blues Tradition;* Michael J. Pfeifer's *Rough Justice: Lynching and American Society, 1874–1947;* Mason Stokes's *The Color of Sex: Whiteness, Heterosexuality, and the Fictions of White Supremacy;* Stewart E. Tolnay and E. M. Beck's *A Festival of Violence: An Analysis of Southern Lynchings, 1882–1930;* and Ida B. Wells-Barnett's *On Lynching.*

18. See Lévi-Strauss's *The Savage Mind.*

19. Regarding this blend of religions, Raboteau writes that "it should be emphasized

that it is the continuity of perspective that is significant, more so than the fact that cultures of particular African gods, such as Shango or Elegba, have been transmitted to the New World. For new as well as old gods have come to be worshiped by Afro-Americans, but the new, like the old, have been perceived in traditionally African ways" (16).

20. See Lageure on the connections between these secret societies and Haitian politics.

21. On African American religion and its magical inflections, see Timothy J. Nelson's *Every Time I Feel the Spirit: Religious Experience and Ritual in an African American Church;* George E. Simpson's *Black Religions in the New World;* Theophus H. Smith's *Conjuring Culture: Biblical Formulations of Black America;* and the essays in *Conjuring: Black Women, Fiction, and Literary Tradition* (edited by Marjorie Pryse and Hortense J. Spillers).

22. Secrecy informs less exotic forms of black religion than voodoo. Evelyn Brooks Higginbotham points out that "[c]hurches and households, both rejecting the worldly pleasure of the male turf, represented female areas" (59). Of course, this space was also ostensibly under the control of black men; one might recall Nanny's saying in Hurston's *Their Eyes Were Watching God,* "Ah wanted to preach a great sermon about colored women sittin' on high, but they wasn't no pulpit for me" (16). Still, religion and its many magical incarnations inundate and are inundated by black women, as Valerie Lee argues in *Granny Midwives and Black Women Writers.*

23. This "peculiar marginality" is matched by a fraught group makeup that makes it impossible to speak of black women as a group in a simple way. Theorists have long been struggling to define black women without essentializing them, from Collins's focusing on the "distinctive contours" (*Black Feminist Thought* 22) of a "Black *women's* collective standpoint" (28) to Kevin Everod Quashie's appropriation of a Spivakian "useful essentialism" (6) to address the complexities of black womanhood. Quashie, in fact, notes "the conundrum of essentialism: the subject is fluid and even fails to appear, though the outlines and meanings of its corpus are well known, even definitive" (3). For further discussion, see also Collins's *Fighting Words: Black Women and the Search for Justice* as well as (and this list only begins to enumerate the many works on this topic) the books by bell hooks and the essays in *All the Women Are White, All the Blacks Are Men, But Some of Us Are Brave: Black Women's Studies* (edited by Gloria T. Hull, Patricia Bell Scott, and Barbara Smith), and *Changing Our Own Words: Essays on Criticism, Theory, and Writing by Black Women* (edited by Cheryl A. Wall).

24. Regarding women's role in the Harlem Renaissance, see along with Hull, Cheryl A. Wall's *Women of the Harlem Renaissance.* On groups of African Americans writers, see Elizabeth McHenry's *Forgotten Readers: Recovering the Lost History of African American Literary Societies.* For discussion of various aspects of the Harlem Renaissance, see Jervis Anderson's *This Was Harlem;* Arna Bontemps's *The Harlem Renaissance Remembered;* James de Jongh's *Vicious Modernism: Black Harlem and the Literary Imagination;* Nathan Irvin Huggins's *Harlem Renaissance;* Bruce Kellner's *The Harlem Renaissance: A Historical Dictionary for the Era;* Steven Watson's *The Harlem Renaissance: Hub of African-American Culture, 1920–1930;* Cary D. Wintz's *Black Culture and the Harlem Renaissance;* and the essays in Victor Kramer and Robert A. Russ's *The Harlem Renaissance Re-examined* and Amritjit Singh, William S. Shiver, and Stanley Brodwin's *The Harlem Renaissance: Reevaluations.*

25. Not to suggest that Johnson always kept Locke at arm's length; as Jeffrey C. Stewart has shown, Johnson and Locke came to be quite close.

26. Other champions of these playwrights whose books address these writers are Carol Allen, Elizabeth Brown-Guillory, Martha Bower Gilman, Gloria T. Hull, and David Krasner (in *A Beautiful Pageant*). Samuel Christian and Jasmin L. Lambert's dissertations undertake systematic explorations of these women's works as a distinct and exclusive group. For articles dealing with these authors in various groupings, see Doris E. Abramson, Jeanne-Marie A. Miller, and Andrea Nouryeh.

The One-Acts

1. On African American theater, see Genevieve Fabre's *Drumbeats, Masks, and Metaphor: Contemporary Afro-American Theatre*; James V. Hatch and Ted Shine's *Black Theater U.S.A.: Forty-Five Plays by Black Americans, 1847–1974*; Errol G. Hill and James V. Hatch's *A History of African American Theatre*; David Krasner's *A Beautiful Pageant: African American Theatre, Drama, and Performance in the Harlem Renaissance, 1910– 1927* and *Resistance, Parody, and Double Consciousness in African American Theatre, 1895–1910*; and Lofton Mitchell's *Black Drama: The Story of the American Negro in Theatre.*

2. See Bernard L. Peterson's *The African American Theatre Directory, 1816–1960: A Comprehensive Guide to Early Black Theatre Organizations, Companies, Theatres, and Performing Groups* for details on the Little Theater Movement.

3. Regarding secrecy and mystery writing, see also Dennis Porter's *The Pursuit of Crime: Art and Ideology in Detective Fiction*; Peter Thoms's *Detection and Its Design: Narrative and Power in 19th-Century Detective Fiction*; and the other essays (along with Hühn's) in *Theory and Practice of Classic Detective Fiction* (edited by Jerome H. Delamater and Ruth Prigozy).

4. Thus providing an instant "secrecy of the archive."

5. For a recent detailed discussion of depictions of African American dialect, see Lisa Cohen Minnick's *Dialect and Dichotomy: Literary Representations of African American Speech.*

6. Helene Keyssar particularly considers the importance and complexity of audience composition in African American drama.

7. She also notes that at the same time that understanding the hidden transcript "is solely dependent and indicative of the individual audience members' cultural competence" (102), African American Theater also "as a secure social space no matter how sequestered, offers a social side where the hidden transcript can readily be employed under the very nose of those who dominate" (105).

8. Further discussion of these figurations of Satan, goats, and blackness may be found in *A History of the Devil and the Idea of Evil from the Earliest Times to the Present Day*, by Paul Carus; *The Devil in the New World: The Impact of Diabolism in New Spain*, by Fernando Cervantes; *A History of the Devil*, by Gerald Messadié; and *A History of the Devil*, by William Woods. For further discussion of racist assignment of signifiers of blackness, see George M. Fredrickson's *The Black Image in the White Mind; The Debate on Afro-American Character and Destiny, 1817–1914*; Robert E. Hood's *Begrimed and Black: Christian Traditions on Blacks and Blackness*; and Peter Rigby's *African Images: Racism and the End of Anthropology.* And for treatment of the development of concepts of blackness in America from the goat/Satan/blackness figuration to the "Black Beast" and twentieth-century depictions, see Bruce Dain's *A Hideous Monster of the Mind:*

American Race Theory in the Early Republic; Adam Lively's *Masks: Blackness, Race, and the Imagination;* Mason Stokes's *The Color of Sex: Whiteness, Heterosexuality, and the Fictions of White Supremacy;* and the essays in Seymour L. Gross and John Edward Hardy's *Images of the Negro in American Literature* and Janis Faye Hutchinson's *Cultural Portrayals of African Americans: Creating an Ethnic/Racial Identity.*

9. The set is thus twice doubled, and done so in a way that is difficult to conceptualize. Is the "landscape" of the "Scene" to be installed on the upper level of the Skin-of-Civilization? Or should it somehow overlay both divisions? Obviously, a director may choose how to negotiate this matter. What is significant is that there should exist the doubled doubling in the set, a spatiality that seems distinctly that of African Americans during the Harlem Renaissance.

10. Quotes will be taken from *The Plays of Georgia Douglas Johnson* (edited by Judith L. Stephens) instead of *Selected Works of Georgia Douglas Johnson* (edited by Claudia Tate) in the interest of using the more recently published and inclusive text.

11. Bower writes that Mrs. Temple "must live with a husband who can never know the secret—a phenomenon that will contribute to a lifelong inability to achieve authenticity of self. Both women must present false selves to the world" (23).

12. The latter especially informs this play as it was a cabinet that concealed an expert chess player who would direct the movements of a mannequin. See Cook for an especially provocative presentation of the history of the Automaton Chess Player.

13. For what it is worth in the context of secrecy, Miller occasionally wrote under the pen name "Jean Ray."

14. In writing about the history of magic, During cites the rods of Moses and Aaron changing to serpents and their juxtaposition with the Egyptian magicians' similar tricks.

15. Ethyl A. Young-Minor observes that Sabena speaks to Catherine in coded language (such coding being emblematic in her singing the spiritual "Go Down, Moses") in order to ascertain her trustworthiness as one to whom she can reveal the secret of Harriet's location. Young-Minor observes that Miller "writes black community as a complicated organism, with its own rules, regulations, insiders, and outsiders" (43–44), noting that Catherine is an outsider to Harriet's group and showing that her failure to discern Sabena's codes "demonstrates the tragic results when a member of the community cannot successfully engage in the call-and-response codes of black female dialogue" (41).

16. Like Sandy, Henry remains the spoilsport in all the game configurations in the play. The play closes with the boys surrounding Henry raising "*their voices threateningly*" (333).

17. Regarding Christophe, see Elizabeth Abbott's *Haiti: The Duvaliers and Their Legacy;* Hubert Cole's *Christophe: King of Haiti;* Sibylle Fischer's *Modernity Disavowed: Haiti and the Cultures of Slavery in the Age of Revolution;* Philippe R. Girard's *Paradise Lost: Haiti's Tumultuous Journey from Pearl of the Caribbean to Third World Hot Spot;* and David Nicholls's *From Dessalines to Duvalier: Race, Colour, and National Independence in Haiti.*

18. Spence literally represents the perfect exemplar of the importance of speech, as one of her prime fields of study was elocution in her courses and activities in college, especially at Columbia. Numerous playbills list her as "elocutionist" as well as "actress" (SCRBC).

19. Allen refers to him as "the white absentee owner" (99) while Shafer writes that

he is "an avaricious white man [who] is punished for his cruelty to his Philippino wife" (273).

20. The spatiality of this play's original performance conditions speaks to the confines of black female space, as it was performed in the basement of the 135th Street Branch of the New York Public Library, where the audience for the performances (held January 10, 19, and 24 of 1927 at 8:30 P.M.) were limited to two hundred, and tickets were to be bought from "Miss Louise Latimer at the 'Brown Bunny,' 2354 Seventh Avenue" (SCRBC).

21. Spence writes that Walter "opens the door and with a well aimed kick sends the Jew sprawling" (49).

22. In fact, dismantling dance and other things seen as being markers of essentialized blackness is part of another of Hurston's one-acts entitled *The First One,* which will be discussed later. It might also be noted that John and Emma drop the "ah" for "I" pronunciation in their speech.

23. Kraut notes that the play "demonstrate[s] more precisely how dance has the power to both unite and fracture groups" (34). Drawing a connection between difficulties in Hurston's childhood (resulting from her father's being mulatto [and showing favoritism to her sister] and her mother's dying when Hurston was thirteen) and Emma's obsession with skin color, Bower writes that the play "expresses the serious problems that accompany the objects of a gaze that 'caint see,' like Emma, beyond the surface of skin color" (46). "As the play *Color Struck* proceeds," Bower observes, "so does the anger, the low self-esteem, the paranoia, and finally the schizophrenia of Emma" (41). Allen notes that the play "is about an issue that challenges cooperative advancement: a couple is pulled apart by color politics . . . [resulting from the fact that] Emmaline internalizes messages that uplift whiteness" (121). At the same time, the uniting "structure of the ring dance [enacted on the train] contains what playwright August Wilson would call 'two trains running,' or the ability to foster personal dynamics and still maintain group directives by upholding a tradition that declares diversity" (132). Sandra Richards notes "the physical-psychological momentum of dance that gradually envelops all the characters in the construction of the community" that heightens "the inverse process by which Emmaline isolates herself and further internalizes a sense of racial inferiority" (78). David Krasner writes that "Emma turns against the big city. . . . Instead, she looks toward the provincial, inner world of her rural black community for spiritual sustenance. Yet her own community, as portrayed in the play, rejects Emma as well" (*A Beautiful Pageant* 123). For further discussion of the play, see Carson, Classon, Hill, North, Peters, and Plant.

24. Krasner also notes the ellipses, dashes, etc., seeing them as examples of Emma's identity-fragmentation.

25. "Dance no less than song could become an instrument of satire at the expense of whites," Levine points out, noting too that the "basic characteristics of American dance" differed from Europe-derived dances/dancers (16–17).

26. Staging again becomes important. It is difficult to imagine what sort of technology Graham imagined could make the mistletoe alight perfectly on the girl's face. A director might choose to have it manipulated by a string or even by a character. If the white soldier were to be brought back on stage to manipulate the mistletoe, then the underlying irony of Emancipation's ultimate disappointment could be well foregrounded.

27. This negative and oppressive aspect of silence is that which Jenny Sharpe

addresses in her essay "Unspeakable Limits of Rape: Colonial Violence and Counter-Insurgency." In the plays that dealt with rape discussed earlier, silence was something that could be empowering, and Irigaray seizes upon silence as an important desirable thing in *To Be Two*, writing that "I find myself wondering whether the work of love that the book transmits has conveyed the fact that to love each other between us, woman and man, women and men, requires the protection of a space, a place of silence" (62). This space of silence "is at least *three*" (63), and Irigaray explains this "third space" (to evoke Bhabha) when she argues that two should strive for "perception" instead of "sensation" because where "perception can assist in the construction of intersubjectivity, sensation tends to erase one of the two subjects or reduce them both to a game between forces that are more or less individuated and controlled" (43). This perception establishes advantageous spaces, for through it "we can each become, the one for the other, a bridge towards a becoming which is yours, mine, and ours. I can be a bridge for you, as you can be one for me. This bridge can never become the property of either. The bridge which I am for you will never be mine or 'to me.' I perceive you, I create an idea of you, I preserve you in my memory—in affect, in thought—in order to assist you in your becoming. While I become me, I remember you. This should be a double gesture: you should be a bridge for me, as I should be one for you" (43). Thus, Irigaray writes, perceiving "you is a way of approaching us," and "I who am visible to you must also protect a certain reserve. Within the intention of appearing to you, there must also exist the intention of remaining invisible, of covering life and love with the shadow of a secret. The eyes are a bridge between us, the gestures express a desire, but this shows itself by hiding itself" (47).

28. Mandy greatly resembles the sort of "Granny" healer-figure that Valerie Lee describes.

29. Again, a change from the source material—in this case, a true move to empower a black woman—for the real William himself got the clothes from different places in Savannah, Georgia. Mandy, here, colonizes her master's clothes (fetish items for his body) to help Ellen pass.

30. Writing about Johnson's lynching plays, Trudier Harris asserts that the "black female body in ill health . . . is not only a metaphor for American racism but a sympathetic response to the continuing destruction of the black male body" ("Before the Strength, the Pain" 40–41).

31. Stephens discusses the role of spirituals in these plays, but in light of Gussow's argument, it seems just as vital to note the blues forms (see Stephens's "Art, Activism, and Uncompromising Attitude in Georgia Douglas Johnson's Lynching Plays" and "Politics and Aesthetics, Race and Gender: Georgia Douglas Johnson's Lynching Dramas as Black Feminist Cultural Performance").

32. Another part of the nuance of this version of the play is Johnson's spelling "nurse" as "nuse," which greatly resembles "noose," which more accurately describes the inevitable effect of any contact with white people.

33. Derrida's comments on "the safe" illumine the play's closing in an interesting light. "Constructing a system of partitions," he writes, "with their inner and outer surfaces, the cryptic enclave produces a cleft in space. . . . Within this forum, a place where the free circulation and exchange of objects and speeches can occur, the cryptic constructs another, more inward forum like a closed rostrum or speaker's box, a *safe*: sealed, and thus internal to itself, a secret interior within the public square, but, by the same token, outside it, external to the interior. . . . The inner forum is (a) safe, an out-

cast outside inside the inside. That is the condition, and the stratagem, of the cryptic enclave's ability to isolate, to protect, to shelter from any penetration. . . . The crypt can constitute its secret only by means of its division, its fracture. 'I' can *save* an inner safe only by putting it inside 'myself,' *beside(s)* myself, outside. What is at stake here is what takes place secretly, or takes a secret place, in order to keep itself *safe* somewhere in the self" (xiv).

34. For example, where *And Yet They Paused* keeps the white empowered space of congress invisible but audible, *A Bill to Be Passed* layers the invisible congressional proceedings with silence and the mediation of a black male voice. In addition to the essays on these plays by Stephens, see Perkins and Stephens's introduction to *Strange Fruit* as well as Fletcher, O'Brien, and Sullivan.

35. The use of Thomas Jefferson's name suggests a famous "secret" of a man's begetting black children.

36. Bill Sturgeon, former editor of *Elevator World: The Publisher for the International Building Transportation Industry,* explains the role of the starter, writing that at the time of the play's action,

> Automatic Traffic Control had not been invented and all elevators had human operators. It was necessary to space the elevators in the shaft way for maximum efficiency and a "starter" was positioned in a lobby served by a bank of elevators. He would motion to one of the operators to start up to the top, or perhaps use a clicker. He was aware of when the maximum influx or exiting of the tenants took place and situated his elevators strategically to fill or empty the building expediciously [*sic*]. Lunch time was another period when he was active in allocating elevator cars. Later, when the elevators were automatically spaced in the hoist way by computer and positions were pictured on the lobby main station he often was used to move people to the next available car so they would enter quickly. The starters represented the first impression upon visitors and wore a snappy uniform. It helped if he was good-natured!

37. Johnson's play is based on Douglass's writing that he "had a number of warm-hearted friends in Baltimore . . . and the thought of being separated from them forever was painful beyond expression" (*Narrative* 142) as well as his sending for and marrying Anna Murray, a free woman in Baltimore, once he has escaped to New York. Johnson does, however, take a number of liberties with the text that are worthy of note. First, she refers to Anna as "Ann" and identifies Douglass himself as "Fred Douglass," whom she calls a "young slave man" (85). Her text is apocryphal, attempting to access Douglass before he was "Frederick Douglass" (as a matter of fact, Douglass makes no mention of having taken or even thought of taking the name "Douglass" before his escape from slavery).

38. Again, this story departs from Douglass's account. First, Douglass was at the time with Master Hugh Auld, not Tom Auld. Second, Douglass makes no mention himself of having withheld some of his funds from his master.

39. Upon first arriving in Baltimore, his master's wife begins to teach him how to read and write but is soon forbidden by her husband to do so anymore. To counteract this move and learn the empowering secret of writing, Douglass famously tricks his white companions into teaching him how to write by asking them how to spell words and then copying them (a secrecy-move that will be discussed again later). His move is particularly interesting in light of Derrida's discussion of Lévi-Strauss's story about the

chief of the Nambikwara tribe, who, after watching Lévi-Strauss write, takes upon himself to draw lines on paper in order to show his subjects that he has mastered writing. They cannot read the writing to prove him wrong, but that does not matter because writing's function goes far beyond expression or communication. Indeed, as Derrida writes, "since the Chief used writing effectively without knowing either the way it functioned or the content signified by it, the end of writing is political and not theoretical" (127). The chief's utilization of inscription mystifies his power in an erasure that establishes a secret that controls his subjects, imitating the power of the center to strengthen his own reign.

40. Johnson creates these details partly from factual account and partly from imagination. As Douglass notes in *Life and Times,* a friend has provided him with a sailor's suit and sailor's protection (a paper describing his friend who did not even resemble Douglass). However, Douglass explains that he had neither train pass nor tickets but rather jumped on the train hoping his sailor protection paper would pass the conductor's scrutiny, which it did.

41. The similarity of names and themes between this play and *Color Struck* are striking.

42. For discussion of the role of the goat in Greek drama, see Francisco R. Abrados's *Festival, Comedy and Tragedy: The Greek Origins of Theatre;* Gerald F. Else's *The Origin and Early Form of Greek Tragedy;* John Ferguson's *A Companion to Greek Tragedy;* A. W. Pickard's *Dithyramb Tragedy and Comedy;* and Sir William Ridgeway's *The Origin of Tragedy.*

43. Gubar writes regarding this situation that "[a]s a statement about the psychology of bondage, Hurston's play suggests that paternal anxiety about potency as well as genealogical claims to legitimacy and property motivate racial subjugation. Laughing at the phallus is the outrage; disrespect for the father (even when the father has earned it) will be punished in the patrilineal, part-centered ancient world. Slavery or white supremacy is the result of the law of the (insecure, out-of-control) father outraged and determined to assert authority and control over his family, his property, and his future" (129).

44. Cora Bresciano, a student in one of my recent graduate seminars, has made the provocative suggestion that the actor portraying Ham might not look any different at all after the curse, thus highlighting race as a set of beliefs unconnected with biology.

45. John Lowe writes, "Two things are worth noting about this play. First is that the origin of a race is in its founding father's joke. Second, the ending suggests that 'The First [Black] One,' a being who knows the true value of life, is superior to whites. Thus Hurston's playlet both embraces and inverts the traditional interpretation of the biblical passage upon which it is based" (67).

46. I am indebted to Trevor W. McKeown, Curator of Library and Archives Board of Trustees, Grand Lodge of British Columbia and Yukon, who was kind enough to inform me that the phrase "[r]iding the goat has been a jocular, and sometimes malicious, euphemism for masonic or fraternal initiation since at least the early 19th century and the Benevolent and Protective Order of Elks are claimed by their current official historian, Mike Kelly, to have actually used a goat in their initiation from 1868 up until 1952." In my earlier published treatment of this play, I assumed that a goat was being ridden in the offstage march later in the play, but, as McKeown has pointed out, it is not explicitly stated that a goat is used. It is likely a horse, although the possibility that the deception is carried out on the back of a goat would further develop the treatment of the goat-as-signifier in the play.

47. The stage directions describing the tomb note that "[o]*ne instinctively thinks of 'I dreamed I dwelt in marble halls' and realizes that there is a new interpretation*" (145).

48. Once again, it might be noted that in this context of lynching and conflict, the black speaker evokes the blues form, which Freddy King would later incorporate in his song, "I'm Tore Down," which features the lines "I'm tore down / I'm almost level with the ground." See Gussow for discussion of the implications of this line.

Works Cited

Abbott, Elizabeth. *Haiti: The Duvaliers and Their Legacy.* London: Robert Hale, 1991.

Abrados, Francisco R. *Festival, Comedy and Tragedy: The Greek Origins of Theatre.* Leiden: E. J. Brill, 1975.

Abraham, Nicolas, and Maria Torok. *The Wolf Man's Magic Word: A Cryptonomy.* Trans. Nicholas Rand. Theory and History of Literature 37. Minneapolis: University of Minnesota Press, 1986.

Abramson, Doris E. "Angelina Weld Grimké, Mary T. Burrill, Georgia Douglas Johnson, and Marita O. Bonner: An Analysis of Their Plays." *Sage* 2.1 (1985): 9–13.

Allen, Carol. *Peculiar Passages: Black Women Playwrights, 1875–2000.* New York: Peter Lang, 2005.

Allen, Theodore W. *The Invention of the White Race,* vol. 2, *The Origin of Racial Oppression in Anglo-America.* The Haymarket Series. New York: Verso, 1997.

Anderson, Jervis. *This Was Harlem.* New York: Noonday, 1981.

Artaud, Antonin. *The Theatre and Its Double.* Trans. Mary Caroline Richards. New York: Grove Press, 1958.

Auslander, J. L. *From Acting to Performance: Essays in Modernism and Postmodernism.* London: Routledge, 1997.

———. *Liveness: Performance in a Mediatized Culture.* London: Routledge, 1999.

Awkward, Michael. *Negotiating Difference: Race, Gender, and the Politics of Positionality.* Chicago: University of Chicago Press, 1995.

Ayres, Edward L. *Vengeance and Justice: Crime and Punishment in the Nineteenth-Century South.* New York: Oxford University Press, 1984.

Baker, Houston A., Jr. *Modernism and the Harlem Renaissance.* Chicago: University of Chicago Press, 1987.

———. *Workings of the Spirit: The Poetics of Afro-American Women's Writing.* Chicago: University of Chicago Press, 1991.

Baol, Augusto. *Theater of the Oppressed.* Trans. Charles A. McBride and Maria-Odilia Leal McBride. London: Pluto Press, 1979.

Barthes, Roland. *Mythologies.* Trans. Annette Lavers. New York: Hill and Wang, 1972.

Baudrillard, Jean. *Simulacra and Simulation.* Trans. Sheila Faria Glaser. Ann Arbor: University of Michigan Press, 1994.

Bean, Annemarie, James V. Hatch, and Brooks McNamara, eds. *Inside the Minstrel Mask: Readings in Nineteenth-Century Blackface Minstrelsy.* Hanover, NH: Wesleyan University Press, 1996.

Beaujour, Michel. "The Game of Poetics." In *Game, Play, Literature,* ed. Jacques Ehrmann, 58–67. Boston: Beacon Press, 1971. Special issue of *Yale French Studies* 41 (1968).

Beckerman, Bernard. *Dynamics of Drama: Theory and Method of Analysis.* New York: Knopf, 1970.

Bennett, Susan. *Theatre Audiences.* 2nd ed. London: Routledge, 1997.

Bentley, Eric, ed. *The Theory of the Modern Stage: An Introduction to Modern Theatre and Drama.* New York: Penguin, 1968.

Berg, Allison, and Merideth Taylor. "Enacting Difference: Marita Bonner's *Purple Flower* and Ambiguities of Race." *African American Review* 32 (1998): 469–80.

Bhabha, Homi K. *The Location of Culture.* London: Routledge, 1998.

Bland, Sterling Lecater, Jr. *Voices of the Fugitives: Runaway Slave Stories and Their Fictions of Self-Creation.* Westport, CT: Greenwood Press, 2000.

Bok, Sissela. *Secrets: On the Ethics of Concealment and Revelation.* New York: Pantheon, 1982.

Bonner, Marita. *Frye Street and Environs: The Collected Works of Marita Bonner.* Ed. Joyce Flynn and Joyce Occomy Stricklin. Boston: Beacon Press, 1987.

Bontemps, Arna. *The Harlem Renaissance Remembered.* New York: Dodd, Mead, and Co., 1972.

Bourdieu, Pierre. *Outline of a Theory of Practice.* Trans. Richard Nice. Cambridge: Cambridge University Press, 1977.

Bower, Martha Gilman. *"Color Struck" Under the Gaze: Ethnicity and the Pathology of Being in the Plays of Johnson, Hurston, Childress, Hansberry, and Kennedy.* Contributions in Afro-American and African Studies. Westport, CT: Praeger, 2003.

Brissett, Dennis, and Charles Edgley. *Life as Theater: A Dramaturgical Sourcebook.* Chicago: Aldine, 1995.

Brown-Guillory, Elizabeth. *Their Place on the Stage: Black Women Playwrights in America.* Contributions in Afro-American and African Studies 117. New York: Greenwood Press, 1988.

———, ed. *Wines in the Wilderness: Plays by African American Women from the Harlem Renaissance to the Present.* Contributions in Afro-American and African Studies. New York: Greenwood Press, 1990.

Brundage, W. Fitzhugh. *Under Sentence of Death: Lynching in the South.* Chapel Hill: University of North Carolina Press, 1997.

Buckton, Oliver. *Secret Selves: Confession and Same-Sex Desire in Victorian Autobiography.* Chapel Hill: University of North Carolina Press, 1998.

Budick, Emily Miller. *Blacks and Jews in Literary Conversation.* Cambridge: Cambridge University Press, 1998.

Bull, Malcolm. *Seeing Things Hidden: Apocalypse, Vision and Totality.* London: Verso, 1999.

Burton, Jennifer. Introduction to *The Prize Plays and Other One-Acts Published in Periodicals,* ed. Henry Louis Gates Jr., xix–lx. African-American Women Writers, 1910–1940. New York: G. K. Hall, 1996.

Butler, Judith. *Bodies that Matter: On the Discursive Limits of Sex.* New York: Routledge, 1993.

Carlson, Marvin A. *Places of Performance: The Semiotics of Theatre Architecture.* Ithaca, NY: Cornell University Press, 1989.

Carson, Warren J. "Hurston as Dramatist: The Florida Connection." In *Zora in Florida,* ed. Steve Glassman and Kathryn Lee Seidal, 121–29. Orlando: University of Central Florida Press, 1991.

Carus, Paul. *The History of the Devil and the Idea of Evil from the Earliest Times to the Present Day.* New York: Bell, 1969.

Certeau, Michel de. *The Practice of Everyday Life.* Trans. Steven F. Rendall. Berkeley: University of California Press, 1984.

Cervantes, Fernando. *The Devil in the New World: The Impact of Diabolism in New Spain.* New Haven, CT: Yale University Press, 1994.

Chaudhuri, Una. *Staging Place: The Geography of Modern Drama.* Ann Arbor: University of Michigan Press, 1995.

Chick, Nancy. "Marita Bonner's Revolutionary Purple Flowers: Challenging the Symbol of White Womanhood." *Langston Hughes Review* 13.1 (1994–1995): 21–32.

Chireau, Yvonne Patricia. "Hidden Traditions: Black Religion, Magic and Alternative Spiritual Beliefs in Womanist Perspective." In *Perspectives on Womanist Theology,* ed. Jacquelyn Grant, 65–88. Black Church Scholars Series. Atlanta: ITC Press, 1995.

Christian, Lynda G. *Theatrum Mundi: The History of an Idea.* New York: Garland, 1987.

Christian, Samuel. "Four African American Female Playwrights, 1910–1950: The Narratives of Their Historical, Genteel, and Black Folk Voodoo Plays." PhD diss., City University of New York, 1995.

Classon, H. Lin. "Re-evaluating *Color Struck:* Zora Neale Hurston and the Issue of Colorism." *Theatre Studies* 42 (1997): 5–18.

Cockrell, Dale. *Demons of Disorder: Early Blackface Minstrels and Their World.* Cambridge Studies in American Theatre and Drama. Cambridge: Cambridge University Press, 1997.

Cole, Hubert. *Christophe: King of Haiti.* New York: Viking, 1967.

Collins, Patricia Hill. *Black Feminist Thought: Knowledge, Consciousness, and the Politics of Empowerment.* 2nd ed. New York: Routledge, 2000.

———. *Fighting Words: Black Women and the Search for Justice.* Minneapolis: University of Minnesota Press, 1998.

Cook, James W. *The Arts of Deception: Playing with Fraud in the Age of Barnum.* Cambridge, MA: Harvard University Press, 2001.

Craft, William. *Running a Thousand Miles for Freedom; Or, The Escape of William and Ellen Craft from Slavery.* 1860. Reprint, Miami, FL: Mnemosyne Pub. Co., 1967.

Crawford, George Williamson. *Prince Hall and His Followers; Being a Monograph on the Legitimacy of Negro Masonry.* New York: The Crisis, 1971.

Cutler, James E. *Lynch Law: An Investigation into the History of Lynching in the United States.* Montclair, NJ: Patterson Smith, 1969.

Dain, Bruce. *A Hideous Monster of the Mind: American Race Theory in the Early*

Republic. Cambridge, MA: Harvard University Press, 2002.

Daraul, Arkon. *Secret Societies: A History*. New York: MJF Books, 1989.

Davis, Morton D. *Game Theory: A Nontechnical Introduction*. Mineola, NY: Dover Publications, 1983.

Davis, Tracy C., and Thomas Postlewait. *Theatricality*. Theatre and Performance Theory. Cambridge: Cambridge University Press, 2003.

de Jongh, James. *Vicious Modernism: Black Harlem and the Literary Imagination*. Cambridge: Cambridge University Press, 1990.

Delamater, Jerome H., and Ruth Prigozy. *Theory and Practice of Classic Detective Fiction*. Westport, CT: Greenwood Press, 1997.

Derrida, Jacques. "Foreword: *Fors:* The Anglish Words of Nicolas Abraham and Maria Torok." In *The Wolf Man's Magic Word: A Cryptonomy*, by Nicolas Abraham and Maria Torok, trans. Nicholas Rand, xi–xlviii. Theory of History and Literature 37. Minneapolis: University of Minnesota Press, 1986.

———. *Geneses, Genealogies, Genres, and Genius: The Secrets of the Archive*. Trans. Beverly Bie Brahic. New York: Columbia University Press, 2003.

———. *Of Grammatology*. Trans. Gayatri Chakravorty Spivak. Baltimore: Johns Hopkins University Press, 1976.

Douglass, Frederick. *Life and Times of Frederick Douglass, Written By Himself; His Early Life as a Slave, His Escape from Bondage, and His Complete History*. New York: Collier, 1962.

———. *Narrative of the Life of Frederick Douglass, an American Slave*. New York: Penguin, 1982.

Dray, Philip. *At the Hands of Parties Unknown: The Lynching of Black America*. New York: Modern Library, 2002.

Du Bois, W. E. B. *The Souls of Black Folk*. New York: Penguin, 1996.

Dunbar-Nelson, Alice. *Give Us Each Day: The Diary of Alice Dunbar-Nelson*. Ed. Gloria T. Hull. New York: Norton, 1984.

During, Simon. *Modern Enchantments: The Cultural Power of Secular Magic*. Cambridge, MA: Harvard University Press, 2002.

Dutta, Prajit K. *Strategies and Games: Theory and Practice*. Cambridge, MA: MIT Press, 1999.

Ehrmann, Jacques, ed. *Game, Play, Literature*. Boston: Beacon Press, 1971. Special issue of *Yale French Studies* 41 (1968).

Ellison, Ralph. *Invisible Man*. New York: Vintage, 1995.

Else, Gerald F. *The Origin and Early Form of Greek Tragedy*. Cambridge, MA: Harvard University Press, 1965.

Fabi, M. Giulia. *Passing and the Rise of the African American Novel*. Urbana: University of Illinois Press, 2001.

Fabre, Genevieve. *Drumbeats, Masks, and Metaphor: Contemporary Afro-American Theatre*. Boston: Harvard University Press, 1983.

Fanon, Frantz. *Black Skin, White Masks*. Trans. Charles Lam Markmann. New York: Grove Press, 1967.

Ferguson, John. *A Companion to Greek Tragedy*. Austin: University of Texas Press, 1973.

Fiedler, Leslie. *Freaks: Myths and Images of the Secret Self*. New York: Touchstone, 1978.

Fischer, Sibylle. *Modernity Disavowed: Haiti and the Cultures of Slavery in the Age of*

Revolution. Durham, NC: Duke University Press, 2004.

Fletcher, Winona. "From Genteel Poet to Revolutionary Playwright: Georgia Douglas Johnson." *Theatre Annual* 30 (1985): 41–64.

Fredrickson, George M. *The Black Image in the White Mind; The Debate on Afro-American Character and Destiny, 1817–1914.* New York: Harper, 1971.

Freud, Sigmund. *Civilization and Its Discontents.* Trans. James Strachey. New York: W. W. Norton, 1961.

———. *The Uncanny.* Trans. David McLintock. New York: Penguin, 2003.

Fuoss, Kirk W. "Lynching Performances: Theatres of Violence." *Text and Performance Quarterly* 19.1 (1999): 1–37.

Gallego, Mar. *Passing Novels in the Harlem Renaissance: Identity Politics and Textual Strategies.* Hamburg: LitVerlag, 2003.

Gates, Henry Louis, Jr. *Figures in Black: Words, Signs, and the "Racial" Self.* New York: Oxford University Press, 1987.

———. *The Signifying Monkey: A Theory of African-American Literary Criticism.* New York: Oxford University Press, 1988.

Ginsberg, Elaine K., ed. *Passing and the Fictions of Identity.* Durham, NC: Duke University Press, 1996.

Girard, Philippe R. *Paradise Lost: Haiti's Tumultuous Journey from Pearl of the Caribbean to Third World Hot Spot.* New York: Palgrave Macmillan, 2005.

Goldsby, Jacqueline. *A Spectacular Secret: Lynching in American Life and Literature.* Chicago: University of Chicago Press, 2006.

Grant, Jacquelyn, ed. *Perspectives on Womanist Theology.* Black Church Scholars Series. Atlanta: ITC Press, 1995.

Gross, Seymour L., and John Edward Hardy, eds. *Images of the Negro in American Literature.* Chicago: University of Chicago Press, 1966.

Gubar, Susan. *Racechanges: White Skin, Black Face in American Culture.* New York: Oxford University Press, 1997.

Gunning, Sandra. *Race, Rape, and Lynching: The Red Record of American Literature, 1890–1912.* New York: Oxford University Press, 1996.

Gussow, Adam. *Seems Like Murder Here: Southern Violence and the Blues Tradition.* Chicago: University of Chicago Press, 2002.

Halm, Ben B. *Theater and Ideology.* Selinsgrove, PA: Susquehanna University Press, 1995.

Hammonds, Evelynn M. "Toward a Genealogy of Black Female Sexuality: The Problematic of Silence." In *Feminist Genealogies: Colonial Legacies, Democratic Futures,* ed. M. Jacqui Alexander and Chandra Talpade Mohanty, 170–81. New York: Routledge, 1997.

Harris, Trudier. "Before the Strength, the Pain: Portraits of Elderly Black Women in Early Twentieth Century Anti-Lynching Plays." In *Black Women Playwrights: Visions on the American Stage,* ed. Carol P. Marsh-Lockett, 25–42. New York: Garland, 1999.

———. *Exorcising Blackness: Historical and Literary Lynching and Burning Rituals.* Bloomington: Indiana University Press, 1984.

Harris, Will. "Early Black Women Playwrights and the Dual Liberation Motif." *African American Review* 28 (1994): 205–21.

Harrison, Paul Carter, ed. *Kuntu Drama: Plays of the African Continuum.* New York: Grove Press, 1974.

Hatch, James V., and Ted Shine. *Black Theater U.S.A.: Forty-Five Plays by Black Americans, 1847–1974.* New York: Free Press, 1974.

Higginbotham, Evelyn Brooks. "Beyond the Sound of Silence: Afro-American Women in History." *Gender and History* 1.1 (1989): 50–67.

Hill, Errol G., and James V. Hatch. *A History of African American Theatre.* Cambridge Studies in American Theatre and Drama. Cambridge: Cambridge University Press, 2003.

Hill, Lynda Marion. *Social Rituals and the Verbal Art of Zora Neale Hurston.* Washington, DC: Howard University Press, 1996.

Hood, Robert E. *Begrimed and Black: Christian Traditions on Blacks and Blackness.* Minneapolis: Fortress, 1994.

hooks, bell. *Ain't I a Woman: Black Women and Feminism.* Boston: South End Press, 1981.

———. *Feminist Theory: From Margin to Center.* 2nd ed. Boston: South End Press, 2000.

———. *Yearning: Race, Gender, and Cultural Politics.* New York: Oxford University Press, 1990.

Huggins, Nathan Irvin. *Harlem Renaissance.* New York: Oxford University Press, 1971.

Huizinga, Johan. *Homo Ludens: A Study of the Play Element in Culture.* New York: Harper and Row, 1970.

Hull, Gloria T. *Color, Sex, and Poetry: Three Women Writers of the Harlem Renaissance.* Bloomington: Indiana University Press, 1987.

Hull, Gloria T., Patricia Bell Scott, and Barbara Smith, eds. *All the Women Are White, All the Blacks Are Men, But Some of Us Are Brave: Black Women's Studies.* New York: Feminist Press, 1982.

Hurston, Zora Neale. "Characteristics of Negro Expression." In *Negro: An Anthology,* ed. Nancy Cunard, 24–31. New York: Continuum, 1996.

———. *Mules and Men.* 1935. Reprint, New York: Harper and Row, 1990.

———. *Tell My Horse: Voodoo and Life in Haiti and Jamaica.* 1938. Reprint, New York: Harper and Row, 1990.

———. *Their Eyes Were Watching God.* New York: Perennial, 1998.

———, et al. *The Prize Plays and Other One Acts Published in Periodicals.* African-American Women Writers, 1910–1940. Ed. Henry Louis Gates Jr. New York: G. K. Hall, 1996.

Hutchinson, George. *The Harlem Renaissance in Black and White.* Cambridge, MA: Belknap Press of Harvard University Press, 1995.

Hutchinson, Janis Faye, ed. *Cultural Portrayals of African Americans: Creating an Ethnic/Racial Identity.* Westport, CT: Bergin and Garvey, 1997.

Hyatt, Harry Middleton. *Hoodoo—Conjuration—Witchcraft—Rootwork: Beliefs Accepted by Many Negroes and White Persons These Being Orally Recorded among Blacks and Whites.* 2 vols. Washington, DC: Distributed by American University Bookstore, 1970 (Hannibal, MO: Western Publishing).

Irigaray, Luce. *This Sex Which Is Not One.* Trans. Catherine Porter and Carolyn Burke. Ithaca, NY: Cornell University Press, 1985.

———. *To Be Two.* Trans. Monique M. Rhodes and Marco F. Cocito-Monoc. New York: Routledge, 2001.

Johnson, E. Patrick. *Appropriating Blackness: Performance and the Politics of Authenticity.* Durham, NC: Duke University Press, 2003.

Johnson, Georgia Douglas. *The Plays of Georgia Douglas Johnson: From the New Negro Renaissance to the Civil Rights Movement.* Ed. Judith L. Stephens. Urbana: University of Illinois Press, 2006.

———. *Selected Works of Georgia Douglas Johnson.* Ed. Claudia Tate. New York: G. K. Hall, 1997.

Kaup, Monika, and Debra J. Rosenthal, eds. *Mixing Race, Mixing Culture: Inter-American Literary Dialogues.* Austin: University of Texas Press, 2002.

Kellner, Bruce. *The Harlem Renaissance: A Historical Dictionary for the Era.* Westport, CT: Greenwood Press, 1984.

Kermode, Frank. *The Genesis of Secrecy: On the Interpretation of Narrative.* Cambridge, MA: Harvard University Press, 1979.

Kershaw, Baz. *The Politics of Performance: Radical Theatre as Cultural Intervention.* London: Routledge, 1992.

Keyssar, Helene. *The Curtain and the Veil: Strategies in Black Drama.* New York: Burt Franklin, 1981.

King, Martin Luther, Jr. "I Have a Dream." American Rhetoric, May 4, 2008. http://www.americanrhetoric.com/speeches/mlkihaveadream.htm.

Knowles, Ric. *Reading the Material Theatre.* Theatre and Performance Theory. Cambridge: Cambridge University Press, 2004.

Kramer, Victor, and Robert A. Russ, eds. *The Harlem Renaissance Re-examined.* New York: AMS Press, 1987.

Krasner, David. *A Beautiful Pageant: African American Theatre, Drama, and Performance in the Harlem Renaissance, 1910–1927.* New York: Palgrave Macmillan, 2002.

———. *Resistance, Parody, and Double Consciousness in African American Theatre, 1895–1910.* New York: St. Martin's Press, 1997.

Kraut, Anthea. "Reclaiming the Body: Representations of Black Dance in Three Plays by Zora Neale Hurston." *Theatre Studies* 43 (1998): 23–36.

Kristeva, Julia. *Powers of Horror: An Essay on Abjection.* Trans. Leon S. Roudiez. European Perspectives: A Series of the Columbia University Press. New York: Columbia University Press, 1982.

———. *Revolution in Poetic Language.* Trans. Margaret Waller. New York: Columbia University Press, 1984.

Kroeger, Brooke. *Passing: When People Can't Be Who They Are.* New York: Public Affairs, 2003.

Laguerre, Michel S. *Voodoo Politics in Haiti.* New York: St. Martin's Press, 1989.

Lambert, Jasmin L. "Resisting the 'Hottentot' Body: Themes of Sexuality and Femininity in Select Plays by Female Playwrights from the Harlem Renaissance." PhD diss., Bowling Green State University, 1998.

Lee, Valerie. *Granny Midwives and Black Women Writers: Double-Dutched Readings.* New York: Routledge, 1996.

Lévi-Strauss, Claude. *The Savage Mind.* Trans. George Weidenfeld. Chicago: University of Chicago Press, 1966.

———. *Tristes Tropiques.* Trans. John and Doreen Weightman. New York: Modern Library, 1997.

Levine, Lawrence W. *Black Culture and Black Consciousness: Afro-American Folk Thought from Slavery to Freedom.* New York: Oxford University Press, 1977.

Lewis, David Levering. *When Harlem Was in Vogue.* New York: Oxford University Press, 1981.

Lhamon, W. T., Jr. *Raising Cain: Blackface Performance from Jim Crow to Hip Hop.* Cambridge, MA: Harvard University, 1998.

Lillo, George. *The London Merchant.* Lincoln: University of Nebraska Press, 1965.

Lively, Adam. *Masks: Blackness, Race, and the Imagination.* Oxford: Oxford University Press, 2000.

Locke, Alain, and Montgomery Gregory, eds. *Plays of Negro Life: A Source-Book of Native American Drama.* Westport, CT: Negro University Press, 1927.

Lorde, Audre. *Sister Outsider.* Trumansburg, NY: Crossing Press, 1984.

Lott, Eric. *Love and Theft: Blackface, Minstrelsy and the American Working Class.* Race and American Culture. New York: Oxford University Press, 1993.

Lowe, John. "From Mule Bones to Funny Bones: The Plays of Zora Neale Hurston." *Southern Quarterly: A Journal of the Arts in the South* 33.2–3 (1995): 65–78.

MacKenzie, Norman. *Secret Societies.* New York: Crescent Books, 1968.

Mahar, William J. *Behind the Burnt Cork Mask: Early Blackface Minstrelsy and Antebellum American Popular Culture.* Music in American Life. Urbana: University of Illinois Press, 1999.

Mance, Ajuan Maria. *Inventing Black Women: African American Women Poets and Self-Representation, 1877–2000.* Knoxville: University of Tennessee Press, 2007.

Manuel, Carme. "*Mule Bone:* Langston Hughes and Zora Neale Hurston's Dream Deferred of an African-American Theatre of the Black Word." *African American Review* 35 (2001): 77–92.

Marsh-Lockett, Carol P., ed. *Black Women Playwrights: Visions on the American Stage.* Studies in Modern Drama. New York: Garland, 1999.

McCullough, Christopher, ed. *Theatre Praxis: Teaching Drama through Practice.* New York: St. Martin's Press, 1998.

McHenry, Elizabeth. *Forgotten Readers: Recovering the Lost History of African American Literary Societies.* Durham, NC: Duke University Press, 2002.

McKay, Nellie. "'What Were They Saying?' Black Women Playwrights of the Harlem Renaissance." *The Harlem Renaissance Re-examined: A Revised and Expanded Edition,* ed. Victor A. Kramer and Robert A. Russ, 151–66. Troy: Whitston, 1997.

McKeown, Trevor W. E-mail message to author, May 4, 2006.

MELUS: The Journal of the Society for the Study of the Multi-Ethnic Literature of the United States 32.2 (2007).

Messadié, Gerald. *A History of the Devil.* Trans. Marc Romano. New York: Kodansha, 1996.

Métraux, Alfred. *Voodoo in Haiti.* Trans. Hugo Charteris. New York: Schocken Books, 1972.

Miller, D. A. *The Novel and the Police.* Berkeley: University of California Press, 1988.

Miller, Jeanne-Marie A. "Georgia Douglass Johnson and May Miller: Forgotten Playwrights of the New Negro Renaissance." *CLA Journal* 33 (1990): 349–66.

Minnick, Lisa Cohen. *Dialect and Dichotomy: Literary Representations of African American Speech.* Tuscaloosa: University of Alabama Press, 2004.

Mitchell, Lofton. *Black Drama: The Story of the American Negro in Theatre.* New York: Hawthorn, 1967.

Morrison, Toni. *Playing in the Dark: Whiteness and the Literary Imagination.* Cambridge, MA: Harvard University Press, 1992.

Nelson, Timothy J. *Every Time I Feel the Spirit: Religious Experience and Ritual in an African American Church.* Qualitative Studies in Religion. New York: New York University Press, 2005.

Nicholls, David. *From Dessalines to Duvalier: Race, Colour, and National Independence in Haiti.* New Brunswick, NJ: Rutgers University Press, 1979.

North, Michael. *The Dialect of Modernism: Race, Language, and Twentieth-Century Literature.* New York: Oxford University Press, 1994.

Nouryeh, Andrea. "Twice Silenced, Twice Oppressed: African American Women Playwrights of the 1930s." *New England Theatre Journal* 13 (2002): 99–122.

O'Brien, C. C. "Cosmopolitanism in Georgia Douglas Johnson's Anti-Lynching Literature." *African American Review* 38 (2004): 571–87.

Page, Thomas Nelson. "No Haid Pawn." *In Ole Virginia, Or, Marse Chan and Other Stories.* Nashville, TN: J. S. Sanders, 1991.

Perkins, Kathy A., ed. *Black Female Playwrights: An Anthology of Plays before 1950.* Bloomington: Indiana University Press, 1990.

———. E-mail message to author, November 14, 2006.

Perkins, Kathy A., and Judith L. Stephens, eds. *Strange Fruit: Plays on Lynching by American Women.* Bloomington: Indiana University Press, 1998.

Peters, Pearlie Mae. *The Assertive Woman in Zora Neale Hurston's Fiction, Folklore, and Drama.* New York: Garland 1998.

Peterson, Bernard L., Jr. *The African American Theatre Directory, 1816–1960: A Comprehensive Guide to Early Black Theatre Organizations, Companies, Theatres, and Performing Groups.* Westport, CT: Greenwood Press, 1997.

———. *Early Black American Playwrights and Dramatic Writers: A Biographical Directory and Catalog of Plays, Films, and Broadcasting Scripts.* New York: Greenwood Press, 1990.

———. *Profiles of African American Stage Performers and Theatre People, 1816–1960.* Westport, CT: Greenwood Press, 2001.

Pfeifer, Michael J. *Rough Justice: Lynching and American Society, 1874–1947.* Urbana: University of Illinois Press, 2004.

Pfeiffer, Kathleen. *Race Passing and American Individualism.* Amherst: University of Massachusetts Press, 2003.

Phelan, Peggy. *Unmarked: The Politics of Performance.* London: Routledge, 1993.

Pickard, A. W. *Dithyramb Tragedy and Comedy.* Oxford: Clarendon Press, 1927.

Pinn, Anthony B. *Varieties of African American Religious Experience.* Minneapolis, MN: Fortress Press, 1998.

Plant, Deborah G. *Every Tub Must Sit on Its Own Bottom: The Philosophy and Politics of Zora Neale Hurston.* Urbana: University of Illinois Press, 1995.

Plato. *The Republic of Plato.* Trans. Allan Bloom. New York: Basic Books, 1968.

———. *Timaeus* and *Critias.* Trans. Desmond Lee. New York: Penguin, 1977.

Porter, Dennis. *The Pursuit of Crime: Art and Ideology in Detective Fiction.* New Haven, CT: Yale University Press, 1981.

Pryse, Marjorie, and Hortense J. Spillers. *Conjuring: Black Women, Fiction, and Literary Tradition.* Everywoman: Studies in History, Literature, and Culture. Bloomington: Indiana University Press, 1985.

Quashie, Kevin Everod. *Black Women, Identity, and Cultural Theory: (Un)Becoming the Subject.* New Brunswick, NJ: Rutgers University Press, 2004.

Raboteau, Albert J. *Slave Religion: The "Invisible Institution" in the Antebellum South.* Oxford: Oxford University Press, 2004.

Raynor, Sharon D. "The World of Female Knowing According to Georgia Douglas Johnson, Playwright." *CLA Journal* 45 (2001): 231–42.

Regan, Robert E. *Professional Secrecy in the Light of Moral Principles: With an Applica-*

tion to Several Important Professions. Washington, DC: Augustinian Press, 1943.

Reinelt, Janelle G., and Joseph R. Roach, eds. *Critical Theory and Performance.* Ann Arbor: University of Michigan Press, 2007.

Richards, Sandra L. "Writing the Absent Potential: Drama, Performance, and the Canon of African-American Literature." In *Performativity and Performance,* ed. Andrew Parker and Eve Kosofsky Sedgwick,. 64–88. New York: Routledge, 1995.

Richardson, Willis, ed. *The Plays and Pageants from the Life of the Negro.* Washington, DC: Associated Publishers, 1930.

Richardson, Willis, and May Miller, eds. *Negro History in Thirteen Plays.* Washington, DC: Associated Publishers, 1935.

Ridgeway, Sir William. *The Origin of Tragedy.* New York: Benjamin Blom, 1966.

Ridley, Jasper Godwin. *The Freemasons: A History of the World's Most Powerful Secret Society.* New York: Arcade, 2001.

Rigby, Peter. *African Images: Racism and the End of Anthropology.* Oxford: Berg, 1996.

Roach, Joseph R. *The Player's Passion.* Ann Arbor: University of Michigan Press, 1985.

Robertson, Sarah. *The Secret Country: Decoding Jayne Anne Phillips' Cryptic Fictions.* Amsterdam: Rodopi, 2007.

Ross, Sonya. "Bill Clinton is no brother." On Deadline, April 4, 2008. http://news.yahoo.com/s/ap_campaignplus/20080425/ap_ca/on_deadline_race_2.

Russell, Jeffrey Burton. *Lucifer: The Devil in the Middle Ages.* Ithaca, NY: Cornell University Press, 1984.

Sachs, Andrea. "10 Questions for Toni Morrison." *Time,* May 7, 2008. http://www.time.com/time/arts/article/0,8599,17383003,00.html

Samuelson, Larry. *Evolutionary Games and Equilibrium Selection.* Cambridge, MA: MIT Press, 1997.

Sánchez, María Carla, and Linda Schlossberg, eds. *Passing: Identity and Interpretation in Sexuality, Race, and Religion.* New York: New York University Press, 2001.

Schechner, Richard. *Between Theater and Anthropology.* Philadelphia: University of Pennsylvania Press, 1985.

———. *Performance Theory.* New York: Routledge, 1988.

Schechner, Richard, and Mady Schuman. *Ritual, Play and Performance: Readings in the Social Sciences/Theatre.* New York: Seabury, 1976.

Sedgwick, Eve Kosofsky. *Epistemology of the Closet.* Berkeley: University of California Press, 1990.

Shafer, Yvonne. *American Women Playwrights: 1900–1950.* New York: Peter Lang, 1995.

Sharpe, Jenny. "The Unspeakable Limits of Rape: Colonial Violence and Counter-Insurgency." In *Colonial Discourse and Postcolonial Theory: A Reader,* ed. Patrick Williams and Laura Chrisman, 221–43. New York: Columbia University Press, 1994.

Shils, Edward A. *The Torment of Secrecy: The Background and Consequences of American Security Politics.* Glencoe, IL: Free Press, 1956.

Simmel, George. "The Secret and the Secret Society." *The Sociology of George Simmel.* Ed. And trans. K. W. Wolff. New York: Free Press, 1950.

Simonson, Lee. *The Stage Is Set.* New York: Harcourt, Brace, 1932.

Simpson, George Eaton. *Black Religions in the New World.* New York: Columbia University Press, 1978.

Singh, Amritjit, William S. Shiver, and Stanley Brodwin, eds. *The Harlem Renaissance: Reevaluations.* New York: Garland Press, 1989.

Smith, Barbara. "Toward a Black Feminist Criticism." In *African American Literary Theory: A Reader,* ed. Winston Napier, 132–46. New York: New York University Press, 2000.

Smith, Theophus H. *Conjuring Culture: Biblical Formulations of Black America.* New York: Oxford University Press, 1994.

Sollar, Werner. *Neither Black nor White and Yet Both: Thematic Explorations of Interracial Literature.* New York: Oxford University Press, 1997.

Southern, Eileen. *The Music of Black Americans: A History.* 2nd ed. New York: Norton, 1983.

Speisman, Barbara. "From 'Spears' to *The Great Day:* Zora Neale Hurston's Vision of a Real Negro Theater." *Southern Quarterly* 36.3 (1998): 34–46.

Stafford, Barbara Maria. *Artful Science: Enlightenment Entertainment and the Eclipse of Visual Educations.* Cambridge, MA: MIT Press, 1994.

Stephens, Judith L. "The Anti-Lynch Play: Toward an Interracial Feminist Dialogue in Theatre." *Journal of American Drama and Theatre* 2.3 (1990): 59–69.

———. "Anti-Lynch Plays by African American Women: Race, Gender, and Social Protest in American Drama." *African American Review* 26 (1992): 329–39.

———. "Art, Activism, and Uncompromising Attitude in Georgia Douglas Johnson's Lynching Plays." *African American Review* 39 (2005): 87–102.

———. "The Harlem Renaissance and the New Negro Movement." In *American Women Playwrights,* ed. Brenda Murphy, 98–117. Cambridge: Cambridge University Press, 1999.

———. "Lynching, American Theatre, and the Preservation of a Tradition." *Journal of American Drama and Theatre* 9.1 (1997): 54–65.

———. "Politics and Aesthetics, Race and Gender: Georgia Douglas Johnson's Lynching Dramas as Black Feminist Cultural Performance." *Text and Performance Quarterly* 3 (2000): 251–67.

———. "Racial Violence and Representation: Performance Strategies in Lynching Dramas of the 1920s." *African American Review* 33 (1999): 655–71.

Stewart, Jeffrey C. "Alain Locke and Georgia Douglas Johnson, Washington Patrons of Afro-American Modernism." *George Washington University Washington Studies* 12 (1986): 37–44.

Stoelting, Winifred. "May Miller." In *Afro-American Poets since 1955,* ed. Thadious M. Davis and Trudier Harris, 241–47. Dictionary of Literary Biography 41. Detroit: Gale, 1985.

Stokes, Mason. *The Color of Sex: Whiteness, Heterosexuality, and the Fictions of White Supremacy.* Durham, NC: Duke University Press, 2001.

Straffin, Philip D. *Game Theory and Strategy.* Washington, DC: Mathematical Association of America, 1993.

Sturgeon, Bill. E-mail message to the author, September 26, 2007.

Sullivan, Megan. "Folk Plays, Home Girls, and Back Talk: Georgia Douglas Johnson and Women of the Harlem Renaissance." *CLA Journal* 38.4 (1995): 404–19.

Tefft, Stanton K. "Secrecy, Disclosure and Social Theory." In *Secrecy,* ed. Tefft, 35–74.

———, ed. *Secrecy: A Cross-Cultural Perspective.* New York: Human Sciences Press, 1980.

Thoms, Peter. *Detection and Its Design: Narrative and Power in 19th-Century Detective Fiction.* Athens: Ohio University Press, 1998.

Toll, Robert C. *Blacking Up: The Minstrel Show in Nineteenth-Century America.* New

York: Oxford University Press, 1974.

Tolnay, Stewart E., and E. M. Beck. *A Festival of Violence: An Analysis of Southern Lynchings, 1882–1930*. Urbana: University of Illinois Press, 1995.

Totten, Gary. "Southernizing Travel in the Black Atlantic: Booker T. Washington's *The Man Farthest Down*." *MELUS: The Journal of the Society for the Study of the Multi-Ethnic Literature of the United States* 32.2 (2007): 107–31.

Trafton, Scott. *Egypt Land: Race and Nineteenth-Century American Egyptomania*. Durham, NC: Duke University Press, 2004.

Wald, Gayle. *Crossing the Line: Racial Passing in Twentieth-Century U.S. Literature and Culture*. Durham, NC: Duke University Press, 2000.

Wall, Cheryl A., ed. *Changing Our Own Words: Essays on Criticism, Theory, and Writing by Black Women*. New Brunswick, NJ: Rutgers University Press, 1989.

———. *Women of the Harlem Renaissance*. Bloomington: Indiana University Press, 1995.

Wallace, Irving. *The Fabulous Showman: The Life and Times of P. T. Barnum*. New York: Knopf, 1959.

Warren, Carol, and Barbara Laslett. "Privacy and Secrecy: A Conceptual Comparison." Tefft, *Secrecy* 25–34.

Watson, Steven. *The Harlem Renaissance: Hub of African-American Culture, 1920–1930*. New York: Pantheon, 1995.

Wells-Barnett, Ida B. *On Lynching*. Classics in Black Studies. Amherst, NY: Humanity Books, 2002.

White, Luise. "Telling More: Lies, Secrets and History." *History and Theory* 39 (2000): 11–22.

Williams-Witherspoon, Kimmika. *The Secret Messages in African American Theater: Hidden Meanings Embedded in Public Discourse*. Lewiston, NY: Edwin Mellen Press, 2006.

Wing, Adrien Katherine, ed. *Critical Race Feminism: A Reader*. Critical America. New York: New York University Press, 1997.

Wintz, Cary D. *Black Culture and the Harlem Renaissance*. Houston: Rice University Press, 1988.

Woods, William. *A History of the Devil*. New York: Putnam, 1973.

Young-Minor, Ethyl A. "Staging Black Women's History: May Miller's *Harriet Tubman* as Cultural Artifact." *CLA Journal* 46 (2002): 30–47.

Index